D1631405

AD 03762582

Eagles and Bulldogs
in
Normandy, 1944

EAGLES AND BULLDOGS

IN

NORMANDY, 1944

THE AMERICAN 29th INFANTRY DIVISION

FROM OMAHA BEACH TO ST LÔ

AND

THE BRITISH 3rd INFANTRY DIVISION

FROM SWORD BEACH TO CAEN

by

Michael Reynolds

SPELLMOUNT
Staplehurst

British Library Cataloguing in Publication Data:
A catalogue record for this book is available
from the British Library

Copyright © Michael Reynolds 2003
Maps copyright © Jay Karamales 2003

ISBN 1-86227-201-8

First published in the UK in 2003 by
Spellmount Limited
The Old Rectory
Staplehurst
Kent TN12 0AZ

Tel: 01580 893730
Fax: 01580 893731
E-mail: enquiries@spellmount.com
Website: www.spellmount.com

1 3 5 7 9 8 6 4 2

Typeset in Palatino by MATS, Southend-on-Sea, Essex
Printed in Great Britain by
TJ International Ltd, Padstow, Cornwall

Contents

List of Maps

(The maps can be found on pages 233–250)

Publisher's Note

It is regretted that for commercial reasons it has not been possible to include coloured or pull-out maps in the book; however, for those purists who enjoy knowing the exact location of the places mentioned and their relationship to each other, it is suggested that they photocopy and enlarge the maps provided and have them to hand when reading. This will also enable them to insert the thrust and defensive lines, etc., that particularly interest them.

Introduction and Acknowledgements

I first stood on SWORD beach in the summer of 1960 during a British Command and Staff College Battlefield Tour of Normandy. I well remember one veteran breaking down in tears as he told us how some of his comrades had died – it was his first return visit. And I remember too that the French authorities would not allow former German officers to address us; instead we had to listen to their recorded accounts of events. I was a 30-year-old infantry captain at the time and although I found the Tour fascinating and instructive, it was to be another thirty-one years before I returned to the Normandy battlefields. And I am embarrassed to admit that my first visit to OMAHA beach was not until June 1994.

There were many reasons for my absence from Normandy over this long period: a busy career, a family desire for holidays in the sun of Italy and the French Riviera and later on, a fascination with another campaign – the Battle of the Bulge. In fact it was my study of one of the German Divisions that played a major part in the 1944 German Ardennes Offensive that led me back to Normandy – the 1st SS Panzer Division Leibstandarte Adolf Hitler. It had already fought in Normandy in the summer of 1944.

In the past eight years I have been back to SWORD six times and to OMAHA nine times. It is best to go out of season and during school term time; then, during a quiet walk along the beaches, one can more easily visualise the terrible events of 6 June 1944. It is not easy though because everything is now so peaceful and on SWORD one can easily be distracted by the graffiti-covered sea walls. But as one drives inland from either beach, one is constantly amazed how little the landscape has changed. The war-torn villages have of course been rebuilt, fortunately in their original style and in most cases with local stone, and the roads are refreshingly free of traffic. Cemeteries, memorials and museums abound – some like Le Mémorial in Caen and the American Cemetery at Colleville-sur-Mer are 'musts'. Caen and St Lô have of course grown out of all recognition. They are crowded and noisy and choked with traffic – one needs a very fertile imagination to think of them as they were fifty-nine years ago. And in the American sector, even with a modern map, it is not easy to follow the paths taken by the men of the 29th Infantry – but it's well worth the effort even if, as they did, one occasionally gets lost!

This has not been an easy book to write. I have often been dismayed and depressed by what I have discovered; for the closer one gets to the men on the ground the more conscious one becomes of the cost in human terms and of the inadequacies of some of the leaders. But war has always been like that and always will be. One can only hope that this and future generations will be worthy of the freedoms gained by the men of these and other WWII Allied divisions and that they will not, as seems to be the case as I write this Introduction, abuse them.

I am greatly indebted to the following for their help during another year of research and writing:

British

Jamie Wilson, my publisher, for his valuable friendship and for meeting nearly all my requests.

Brigadier Tony Baxter and John Hampson for reading my first drafts and making some very useful suggestions.

Penelope Cameron, General 'Bolo' Whistler's eldest daughter, for allowing me to quote from her father's unpublished diary.

Colonel Mike Chilcott, who lives in Normandy and is a great expert on the D-Day landings, for information on specific points and the loan of books.

Charles Markuss and Ian Daglish for information on military equipment.

David Miller for allowing me to quote from his father's unpublished account of the SWORD beach landings.

Detective Inspector Martin McIntyre of the Thames Valley Police for providing me with the relative part of Brigadier K P Smith's little known autobiography.

The Regimental Secretaries and Museum curators of the British Regiments featured in this book; particularly Peter Duckers of the Shropshire Regimental Museum, Kate Thaxton of the Royal Norfolk Museum, Lieutenant Colonel John Downham, the Regimental Secretary of the Queen's Lancashire Regiment, and not least my old friend Brigadier Brian Burditt for information on the 2nd Battalion The Royal Warwickshire Regiment.

Desmond Seward, the well known author, for suggesting the title of this book.

American

Richard Anderson of the Dupuy Institute, Annandale, Virginia, for providing detailed casualty figures derived from numerous American and British official and semi-official sources.

Jay Karamales for turning my Maps and Appendices into 'finished' products and for spending hours in the US National Archives on my behalf searching for photographs and documents.

Frank Natoli for providing me with the American Official Histories.

Chris Ubik for photographic research and scanning.

French

André Heintz, a citizen of Caen and a former member of the Resistance, for giving me so much of his time and for providing me with invaluable information about events in Normandy in 1944.

Maurice Lantier, a citizen of St Lô, for providing details of events in that city.

I must also thank my wife Anne, my daughter Deborah and many friends who have encouraged me to go on researching and writing. It is a wonderful hobby which has brought me many new friends and taken me to some fascinating places.

Lastly, I would like to dedicate this book to the memory of the GIs and Tommies who fought in these battles and in particular to Captain, later Colonel, Eric Lummis of the Suffolk Regiment. He contacted me after he read my first book on the Normandy campaign, *Steel Inferno*, and we subsequently became good friends. I knew he was writing a book about the 3rd Infantry Division in the Second World War but in June 1999 when I telephoned to ask him how it was going, I was saddened to hear that he had just died. Two years later the basic idea for this book came into my mind and his daughter Diana very kindly gave me her father's draft, *Sword to the Seine*, and permission to use and quote from it as I wished. I am very grateful.

MFR
Sussex, England
January 2003

Preface

By the beginning of June 1941, Hitler controlled Europe from the North
Cape to the Pyrenees and from the English Channel and North Sea coasts
to the borders of the Soviet Union and Turkey. Only the British Empire
and Commonwealth remained at war with Germany and Italy. Exactly
three years later the Americans, British, Canadians and Poles had
assembled the necessary forces to embark on their crusade to destroy the
Third Reich from the west, whilst Stalin's armies advanced relentlessly
from the east.

The crusade began shortly after midnight on 6 June 1944 in Normandy,
when a small glider-borne force of some 200 men from the British 6th
Airlanding Brigade seized the bridges over the Caen canal and Orne river
at Ranville. By 0240 hours 1,200 transport aircraft and 700 gliders had
delivered nearly 24,000 American and British paratroopers to the flanks of
the planned 80km-wide beachhead in northern France.

Offshore in rough seas, nine Allied battleships, twenty-three cruisers
and seventy-three destroyers stood ready to commence their bombardment of the German defences and a further thirty-one destroyers and
seventy-one corvettes were protecting nearly 6,500 converted liners,
merchantmen and tank landing craft with the 150,000 soldiers and 800
tanks due to be put ashore before the day was ended.

Onshore, in the immediate invasion area, five unsuspecting German
infantry divisions and one parachute regiment were positioned behind
the so-called 'Atlantic Wall'. Many of the German commanders responsible for the defence of the Channel coast were not even present in their
Headquarters. The only armour within immediate striking distance of the
coast was the famous 21st Panzer Division, but it could not be released for
action without the personal permission of the Commander of Army
Group 'B', Field Marshal Erwin Rommel, and he was nearly 1,000km
away near Ulm in Germany.

At 0630 hours the first American troops waded ashore on UTAH and
OMAHA beaches and at 0725 hours British mine-clearing tanks touched
down on SWORD beach on the eastern flank. Fighters and fighter-
bombers of the Allied Tactical Air Forces roared overhead in support.

Post-WWII historians and commentators have argued continually about the strategy pursued by the Allies during the Normandy campaign and in particular the strategy set out by the land forces commander himself, Bernard Montgomery, before D-Day, during the fighting and after the war. Sadly for the latter, his claim that the whole campaign had been conducted in exact accordance with his master plan has been disproved by many historians and has done much to damage the reputation of a great soldier and general who, as Carlo D'Este puts it in his brilliant book *Decision in Normandy*, 'masterminded the most successful invasion in the history of warfare'.

Less controversial and more relevant to this book are the initial tasks for each of his Armies detailed by Montgomery in London on Good Friday, 7 April 1944, before all the senior generals, admirals and air marshals involved in Operation OVERLORD, and attended by his superior, General Eisenhower. He made it clear that the primary task of Bradley's First US Army was to capture the port of Cherbourg. Dempsey's Second British Army was, at the same time, to secure Caen and the strategically vital ground to its south-east in order to protect the American eastern flank during the Cherbourg operation. Both Armies were then to advance in a generally southern direction – the First US Army through the St Lô sector and the Second British Army towards Falaise. Montgomery went on to describe his intentions for subsequent phases of the campaign – phases that need not concern us. What *does* concern us in this narrative is that in order to achieve a sufficiently secure and large enough lodgement area for a breakout towards the Seine and eventually the borders of the Third Reich itself, the cities of St Lô and Caen, both hubs of the Normandy road network, had to be captured. St Lô, 33km from the coast even as the crow flies, was clearly too far inland to be an early objective for Bradley's men but Caen, a mere 16km from the coast, became the primary D-Day objective for Dempsey's Second Army.

Two infantry Divisions, one American and one British, were to be associated forever with the capture of these two cities – the American 29th and the British 3rd. Other formations and units would inevitably make important and indeed vital contributions, particularly in the case of Caen, where the Canadians played a major role, but the men of the 'Blue and Gray' and 'Iron' Divisions would be more directly involved than any others. This is their story – and to a lesser extent the story of the unfortunate inhabitants of the two cities. As the separate stories unfold, the reader will be able to compare and contrast the ways in which the men of these two very different Divisions were led and achieved their missions and the suffering they had to endure in doing so.

Author's Note

For readers who wish to follow the fortunes of one particular Division without interruption, they are invited to read the first seven chapters and then chapters with the relevant title.

In 1944 Continental Europe was using Central European Time; the Allies, however, were on Double British Summer Time, which was one hour ahead. In the interests of simplicity, all times quoted from German and French documents and books have been adjusted to equate to those used by the Allies. Many previous descriptions of the Normandy fighting have failed to take this significant time difference into account.

Perfectionists will note that the abbreviated titles given to certain British infantry Battalions and Regiments are not the ones listed in the official Army List. This is deliberate – the ones used in this account are those used by British soldiers in 1944.

Guide to Abbreviations

13/18 H	13th/18th Royal Hussars
A/tk	anti-tank
AA	Anti-aircraft
AAA	Anti-aircraft artillery
AAR	After Action Report
Abn	Airborne
AEAF	Allied Expeditionary Air Forces
Appx	Appendix
Armd	Armoured/Armored
Arty	Artillery
Aslt	Assault
ATAF	Allied Tactical Air Force
AVRE	Armoured Vehicle Royal Engineers
BAR	Browning Automatic Rifle
bazooka	US hand-held anti-tank rocket launcher
Bde	Brigade
Bn	Battalion
Bren	British section light machine-gun
Brig	Brigadier
Bty	Battery
Capt	Captain
Cav	Cavalry
CCA/B/R	Combat Command A/B/R
Cdn	Canadian
CinC	Commander-in-Chief
CMH	Center of Military History
CO	commanding officer
Col	Colonel
Coy	Company
CP	Command Post
Cpl	Corporal
CT	Combat Team

Dandy Fifth	The 175th Infantry Regiment
DD	Duplex-Drive Sherman amphibious tank
Div	Division
DSO	Distinguished Service Order
DUKW	Duplex-Drive amphibious truck
DZ	drop zone
East Yorks	2nd Battalion The East Yorkshire Regiment
Engr	Engineer
ETHINT	European Theatre Historical Interrogations
FA	field artillery
Fd	field
Flail	chains attached to a revolving drum mounted on a tank; used for mine clearing
Flak	anti-aircraft
FSD	Parachute Division
G-2	Intelligence Branch in a division or above
G-3	Operations Branch in a division or above
G-4	Supply Branch in a division or above
Gds	Guards
Gen	General
GI	US infantryman
Gp	Group
HE	High explosive
Heer	German Army
H-Hour	Precise time of an attack
HMG	heavy machine-gun
How	howitzer
HQ	Headquarters
hr	hour
Hy	heavy
Indep	Independent
Inf	Infantry
IWM	Imperial War Museum
JgPz	Jagdpanzer (hunter tank)
KG	Kampfgruppe (Battle Group)
km	kilometre(s)
KOSB	1st Battalion The King's Own Scottish Borderers

KSLI	2nd Battalion The King's Shropshire Light Infantry
LAA	light anti-aircraft
LCA	Landing Craft Assault
LCI	Landing Craft Infantry
LCT	Landing Craft Tank
LCVP	Landing Craft Vehicle and Personnel
Lincolns	2nd Battalion The Lincolnshire Regiment
LST	Landing Ship Tank
Lt Col or LTC	Lieutenant Colonel
Lt	Lieutenant or light
m	metre(s)
Maj	Major
MC	Military Cross
med	medium or medical
MG	machine-gun
Mk	Mark
MLR	main line of resistance
mm	millimetre(s)
MM	Military Medal
MMG	medium machine-gun
Mor	mortar
Mot	motorized
MP	Military Police
Ms	Manuscript
NCO	Non Commissioned Officer
Norfolks	1st Battalion The Royal Norfolk Regiment
OKH	Supreme Headquarters of the German Army
OKW	Supreme Headquarters of the German Armed Forces
Op	Operation
OP	Observation Post
Panzerfaust	German hand-held anti-tank weapon
Pdr	pounder
Petard	Tank-mounted heavy mortar
PIAT	British Projector Infantry Anti-tank
Pl	Platoon
Pnr	Pioneer (German engineer)
POW or PW	prisoner of War
PRO	Public Record Office
Pz	Panzer

Pz-Gren	Panzer-Grenadier (armoured infantry)
PzJg	Panzerjäger (tank hunter)
RAC	Royal Armoured Corps
RASC	Royal Army Service Corps
RCT	Regimental Combat Team
RE	Royal Engineers
Recce or Recon	reconnaissance
Regt	Regiment
RM	Royal Marine
RTR	Royal Tank Regiment
S-3	Operations Branch in a regiment or below
SBG	Small box girder (bridge)
Sgt	Sergeant
SHAEF	Supreme Headquarters Allied Expeditionary Force
Sigs	Signals
South Lancs	1st Battalion The South Lancashire Regiment
SP	self-propelled
Spitze	vanguard
SPW	open-topped, German half track
Sqn	Squadron
Stonewallers	The 116th Infantry Regiment
StuG	armoured assault gun
Suffolks	1st Battalion The Suffolk Regiment
TD	tank destroyer
TF	Task Force
Tk	tank
Tp	Troop
Tpt	transport
Ulster Rifles	2nd Battalion The Royal Ulster Rifles
VGD	Volks-Grenadier Division
Warwicks	2nd Battalion The Royal Warwickshire Regiment
Wehrmacht	German Armed Forces
Werfer	German mortar
WWI	World War I
WWII	World War II
XO	Executive Officer

CHAPTER I
The American 29th Infantry Division –
'The Blue and Gray'[1]

Early History

The 29th Division was first formed in July 1917, three months after America declared war on Germany. Somewhat surprisingly it was made up of National Guard units from Virginia, Maryland, Delaware, New Jersey and the District of Columbia – surprising since this was a mixture of Southern boys and Yankees and memories of the Civil War, which had only ended just over fifty years before, were still fresh. Nevertheless, a circular blue and gray patch worn on the left sleeve symbolised unity in a time of national crisis and with its new nickname, 'The Blue and Gray', the Division was sent to France in June 1918. It took part in the Meuse–Argonne offensive in October 1918, suffering 5,691 casualties in just twenty-one days of combat. After returning to the States the Division was demobilised on 30 May 1919 and the units reverted to their original National Guard status. For the benefit of non-American readers it is worth describing that status. The National Guard was, and still is, a dual State–Federal force providing to the individual States units trained and equipped to protect life and property, and to the nation units trained, equipped and ready to defend the United States and its interests all over the globe.

Between the World Wars, the Delaware and New Jersey units of the 29th were transferred out of the Division and replaced by a second Virginian Regiment. Thus the 29th drew its recruits from just two States and the District of Columbia and from an area just 250 miles from north to south and 250 miles from east to west.

The Division comprised three Regiments and not surprisingly the men were indoctrinated from Day 1 in the history of their Regiments – the men of the 115th learning that its origin lay in the old 1st Maryland and those of the 116th in the 2nd Virginia Regiment dating back to 1760. The latter called themselves the 'Stonewallers', remembering that at the Battle of First Bull Run the Confederate General, Barnard Bee, seeing Brigadier General Thomas Jackson's Brigade standing fast when the battle seemed lost, had shouted to his men: 'There stands Jackson like a stone wall! Rally behind the Virginians!' The men of the 175th Regiment traced their heritage back to the 'Dandy Fifth' of Maryland, named after its handsome full-dress uniform. They were instructed that their forebears had saved George Washington's Army at the Battle of Long Island in 1776 by charging the British lines!

With the exception of the 175th Regiment, which was recruited and based solely in the city of Baltimore, the companies of the 115th and 116th Regiments were decentralised and located in armories right across Maryland or Virginia – in towns like Annapolis, Westminster, Salisbury, Winchester and Charlottesville. In many ways they were similar to the British Territorial Army with complete companies being recruited from a single community. For example, by the time A Company of the 116th Regiment took part in the invasion of Normandy, it contained forty-six guardsmen from Bedford in Virginia, a village of only 3,000 people.

Military service was unpopular in the late Twenties and Thirties and most National Guard units were understrength and suffered from a lack of training ammunition and modern equipment. The 29th Division came together for collective training only two weeks each year. Inevitably the outbreak of WWII improved recruiting and on 3 February 1941 the Division was inducted into one year's Federal service at Fort Meade, Maryland. Two months later the first draft of conscripts, mainly from Maryland and Virginia, arrived and within a short time they outnumbered the volunteers. However, any ideas that the Division might be sent to fight the Japanese following the attack on Pearl Harbor in December 1941 were soon dashed, and the demoralising cycle of humdrum training and guard duties throughout the East Coast region continued relentlessly. Ammunition was still in short supply and the men still wore WWI steel helmets. Boredom, rather than Japan or Germany, became the biggest enemy and these factors together led to a serious lowering in morale.

On 2 March 1942 the 61-year-old commander of the Blue and Gray was replaced, to the delight of the Division, by a graduate of the Virginia Military Institute, Major General Leonard T Gerow. An officer of the 'old school' but not a martinet, Gerow was popular with his officers and men. He was to go on to command a Corps in the European campaign. Ten days later the 29th was restructured to conform to the triangular organisation of regular army divisions and reduced in size from 22,000 men to 15,500. In essence it comprised three Regiments[2] (each of three infantry Battalions), four artillery Battalions[3], a Cavalry Reconnaissance Troop (company)[4] and an engineer Battalion[5]. The organisational table is at Appendix A.

The Division continued its training during the early summer of 1942 in the Carolinas, before moving to Florida in mid-August. Then, on 6 September, Gerow received orders that his Division was to prepare for an immediate deployment overseas. Within a few days the Blue and Gray was moved by train to Camp Kilmer in New Jersey and on the 26th the bulk of the Division boarded the giant Cunarder, the *Queen Mary*, for an unescorted high-speed crossing of the Atlantic. The balance of the Division followed in her sister ship, the *Queen Elizabeth*, leaving New York on 5 October, bound for Greenock in the Firth of Clyde, Scotland.

England

By 11 October the 29th was complete in England. It was to remain there for nearly two years. It spent the first seven months in a Victorian barracks in Tidworth, in the central-southern part of the country, before being dispersed to various towns in Devon and Cornwall in the West Country – towns like Tavistock, Barnstaple, Bodmin and Okehampton. The Americans found the winter weather depressing and life unlike anything they had experienced previously. They found the British and their way of life puzzling – no ice or refrigerators, no showers, warm beer, vehicles driving on the 'wrong' side of the road, the perils of English pronunciation and so on; keeping warm was a major problem with no central heating in army camps and little or none even in the private houses in which some were billeted and others invited. But some things were familiar and comforting – the language, distances measured in miles, even if nobody knew what a 'block' was, and of course, girls! As General Omar Bradley put it in his book *A Soldier's Story*: 'American troops . . . drained the local pubs of beer and made affectionate union of our British alliance. Indeed, nowhere was amity [friendly relationship] courted with more diligence than in the homes of British fathers with pretty unmarried daughters'.[6] But although the GIs were clearly popular with the local civilians, they were dismayed to find that they were very much less so with their 'comrades' in the British forces. This unpopularity and occasional antagonism stemmed mainly from the cockiness and confidence displayed by the newcomers from the 'New World' and envy – envy of uniforms which were tailored and included shirts with collars and ties for all ranks, envy of less discipline and more freedom, envy of equipment which did not require polishing, and above all, envy over pay. A British private soldier, even with three years' service, was paid only £55 a year in 1944; an American private first class, with the same length of service, earned £200 ($778); a British second lieutenant £200, an American £447 ($1,800); a British lieutenant colonel £785, an American £868 ($3,500).[7] The pay differentials between the ranks in each army are also of interest and tell a story in themselves – the British lieutenant colonel earned 14.25 times the pay of a private, an American only 4.5 times.

By the spring of 1943, the Blue and Gray was still the only US infantry Division in the UK and the men began to wonder if they would ever see action. Their predecessors in Tidworth, the 1st ('Big Red One') Infantry Division, had been sent to North Africa and they were aware that other divisions, including National Guard units, were being sent to that theatre directly from the States. Many of the GIs wondered why they were in Europe at all – after all it was Japan, not Germany, that had attacked their country. The fact that a surprising number were of German origin certainly did not help matters. In the 'Midland' region of the USA, which included Maryland, people of German origin formed up to 70% of the population in some towns.[8]

In July 1943 Major General Gerow was promoted to command V Corps and on the 22nd of that month the new Divisional commander arrived directly from the States. His reputation had preceded him – a West Pointer and a strict disciplinarian of the old school. General Omar Bradley later described him as, 'a peppery 48-year-old cavalryman whose enthusiasm sometimes exceeded his judgment as a soldier'.[9] He was Major General Charles H Gerhardt. Despite his awesome reputation, the new commander started with a highly popular move. Sensing that morale was low and that a seven-day week training programme was leading to staleness and boredom, he immediately ordered a three-day rest period and an extension of the previously very restricted furlough (leave) system. But despite this seemingly generous gesture, Gerhardt soon proved himself a fearsome, though competent, leader. He was a stickler for neatness and immediately made it clear that nothing but the highest standards were acceptable in his Division. And above all he made strenuous efforts to raise the morale of his men to a point where they considered themselves superior not only to the enemy but to all other troops in the US Army. To this end he invented the battle cry: 'Twenty-Nine, Let's Go!' and insisted that his men used it in battle drills, on official correspondence and even on Divisional signposts. Despite some initial scepticism, it soon caught on.

Gerhardt was determined to infuse a new spirit of aggressiveness into his Division and to this end he placed great emphasis on hard physical training, weapon handling and shooting. He even demanded that every man be taught how to swim. And he insisted that any soldier failing to meet his rigorous training standards be transferred out of the Division. This resulted in some infantry companies losing nearly half their original personnel during their time in England.

In September 1943 the Division, nicknamed 'England's Own' by its rivals, was the first to be selected for amphibious training at a new US Army Assault Training Center at Woolacombe in north Devon. Each Regiment, accompanied by its affiliated artillery battalion and engineers, spent three weeks there, rehearsing landings from Landing Craft Infantry (LCIs) and Landing Ship Tank (LSTs) and familiarising themselves with new weapons such as flame-throwers, bangalore torpedoes and recoilless bazookas. The 116th Regiment returned in early 1944 for a refresher course.

It was during this period that Brigadier General Norman Cota joined the 29th as its new assistant Divisional commander, a post recently introduced into the Army. Cota had been Chief of Staff of the 1st Infantry in the North Africa campaign and was a perfect choice for the post. He inspired confidence and was a natural leader. Fortunately, he and Gerhardt got on famously; the latter, known to the men as 'Uncle Charlie', was short and neat to the point of being dapper, the former, known as 'Dutch', tall and often casually dressed. They made a formidable pair.

The nearer D-Day approached the more intense the training became. In December 43 and January 44, the 29th was joined by the 1st Infantry Division, recently returned from action in the Mediterranean, and by tank, artillery and engineer Battalions[10] for landing exercises at Slapton Sands in south Devon. The organisation of the tank unit is shown at Appendix B. Ships bombarded mock pillboxes and both the navy and the assault troops used live ammunition on a lavish scale. The exercise was repeated on 27 April and no one was left in any doubt that they were to be the lead troops in the forthcoming invasion of the European mainland. Fortunately for the 29th its landing exercise was carried out successfully and without the calamity that befell the 4th Infantry Division in the early hours of the following day when German E-boats penetrated the escorted convoy of nine US LSTs, sinking two and damaging a third, with the loss of 198 naval personnel and 551 soldiers.[11]

General Dwight D Eisenhower, the Supreme Allied commander, inspected the Division in February and again in April just before the landing exercise. General Montgomery, the designated commander of the 21st Army Group, had already visited each of the Regiments during January. He proved popular with all ranks. The GIs liked his informality and they were delighted to be commanded by a general who had thrashed Rommel in North Africa.

In mid-May the 29th received a sudden and largely unexpected order to move to special camps between Falmouth and Plymouth. These new camps were isolated, surrounded by barbed wire and guarded by some 2,000 Counter Intelligence Corps personnel. No unauthorised personnel were permitted to leave or enter and camouflage discipline was strictly enforced.

At the time of the move fewer than 200 members of the Division knew any of the details of the invasion plan and it was to be the last week in May before the GIs were briefed on the greatest amphibious operation in the history of warfare and learned that the Stonewallers (the 116th Regiment) were to spearhead the Division's landing on OMAHA beach alongside the 16th Regiment of the 1st Infantry Division. They were to be the only National Guard unit to land in the first wave on D-Day.

General Montgomery personally briefed the Divisional, Regimental and Battalion commanders of the 29th and 1st Divisions in a theatre in Plymouth towards the end of May. He emphasised the urgent need for them to push inland quickly and not to worry about their flanks. General Gerow, the former commander of the 29th and now its Corps commander, visited each of the Regiments, as did General Omar Bradley, commander First US Army. The latter addressed some 3,500 men of the 'Stonewall Brigade' on a hillside near the same city shortly before D-Day. He had been told that Gerhardt's Division 'had been infected with a despondent fear of the casualties it was predicted they would suffer in the assault. Some talked of 90%'.[12] He responded by telling them: 'This stuff about tremendous losses is tommyrot. Some of you won't come back – but it'll be very few.' He went on to tell them that the navy and air force would pave the way for them and ended his speech: 'You men should consider yourselves lucky. You're going to have ringside seats for the greatest show on earth.'[13] In fact his audience would not only have ringside seats – they would be required to enter the ring itself.

Towards the end of the month the Division moved into its final Marshalling Camps where the men and vehicles were organised into shiploads and by 3 June they were embarked.

NOTES

1. Based largely on information provided on the US Army CMH website and Joseph Balkoski's well-researched book, *Beyond the Beachhead*.
2. 115 (Maryland), 116 (Virginia) & 175 (Maryland) Inf Regts.
3. 110 (Maryland), 111 (Virginia), 224 (Maryland) & 227 (Virginia) FA Bns.
4. 29 Cav Recon Tp (Virginia).
5. 121 Engr Bn (Distr of Columbia).
6. Bradley, *A Soldier's Story*, p. 238.
7. *Royal Warrant for the Pay, Appointment, Promotion, and Non-Effective pay of the Army 1940*, HMSO, London; and Ganoe & Lundberg, *The History of the United States Army*, Appendix C. Official exchange rate 1944: $4.03 to £1.
8. *New Encyclopaedia Britannica, Macropaedia*, Vol. 29, p. 191.
9. Bradley, op. cit., p. 236.
10. 743 Tk Bn with fifty-six Shermans & eighteen Stuart lt tks, 58 Armd FA Bn with eighteen 105mm SP guns & 146 Combat Engr Bn.
11. Charles B MacDonald, *Slapton Sands: The 'Cover Up' That Never Was*, Army 38, no. 6 (Jun. 1988): pp. 64–6.
12. Bradley, op. cit., pp. 237–8.
13. Balkoski, op. cit., p.63.

CHAPTER II
The British 3rd Infantry Division – the 'Iron Division'

Early History

The 3rd Division was formed in July 1809 during the Duke of Wellington's campaign against Napoleon in Spain, better known as the Peninsular War, and as one of the first Divisions in the British Army it took part in many well-known battles such as Badajoz and Salamanca. After Spain it continued under Wellington's command for the rest of the war against the French and played a decisive role in the final battle at Waterloo in June 1815.

In less than forty years the 3rd Division was again in action – in the Crimean War against Russia and later, in 1899, in the Boer War in South Africa. Both these nineteenth century wars, however, saw the British Army plagued by inadequate training and administration and in some cases low professional standards. Fortunately, by the time WWI broke out this appalling situation had been rectified and the British Expeditionary Force which went to France in August 1914 and included the 3rd Division, was well trained and properly prepared. The Division spent four years on the Western Front and it was during this war that it was given its nickname the 'Iron Division'.[1] Inevitably the high casualty rates of WWI led to the regular content of the 3rd being diluted and to the need for it to be reinforced, initially with volunteers and later with conscripts.

The 3rd Division spent the period between the World Wars based in the Portsmouth area of England as part of the Southern Command. The commander of one of its Brigades in 1937 was Brigadier Bernard Montgomery. He was promoted to the rank of major general and assumed command of the Division just before Britain declared war on Hitler's Third Reich on 3 September 1939. By that time it was organised into three Brigades – the 7th Guards and 8th and 9th Infantry (each of three infantry Battalions), with three artillery Regiments (battalions) in support. Lest readers should think that the British Army was always one of 'spit and polish' and performing smart parades such as those seen on Horse Guards, it is interesting to note parts of a confidential memorandum issued by Monty to his commanding officers shortly after his Division arrived in France:

1. I am not satisfied with the general standard of discipline, turnout, smartness, soldierly bearing, and so on that I notice in the Division.
2. I see men lounging about in the streets with their tunics open, hats on

the back of their head, cigarettes behind their ears. . . At night . . . a good deal of drunkenness and a great deal of shouting and singing in the streets. We have got to keep the men in hand. . .

I know there are many difficulties; we have many men who have been soldiers only a few weeks, and we have large numbers of reservists who may tend to pull our standard down unless we are careful. But I will not allow any let-up in this matter, whatever the difficulties, and all officers . . . will give this subject their immediate attention.

This they clearly did because in the retreat to Dunkirk in the face of the German Blitzkrieg that began on 10 May 1940, the Iron Division, defending the left flank of the BEF, never lost its cohesion or discipline. As one officer put it: 'It was a great experience to see officers and men turn into veterans of the highest calibre in under three weeks.'

Monty himself took over II Corps in the final stages of the retreat and evacuation from France, but soon after his return to England he reassumed command of his Division, which had suffered serious manpower losses and had lost all its heavy equipment and vehicles during the short campaign. Few people realise that only men came back from France – 2,474 artillery pieces and 63,879 vehicles were destroyed or abandoned.[2] Nevertheless, after only a week's leave all 3rd Division personnel were ordered to report to Frome in the West Country. Then, to the amazement of both officers and men, the Division received not only reinforcements but also a complete replacement of weapons and equipment. There was only enough for just one division at that time and the 3rd received it all. The reason was simple – it was destined to return to north-west France to continue the fight. France, however, capitulated on 17 June, the expedition was cancelled and the Division took up defensive positions on the Sussex coast between Brighton and Littlehampton, ready to resist the expected German invasion.

On 2 July Winston Churchill visited the Division and Monty suggested that the 3rd should be formed into a mobile counter-attack force. This made sense to the Prime Minister and within a month the Division was in central England training in its new role. Soon after this Monty left to command V Corps.

During 1941 the Iron Division was restructured with one of its infantry Brigades being replaced by a Tank Brigade; however, in 1943 it reverted to its original organisation but with the 185th Infantry Brigade replacing the Guards. At about this time the three Infantry Brigades, the three Field Artillery Regiments[3] (battalions) and the 3rd Reconnaissance Regiment (battalion)[4] of the Division were joined by a light Anti-Aircraft (AA) Regiment (battalion)[5], an Anti-Tank (A/tk) Regiment (battalion)[6] and a Machine-Gun (MG) Battalion.[7] The full organisation of the Division is shown at Appendix C.

By mid-1943 the 3rd Division had spent nearly three years at home without firing a shot in anger. It had started training in Scotland for the planned invasion of Sicily, but in the event a Canadian Division was chosen for the operation instead. Morale began to suffer and promises that it would be the first British Division ashore in the forthcoming invasion of Europe were greeted with disbelief. Nevertheless, all infantry companies attended a fortnight's training at the Divisional Battle School at Moffat in south-west Scotland, where they learned assault techniques against fixed defences and the whole Division took part in combined operations on the rugged west coast. In December, when it moved to Inverness on the Moray Firth and began training with 'Force S' of the Royal Navy, it became clear that it would indeed be one of the leading assault Divisions. It was in this new location that a large number of specialist units were placed under its command for the forthcoming landings. These included the 27th Armoured Brigade[8] (see Appendix D), the 1st Special Service (Commando) Brigade, plus an additional Commando from the 4th Special Service (SS) Brigade[9] and an Independent Battery from the Royal Marine Armoured Support Group, a medium Artillery Regiment (battalion)[10], an Assault Regiment (battalion) Royal Engineers[11] and two specialist engineer Companies. In addition a Squadron (company) of mine clearing 'flail' tanks, known officially as Sherman Crabs, was attached.[12] The size of the Division virtually doubled from its official strength of about 17,000.

On Christmas Day 1943 a new commander took over – Major General Tom Rennie. A Highland officer of the Black Watch, Rennie had been captured in France in June 1940 but escaped within ten days and later won a Distinguished Service Order commanding an infantry Battalion at El Alamein in 1942. After promotion to the rank of brigadier he commanded an infantry Brigade in the invasion of Sicily in July 1943. A capable officer and one well suited to planning his Division's D-Day landing, Rennie's temperament could not have been more different to that of his counterpart in the Blue and Gray.

But what of the infantry of the 3rd Division who were to bear the brunt of the fighting and suffer the majority of the casualties? Its 8th Brigade comprised Battalions from northern and eastern England[13], the 9th from northern England, the Scottish Lowlands and Northern Ireland[14], and the 185th from central and eastern England.[15] It was in fact a complete mixture of Battalions from most of the United Kingdom and even its Regiments did not consist wholly of men from the regions and counties whose names they bore. Nevertheless, it is appropriate to point out the preponderance of regular Army units in the Iron Division. Only two of the Regiments[16] had Territorial Army (TA) origins and although there were many changes of personnel in the period between Dunkirk and D-Day, the percentage of regular soldiers remained fairly high – about 30%, and in a few cases as high as 40%. For the benefit of North American readers the TA was, and is, a force of part-time volunteer soldiers, usually formed into combat and specialist units, that can be activated for full-time service alongside or in support of the regular Army in the event of a national emergency.

Between December 43 and March 44 the 3rd Division carried out seven full-scale assault landing exercises in the Moray Firth, some in extremely bad weather, to perfect and test the landing techniques of the whole Divisional group. The planners had found almost exact replicas of the beaches and hinterland that the men would face on D-Day and replica beach defences, based on air and ground reconnaissance, were constructed for familiarisation training. Two of the exercises went so far as to sail the whole force ninety miles across the Firth in order to simulate the voyage from the south coast of England to the Calvados coast in Normandy. Then in April the Division moved into camouflaged camps in Hampshire and Sussex in southern England and began its final preparations for the invasion. Another rehearsal landing was completed on the Sussex coast between Littlehampton and Bognor Regis on 3 and 4 May.

On 13 May General Eisenhower visited the Division and he was followed by King George VI on the 22nd and Monty towards the end of the month. Addressing the men in his usual informal way from the engine cover of a jeep, the latter told the men of his old Division: 'the Germans would have cause to remember the Division they had pushed into the Straits of Dover in 1940'. And then, on 26 May, the camps were sealed with barbed wire and guarded by armed patrols. French francs and phrase books were issued and the men briefed on everything except the real names and locations of their objectives. Some of the briefings took as long as six or seven hours and involved the lavish use of models, air photographs and even wave-top views of the run-ins to the beaches. Real names and the precise locations of unit objectives were not revealed until after embarkation, which began on 30 May and was completed on 3 June.

NOTES

1. The American 28th Inf Div was also known as the 'Iron Division' having been awarded this title by General Pershing in WWI.
2. Smurthwaite, Nicholls & Washington, *Against All Odds: The British Army of 1939–1940*, p.6.
3. 7, 33 & 76 (Highland) Fd Arty Regts Royal Artillery (RA), each with eight M-7s (105mm on Sherman chassis) & sixteen towed 25-pdrs.
4. Twenty-eight personnel half-tracks, twenty-four scout cars & sixty-three tracked Bren-gun carriers. The Regt had been formed from the 8th Bn Royal Northumberland Fusiliers TA.
5. 92 LAA Regt RA with fifty-four 40mm guns, formed from 7th Bn The Loyal Regt TA.

6. 20 A/tk Regt RA with forty-eight guns, mainly towed 17-pdrs but including three troops (pls) of M-10s (3-inch gun on Sherman chassis).
7. 2nd Bn The Middlesex Regt (Middlesex) with thirty-six med MGs & twelve 4.2-inch mortars.
8. 13th/18th Royal Hussars (13/18 H), the East Riding Yeomanry & the StaffordshireYeomanry. A total of 190 Shermans & thirty-three Stuart lt tks.
9. 3, 4, & 6 (Army) Commandos (Cdos) & 45 RM Cdo forming 1 SS Bde and 41 Cdo from 4 SS Bde. Each Cdo had a strength of 464.
10. 53 Med Regt RA.
11. 5 ARRE.
12. A Sqn, 22nd Dragoon Gds (22nd Dragoons) from 79 Armd Div.
13. 1st Bn The Suffolk Regt (Suffolks), 2nd Bn The East Yorkshire Regt (East Yorks), 1st Bn The South Lancashire Regt (South Lancs).
14. 2nd Bn The Lincolnshire Regt (Lincolns), 1st Bn The King's Own Scottish Borderers (KOSB) & 2nd Bn The Royal Ulster Rifles (Ulster Rifles).
15. 2nd Bn The Royal Warwickshire Regt (Warwicks), 1st Bn The Royal Norfolk Regt (Norfolks), 2nd Bn The King's Shropshire Light Infantry (KSLI).
16. 3 Recce Regt & 76 (Highland) Fd Arty Regt RA.

CHAPTER III

The Big Picture – 1944

(Map 1)

With the men of the Blue and Gray and Iron Divisions safely aboard their transport ships, it is time to see how they fitted into the overall plan for the invasion of Normandy.

The Allies had finally agreed, after not a little argument, that their first priority was the defeat of Hitler's Reich and that the main American and British effort would be made on the western coast of Europe – specifically, the Normandy coast. General Dwight D Eisenhower had been appointed Supreme Commander Western Europe, with a British airman as his Deputy and an American Chief of Staff. The British were given command of both the Allied Naval and Air Expeditionary Forces and General Sir Bernard Montgomery was appointed to command all ground forces in the initial stages of the campaign. He had two Armies – Lieutenant General Omar Bradley's First US Army and Lieutenant General Miles Dempsey's Second British Army. It was planned that Eisenhower himself would assume command of all land forces as soon as General George Patton's Third US Army became operational in France. Bradley would then take command of the US 12th Army Group and Lieutenant General Courtney H Hodges replace him at First US Army. It was foreseen that Lieutenant General Henry Crerar's First Canadian Army would be activated at about the same time, giving Montgomery another Army for his 21st Army Group. Although nominally 'Canadian', Crerar's Army would include I British Corps and the 1st Polish Armoured Division.

Monty arrived in England from the Middle East in January 1944 and immediately rejected the invasion plan, code-named OVERLORD. In a letter to Churchill he wrote: 'My first impression is that the present plan is impracticable'.[1] He had seen Eisenhower in Algiers before his return and his future C-in-C had told him that although he had only a sketchy idea of the plan, he was unhappy with its scale. Monty knew therefore that he was in a strong position when he declared that the planned frontage was too narrow and that the assault lacked sufficient force to guarantee a rapid advance inland. When told that what he was demanding was beyond the resources available, he simply told the planners to get more resources or another commander.

We need not go into the final plan for the Normandy invasion in any great detail, except to say that it was very much Monty's plan. Following airborne landings at each end of the proposed beachhead[2], four Allied Corps would land on five beaches[3] and would, hopefully, penetrate to an average depth of about 10km on D-Day, capturing the towns of Isigny, Bayeux and Caen. It was then planned to hold Caen and the high ground immediately to its south whilst American and British Corps secured the line of the high ground running from St Lô, through Caumont, to Villers-Bocage. It was hoped this would be achieved by D+9. As already stated in the Preface, the Americans were tasked with capturing the vital port of Cherbourg in the same time frame.

This then was the plan outlined by Montgomery in front of King George VI, Prime Minister Churchill, General Eisenhower and all the senior commanders in his old school, St Paul's, London, on 15 May. All who attended were left in no doubt about Monty's intentions. Omar Bradley wrote later:

> The British and Canadian armies were to decoy the enemy reserves and draw them to their front on the extreme eastern edge of the Allied beachhead. Thus while Monty taunted the enemy at Caen, we were to make our break on the long roundabout road toward Paris. When reckoned in terms of national pride, this British decoy mission became a sacrificial one, for while we tramped around the outside flank, the British were to sit in place and pin down Germans. Yet strategically it fitted into a logical division of labours, for it was toward Caen that the enemy reserves would race once the alarm was sounded.[4]

Monty ended his presentation with the following statement:

> We must blast our way on shore and get a lodgement before the enemy

can bring up sufficient reserves to turn us out. Armoured columns must penetrate deep inland, and quickly, on D-Day; this will upset the enemy's plans and tend to hold him off while we build up strength. We must gain space rapidly and peg out claims well inland. . . . once we get control of the main enemy lateral Granville–Vire–Argentan–Falaise–Caen and have the area enclosed in it firmly in our possession, then we will have the lodgement area we want and can begin to expand.[5]

On the subject of armoured columns penetrating deeply inland on D-Day, Bradley, with the benefit of hindsight, had this to say:

Monty . . . became increasingly optimistic. Pointing to Falaise, he talked of breaking his tanks free on D-Day 'to knock about a bit down there' . . . [he] urged me to explore the possibility of a similar tank knockabout behind OMAHA beach. Although knowing there was a scant chance of carrying it through, I nevertheless devised such a mission. As I anticipated, we never even tried it. In contrast to Monty, I had foreseen a hard enemy crust on the Normandy coast. [6]

The question of precisely when to make the landings and whether they were to be launched during the hours of darkness or in daylight depended on two basic factors: first, the tides and second, naval and air force support. The naval and air planners wanted the final approaches of the landing craft and troop carrying aircraft to be made in moonlight so that ships and aircraft could navigate with relative certainty. Furthermore, they wanted the beach landings to be made in daylight so that fire support could be provided more accurately. The military planners demanded that the first wave of landing craft should touch down during low tide so that they could reach the beaches unhindered by German obstacles. A low tide landing would also enable the landing craft to back off the beaches and allow Allied engineers several hours to make gaps through the obstacles so that later waves could beach safely during high tide. All these factors taken together dictated that the airborne landings should be carried out shortly after midnight, hopefully during a full moon, and the seaborne landings an hour after low tide and half an hour after sunrise. Only three dates in any particular month satisfied all these requirements. On 17 May Eisenhower selected 5 June as the tentative D-Day.

An essential aspect of Allied strategy and one that would impact strongly on the forthcoming campaign, was air power. Eisenhower, with Montgomery's full support, had insisted that the Allied Strategic Air Forces should be switched from their directed task of crippling German industry to a mission of paralysing rail communications in the invasion area. Inevitably this policy would result in casualties to the French population. Nevertheless, Eisenhower's arguments won the day and in

March 1944 the Combined Chiefs of Staff placed both Air Forces under his operational control.

It is time now to focus our microscope down on to our two specific Divisions – the American 29th and the British 3rd. The 29th Infantry, under General Gerow's V US Corps, was to land, along with the 1st Infantry Division and the 2nd and 5th Rangers, on the most easterly of the American beaches, OMAHA. This landing was to be supported by fire from the battleships *Arkansas* and *Texas*, the cruisers *Glasgow, Montcalm* and *Georges Leygues*, and twelve destroyers.[7] Once a safe lodgement area had been secured, the 29th was to establish a link with the VII Corps troops in the UTAH sector to its west, whilst the 1st Division was to turn east and link up with the British in the Port-en-Bessin area, 9km north-west of Bayeux. The British 3rd Infantry, under General Crocker's I British Corps, was to land with Nos 4, 6 and 41 Commandos on the most easterly of British beaches, SWORD. This landing was to be supported by fire from two battleships, the *Warspite* and *Ramilles,* the monitor HMS *Roberts,* five cruisers and thirteen destroyers. The Division's mission was to drive straight for Caen. Air support across the five beaches was to be provided by 10,585 strategic and tactical air sorties, covered by over 5,000 fighters. With only 119 serviceable German fighters on the Channel front in early June 1944, there was little danger of interference from the enemy.[8]

NOTES

1. Montgomery, *Memoirs*, p. 210.
2. 82 & 101 US Airborne Divs on the western flank & 6 British Airborne on the eastern flank.
3. From west to east: VII US Corps on UTAH, V US Corps on OMAHA, XXX British Corps on GOLD, the Canadians (part of I British Corps) on JUNO & the British element of I British Corps on SWORD.
4. Bradley, *A Soldier's Story*, p. 241.
5. Wilmot, *The Struggle for Europe*, p. 216.
6. Bradley, op. cit., p. 241.
7. CMH Pub 100-11, *Omaha Beachhead*, p.36.
8. Wilmot, op. cit., p. 289.

CHAPTER IV

The Ground and the Objectives

The Blue and Gray Division Sector

(Maps 1 & 2)

OMAHA was a concave, crescent-shaped beach approximately 7km long. Owing to rocks and steep cliffs on its flanks, it was in fact the only place on the 15km coast between the Vire river and Arromanches where it was possible to land a large invasion force. This factor naturally favoured the Germans. The leading Regiment of the 29th Division was allocated the western half of OMAHA and that of the 1st Division the eastern.

The men in the first wave of the Blue and Gray would be faced by some 500m of sand, the last 250m of which was covered with anti-invasion obstacles and then, just short of the high water mark, up to 10m of shingle, often taller than a man. The shingle, now mainly replaced with rocks, ran up to a sea wall averaging 2m in height, very steep and made of wood in some places and sloping to an angle of 40 degrees and made of concrete in others. Just beyond it there was a coast road with a scattering of beach houses and then salt marsh, 50 to 200m deep, before 30m high bluffs covered with low undergrowth and shrubs. These bluffs, varying in steepness from 40 to 90 degrees, were impassable to vehicles but could be climbed, with difficulty, by men on their feet. However, for soldiers laden down with 60lbs of equipment they were significant obstacles, not least because their crests were protected by barbed wire and anti-personnel mines. The bluffs were divided in five places by wooded re-entrants, or draws as the Americans called them, four of which contained tracks leading inland. The most westerly, in the 29th Divisional sector, led to the village of Vierville-sur-Mer and was known as the Vierville draw. The other exit in the 29th's sector, a little to the east, led towards the hamlet of St Laurent-sur-Mer but was known as the les Moulins draw, after a cluster of buildings of that name running inland from the beach. Only the Vierville draw was paved but it was blocked at its seaward end by a 4m-high concrete wall. The two draws in 1st Division sector led towards the hamlet of St Laurent-sur-Mer and the village of Colleville-sur-Mer. A lateral road linked these villages and Vierville with Isigny in the west and Port-en-Bessin in the east. Beyond the road the ground is virtually flat with numerous hedgerows, orchards and small copses, but not 'bocage' in the worst sense. We will come back to 'bocage' when we describe the German beach defences in a later chapter.

Roughly 8km from OMAHA beach and lying across the American line of advance was the Aure river. Although only some 3m wide for most of its course, the Aure lies in a 3km-wide marshy valley only a metre or so above sea level criss-crossed by deep ditches. In 1944 it had been flooded by the Germans to form a major barrier. Not surprisingly, the area was, and remains today, virtually uninhabited. The western flank of the V Corps sector was bounded by the Vire river, the estuary of which had also been flooded by the Germans creating a major obstacle to east-west movement. And then, beyond the Aure valley, the men of the Blue and Gray faced the true 'bocage'. Stretching 25km all the way to their eventual objective of St Lô and crossed by another river, the Elle (Map 14), the 'bocage' was virtually impenetrable for vehicles and was to prove claustrophobic for the men who had to fight their way through it. It comprised irregular small fields, usually little more than 100 square metres in size, separated by high earth banks, on top of which grew dense bushes and trees. Running along these banks were sunken tracks, often overgrown and some so narrow that once in them even tanks could not turn or traverse their guns. Such country resembled a giant, irregular chessboard or gigantic shrubbery and was of course ideal for defence and counter-attack. The scale of the 'bocage' problem can be judged by the fact that in a single aerial photograph of the US sector one can see 3,900 hedged enclosures in an area of less than 20 square km. Although much of the 'bocage' has been cleared since WWII, it can still be seen in its original form in a number of places.

St Lô

Built on a rocky hill on the eastern bank of the Vire and fortified by Charlemagne in the 9th century, St Lô is a rural town ringed by hills. In 1944 it had a population of only 10,985[1] – about the size of today's Williamsburg in Virginia or Newhaven in south-east England. The double-spired cathedral of Notre-Dame dominated the town, standing on ramparts, high above the Vire river. It was an elegant town with numerous schools, a college, theatre, covered market hall and all the normal buildings associated with the capital of a French Department (Administrative District), including a Public Record Office and a prison. The only unique thing about the capital of La Manche was its large stud farm[2] and riding school, located on its eastern edge. It has been described as a 'very tranquil little town'.

Why was it so important as an objective? Principally because it was the hub of a vital communications network, but also because the hills on both sides of the city commanded the Vire valley – a major gateway to the south. Roads from the north connected St Lô with Carentan and Isigny, from the east with Caumont and Bayeux and to the south-west with Coutances. The road running out to the north-west to Périers and Lessay was the principal lateral route behind the German west wing. As the commander of the First US Army, Omar Bradley, put it: 'We desperately needed its roads to exploit the attack.'[3]

Up to June 1944 St Lô had seen little of the violence of war. The Germans arrived in August 1940 and on the 12th of that month organised a grand reception in the city theatre. It is alleged that someone informed London and at 2320 hours British aircraft dropped incendiary bombs, missing the theatre but setting fire to a number of houses.

Although there were some restrictions on movement and the Germans requisitioned a number of buildings, the proximity of St Lô to the countryside meant that there were no serious food shortages and life was able to follow a fairly normal pattern between 1940 and June 1944. The town's isolation made it a relatively safe haven for some of the better off residents of larger and more vulnerable cities like Cherbourg. The most significant happenings were the establishment in the city of General Marcks' LXXXIV Corps Headquarters and the arrival of a new German infantry Division, the 352nd, in November 1943. Formed from the remnants of a Division[4] that had been badly mauled on the Eastern Front, this formation was destined to play a major part in our story.

At 2215 hours on 5 June 1944 the French Resistance heard a coded message broadcast by the BBC saying that the invasion was coming within forty-eight hours and instructing it to activate its members. Then, sometime before 1000 hours on D-Day, Allied aircraft dropped leaflets warning the people that, as an important communications centre, their town was to be subjected to heavy bombing and advising them to leave as a matter of great urgency. The leaflets did not of course say that the presence of General Marcks' LXXXIV Corps Headquarters was another very valid reason for it to be chosen as a target for Allied bombers. In fact most of the leaflets fell well to the east of the city anyway and few people were aware of them. It hardly mattered – the Germans soon issued notices ordering the citizens to stay indoors and off the roads. Life for the citizens of St Lô was about to be literally shattered.

The Iron Division Sector

(Map 3)

SWORD beach appeared on the Allied invasion maps to be almost twice as wide as OMAHA. In reality it was not. A steeply shelving beach in the east, cliffs and off-shore reefs in the west and built up areas in St Aubin-sur-Mer, Luc-sur-Mer, Lion-sur-Mer and particularly towards the port of Ouistreham, meant that there was a mere 1.5km strip of shoreline suitable for landing men and vehicles. And yet, incredible though it may seem, the British plan envisaged putting not only the leading Brigade ashore on this tiny beach, code-named QUEEN, but indeed the whole of the 3rd Division with all its many attachments. Adding to the problem of overcrowding was the fact that the ground immediately to the south of this strip of beach was saturated and formed a 500m-deep natural barrier to vehicles including tanks. There were only two roads leading inland across this soft ground – a metalled one at the western extremity of the beach leading to Hermanville-sur-Mer and a secondary one, really only a track, leading from the eastern extremity to Colleville-sur-Orne. Furthermore, there was no shingle bank just short of the high water mark as at OMAHA, but instead sand dunes and then numerous evacuated houses and other buildings. The latter lay along two parallel, metalled coast roads (Maps 9 and 10) that joined the small beach resorts of Luc-sur-Mer, Lion-sur-Mer and la Brèche[5] to the port of Ouistreham. Running south from Ouistreham and flanking the 3rd Division sector was the Caen canal. The German defences will be described in a later chapter.

Beyond the SWORD beach coastal strip, open rolling country with large cornfields broken by occasional clumps of trees or small woods led to Caen. The area offered little cover from aerial observation. It was well cultivated and abounded with small hamlets, the houses and boundary walls of which were built of strong Caen stone, well able to resist anything other than the largest calibre or very high velocity weapons. 3km south of SWORD lay the Périers ridge from which the ships and landing craft of the invasion force could be seen in one direction and the northern outskirts of Caen in the other. South again, across a 3km valley, lay the villages of Beuville and Biéville and then, after another valley, a further ridge with the village of Hérouville near the east bank of the Caen canal and, a little to the north-west, the hamlet of Lébisey adjoining a large wood. 3km beyond this ridge and roughly 14km from SWORD, lay the centre of Caen.

Caen

Founded by William the Conqueror in the 11th century, Caen stands on the Orne river and is surrounded by low hills. It has always been dominated by the fortress built by William the Conqueror, known as the 'Château', and by the two large and famous abbeys – the Abbaye-aux-Hommes and the Abbaye-aux-Dames, founded by William and his Queen Matilda respectively. The city was captured by the English under Henry V in 1346 and held by them until 1450. His son, Henry VI, founded a university and Caen later became known as the 'Athens of Normandy'. Always an important communications centre, the construction of a 14km canal connecting the city to the sea at Ouistreham in the mid-19th century enabled Caen to become an industrial centre with flourishing iron and steel factories. These were established on the south side of the Orne and were soon joined by chemical plants and lumber mills.

Monty described the strategic importance of Caen in his own *Memoirs*:

It was a vital road and rail centre through which passed the main routes leading to our lodgement area from the east and south-east. As the bulk of the German mobile reserves were located north of the Seine, they would have to approach our bridgehead from the east and thus converge on Caen.[6]

In 1944 the city had a population of only 61,334[7] – about the size of today's Lowestoft in East Anglia or Bethesda in Maryland. Before 1944 it had suffered only three air raids[8] but as part of the general Allied air interdiction plan in the run-up to D-Day, it was bombed on 11, 13 and 17 April. Fifteen people were killed and thirty-six injured in these raids and many private homes, the railway station and a gasometer damaged. As in the case of St Lô, in the late evening of 5 June a coded BBC broadcast alerted members of the Resistance to an invasion within forty-eight hours. Life would never be the same again for the people of Caen.

NOTES

1. The population in 1990 was 21,546.
2. Destroyed in Jun 44. The present National Stud was built just to the east of the original.
3. Bradley, *A Soldier's Story*, p. 295.
4. 321 Inf Div.
5. Brèche means breach or gap. The la Brèche shown on the British invasion maps and on Maps 3 & 9 in this book is over 1.5km to the east of the present day la Brèche d'Hermanville and was just one of ten breaches in the sand dunes between Hermanville and Ouistreham in 1944. Its full name was Brèche à Vaussy. This is an important point for those wishing to visit the area and pinpoint the German strongpoint code-named COD (see Chapter IX).
6. Montgomery, *Memoirs*, p. 254.
7. The population in 1990 was 112,846.
8. On 11 Mar 42 & 10 Feb & 14 Apr 43.

CHAPTER V

The Enemy

(Map 4)

In the summer of 1944 there was no agreed German strategy for countering an Allied invasion of Western Europe. The arguments between

Field Marshal von Rundstedt, Commander-in-Chief (CinC) West, and General Geyr von Schweppenburg, Commander Panzer Group West, on the one hand, and Field Marshal Erwin Rommel, Commander Army Group 'B' on the other, are well known and have been described in most books written about the Normandy campaign. Von Rundstedt was senior to Rommel but he did not have Hitler's confidence and could not overrule the latter's views.

Rommel, with his experience of Allied air power, wanted all available tank forces positioned as close as possible to likely landing areas. He knew the Luftwaffe would be incapable of protecting his armoured columns moving to the battle areas in daylight and that the very short summer hours of darkness would be insufficient for any long distance movement. He reasoned that the Germans would therefore lose the battle of the build-up. Von Rundstedt and von Schweppenburg, correct in theory but wrong in the circumstances pertaining at the time, wanted to hold the armour well back from the coasts and out of range of powerful naval guns until they could see where the main threat was developing and then launch coordinated counter-thrusts against it. The result of all this argument was a disastrous compromise.

To compound matters further, the command system designed to put the strategy into operation was complicated and inefficient. This was in some ways deliberate on the part of Hitler who, as well as mistrusting his army generals, wished to retain supreme command and have the opportunity to intervene at all levels. He therefore operated on a principle of 'divide and rule'.

Von Rundstedt, as CinC West, with his Headquarters at St Germain just outside Paris, had two Army Groups under his command: 'B' commanded by Rommel, responsible for France north of the Loire, Belgium and Holland, and 'G' under Blaskowitz, responsible for France south of the Loire. We need not concern ourselves with Army Group 'G'.

Rommel, with his Headquarters in the luxurious Château La Roche-Guyon near Vernon on the Seine, had two Armies under command: the Seventh, covering from the Loire river to the Orne river in Normandy and the Fifteenth covering from there to Holland. This was relatively tidy, but when it came to the Panzer forces the picture was very different. The argument over where to position these forces led inevitably to a split command structure. Rommel was given command of only half the six available Panzer divisions – the 2nd, 21st and 116th. They were grouped under a new Corps Headquarters, the XLVII, which was in fact just taking over when the Allies landed. Not surprisingly, these divisions were located reasonably near the coast – the 2nd between Abbeville and Arras in the Pas de Calais, the 21st nearest to the sea just to the south of Caen and the 116th to the east of Rouen. These locations reflected Rommel's strategic thinking and his estimate of where the Allies would land. While this seemed a reasonable arrangement, there was one potentially critical problem – none of the Panzer divisions could be committed by the Army or Corps commanders charged with resisting the invasion. Rommel retained ultimate control. The other three Panzer Divisions, 1st SS, 12th SS and Panzer Lehr remained under the operational control of von Rundstedt. 12th SS had its centre of gravity over 100km from the forthcoming battle area, Panzer Lehr over 150km and 1st SS was based in Belgium! The net result of all this over-control and divided strategy was that there was neither a strong immediate armoured reserve in Normandy nor a strong strategic reserve.

(Map 1)

Turning now to the coastal defences on the Calavados coast between Isigny and the Orne river on the eve of D-Day, we find two German Divisions in place under the command of General Erich Marcks's LXXXIV Corps. Lieutenant General Wilhelm Richter's 716th Infantry Division had been in the coastal area since June 1942. It had no combat experience and with strength of only 7,771 it was at best a very mediocre formation containing many foreign conscripts, including former Russian prisoners who had been formed into 'Ost' (East) Battalions, officered by Germans. It consisted of two Grenadier (infantry) Regiments, each of three weak German Battalions and one Ost Battalion, plus an anti-tank Company. There was one additional semi-independent Ost Battalion. Each German infantry Battalion had forty-eight machine-guns, six to nine 80mm mortars and one bicycle mounted company. The Ost Battalions were less well equipped. In support was an artillery Regiment of ten batteries. Two were equipped with French 155mm howitzers and the rest with Czechoslovakian 100mm howitzers. Also in support was a Pioneer (engineer) Battalion of two Companies and a Panzerjäger Battalion with ten heavy anti-tank guns on tracked chassis and eleven towed anti-tank guns, two of which were 88mm and the remainder 75mm.[1] The Divisional organisation is shown at Appendix E.

Originally the 716th Division was responsible for the entire 70km coastal defence line from Carentan to the Orne estuary, but the formation of an additional infantry Division, the 352nd, in the St Lô area eased the over-stretch. This new Division, with an overall strength of 12,734, was commanded by Major General Dietrich Kraiss. It was organised in accordance with the Order of Battle of a Type 44 Infantry Division and had three infantry Regiments, each with two Battalions, an Infantry Gun Company with two 150mm and six 75mm howitzers and an Anti-Tank Company with three 75mm anti-tank guns. In support was an artillery Regiment with twelve Batteries – nine equipped with 105mm and three with 150mm howitzers. The Divisional Panzerjäger Battalion had fourteen

Marder 38s[2], ten StuG IIIs[3] and nine motorised 37mm Flak (AA) guns. In addition there was a Fusilier Battalion with four Companies mounted on bicycles and a Pioneer Battalion of three Companies. The latter was equipped with twenty flame-throwers, thirty-seven machine-guns and six mortars. Pioneer units in the German Army were specially trained for fighting in built-up areas. All the infantry Battalions had sixty light and three heavy machine-guns and twelve 80mm mortars. Most of the officers and NCOs in the Division were veterans of the Eastern Front but the new recruits were only 18 or 19 years old, mainly Hanoverians. The organisation of the 352nd Division is shown at Appendix F.

Following a tour of inspection by Rommel in January 1944, two artillery Battalions from the 352nd Division were placed in support of the 716th and then, on 14 March, it was decided to insert the entire Division into the line in the Bayeux sector. This was achieved by 19 March.[4]

As soon as the 352nd arrived in the 716th Division's western sector, Dietrich Kraiss, its commander, assumed operational control of the four Battalions manning the static defences from Isigny to Arromanches[5] and reinforced them with four of his own Infantry Battalions.[6] He located his Divisional Headquarters in le Molay (Map 2), 14km west of Bayeux, and kept his other two Battalions[7] and the Divisional Fusilier Battalion as a central reserve in the Bricqueville–Colombières area (Map 2), within striking distance of OMAHA and another possible landing area near Arromanches. Thus there were eight Battalions of infantry with significant artillery support in the Isigny–Arromanches sector – four more than the Allies expected.

The other four Battalions of Richter's 716th Division[8] remained responsible for the 25km sector from Arromanches to the Orne river. This latter sector included of course all three beaches allocated to the British Second Army – GOLD, JUNO and SWORD.

How were the German coastal defences organised? The smallest defensive position was called a resistance nest. It was manned by between twelve and thirty men equipped with up to four machine-guns, and comprised fire positions with overhead cover and accommodation dugouts, all inter-connected by tunnels and surrounded by barbed wire and mines. A group of resistance nests was called a strongpoint. Strongpoints were manned by at least a platoon of infantry and sometimes by as many as sixty men. They were usually equipped with machine-guns, mortars, some sort of anti-tank gun and/or an artillery piece and had a local reserve.

According to Lieutenant General Richter there were some forty to fifty strongpoints placed along the coastline like 'a string of pearls'.[9] They were supported by artillery batteries, sited in depth and also protected.

(Map 6)

OMAHA was the most heavily defended of all the invasion beaches. As early as 12/13 September 1942 thirty-one British commandos had been killed there during a raid (Operation AQUATINT) designed to gain intelligence. All five re-entrants leading inland were blocked by mines, concrete obstructions and anti-tanks ditches and at their mouths were strongpoints with fire positions terraced up the slopes on each side and echeloned inland, making them almost impregnable against frontal attack. Five strongpoints covered the eastern OMAHA draws and another six in the western sector would have to be overcome by the men of the Blue and Gray and the Rangers. It has been estimated that two 88mm and six 75mm guns, eighteen 37mm or 75mm anti-tank guns and eighty-five machine-guns were directly covering OMAHA beach on D-Day and twelve 105mm and twelve 155mm guns of the 352nd Division were capable of providing indirect fire.[10] A diagram showing the defences covering the les Moulins draw is shown at Appendix G.[11]

(Map 3)

SWORD beach was defended by Colonel Krug's 736th Grenadier Regiment. His Headquarters and one Company of the 642nd Ost Battalion were located in a massive underground strongpoint, codenamed HILLMAN by the British, 1.5km south-west of Colleville-sur-Orne, and other Companies were manning a series of strongpoints and defensive works running along the coast from Lion-sur-Mer to Ouistreham, where the lock gates were protected by bunkers with armoured cupolas. The holiday beach villas along the coast had been evacuated, mines had been laid between and around them and extensive wire barriers had been erected across the beach exits. Some of the more substantial villas had been turned into strongpoints by the lavish use of concrete. Minefields, which included many dummy mines, had been laid on the beach and behind the coast road. The two strongpoints most likely to affect the 3rd Division's landings, codenamed COD and TROUT by the British, were located at la Brèche and on the western edge of Lion-sur-Mer respectively.

Adjacent to strongpoint HILLMAN, at the junction of the Hermanville and Biéville roads (Point 61), was the underground Headquarters of the 1st Battalion of the 1716th Artillery Regiment. It had four Batteries under command, plus the 1st Battalion of the 155th Artillery Regiment of the 21st Panzer Division and a Battery of coastal artillery on the seafront at Ouistreham.

Lieutenant General Richter's 716th Divisional Headquarters was located in the tunnels of a quarry at Couvrechef on the outskirts of Caen (now part of the Caen Mémorial Peace Museum) and his two Pioneer

Companies, employed on further defensive works, had alarm positions at Mathieu and Hérouville. Artillery support in the SWORD beach sector was provided by two Batteries, each of four 100mm howitzers, at Cresserons and near Colleville-sur-Orne and two of four 155mm howitzers each in the Ouistreham sector. All Batteries had concrete emplacements. In addition the four 100mm and eight 122mm guns of the 1st Battalion of the 21st Panzer Division's 155th Regiment already mentioned were positioned in the Périers-sur-le-Dan–St Aubin-d'Arquenay–Beuville triangle in support of the coastal defences.[12]

In many places, however, Hitler's 'Atlantic Wall' as it was known, was a wall in name only. According to the Chief of Staff of the 352nd Division[13], almost half the strongpoints in his sector had inadequate protection – 45% were only splinter-proof and just 15% bombproof – and most of the infantry resistance nests were 'in poor earth emplacements' and subject to flooding. He claimed too that the minefields, the majority of which had been laid two years before the invasion, were unreliable. Anti-tank mines requested by his Division did not arrive, although some 10,000 new anti-personnel mines had been laid before 6 June. He went on to say that Field Marshal Rommel's demand for stronger coastal defences was impossible due to a lack of concrete and mines. Rommel's idea of a minefield 50km wide and 5km deep would have needed ten million mines and was out of the question. The shortages 'did not allow the realisation of these plans for even one divisional sector in the [entire] Atlantic Wall'. The lack of concrete[14] meant that a second line of strongpoints behind OMAHA and a number in the eastern part of the 716th's Division sector were still in the course of construction in June 1944. Richter quotes those at Blainville, Reviers, Tailleville, Plumetot and Colleville-sur-Orne as examples.[15] Nevertheless, those in the British Second Army's sector, particularly HILLMAN, and two Luftwaffe radar stations located in concrete bunkers just to the west of Douvres and described by Richter as 'heavily fortified', were to cause the British and Canadians significant problems. We shall hear more of them later.

In front of the coastal strongpoints along the whole invasion coast where landings were possible lay the beach obstacles. Those covering OMAHA and SWORD are shown in Appendix G and on Maps 9 and 10 respectively. The obstacles began about 100m beyond the high water line with a belt of 1.5m-high 'hedgehogs' – three steel rails welded together and easily capable of taking out the bottom of a landing craft. These were sited in overlapping rows about 100m long, each containing about fifteen hedgehogs. They would be under water at high tide and invisible. 50m or so farther out was a thick belt of wooden stakes and ramps with mines attached, embedded in the sand and facing out to sea. And then, another 100m to seaward, was a final line of obstacles known as 'C' units or, since they had been invented by the Belgians, as 'Belgian barn doors'. These were wire meshes about 2m across and 3m high, held in place by steel girders or wooden stakes and topped with waterproofed Teller mines. Although these barrier lines were not continuous, the difficulties of manoeuvring landing craft through them, especially in the quantities that will be described shortly and when under fire, can be well imagined.

As we have already seen, there were no German armoured forces within striking distance of OMAHA beach and only one Panzer Division, the 21st, near SWORD. But even this had only one of its Panzer-Grenadier Battalions, its Panzerjäger Battalion[16] and the part of its artillery Regiment previously mentioned, west of the Orne. One Panzer-Grenadier Company, the 7th, is known to have been located near Périers-sur-le-Dan and the twenty-four 88mm guns of the 200th Panzerjäger Battalion were positioned in the area Périers–Plumetot–Mathieu–Beuville.[17] The remainder of the Division was either to the east of the Orne or in the area between Caen and Falaise (Map 1). Nevertheless, 21st Panzer was a very powerful formation with 130 tanks and an overall strength of 16,925[18], and since it was to play a major role in the 3rd Division's part of our story, we should be aware of its composition. In many ways it was unique in that as well as its normal Assault Gun Battalion with sixteen 75mm and twenty-four 105mm guns, it had, as already mentioned, a Panzerjäger Battalion with twenty-four towed 88mm guns. The Division's basic structure, however, comprised a Panzer Regiment of two Battalions, equipped with a total of 104 Mk IV tanks (no Mk V Panthers), and two Panzer-Grenadier Regiments, each with two Grenadier Battalions, an Infantry Gun Company and a Mortar Company. It also had a Panzer Reconnaissance Battalion with five Companies, a Panzer Pioneer Battalion and an Anti-Aircraft Battalion with eight 88mm and seventeen 20mm guns. Artillery support was provided by an integral Regiment with twelve 150mm guns, four 100mm cannons, twenty-four 105mm howitzers and eight 122mm howitzers captured from the Russians.[19] The overall organisation is shown at Appendix H.

In summary, it can be said that the German defences in the OMAHA sector were far more formidable than those to be found on SWORD beach. Once the Americans had scaled the bluffs immediately behind the beach, however, there were no more strongpoints to be overcome and no risk of an immediate armoured counter-attack. The British on the other hand, faced further strongpoints up to 4km inland and the distinct likelihood that they would subjected to an armoured counter-attack within a few hours of landing.

NOTES

1. All details from Zetterling, *Normandy 1944*, pp. 297–300.
2. Tk hunter mounting a 75mm gun.
3. A 75mm assault gun.
4. Seventh Army War Diary 19 Mar 44.
5. 726 Inf Regt including 439 Ost Bn.
6. 914 & 916 Regts.
7. 915 Regt.
8. 736 Regt plus 441 Ost Bn. 642 Ost Bn was engaged in construction work east of the Orne.
9. Richter, MS # B-621.
10. The French memorial at les Moulins says there were thirty-five concrete bunkers in the immediate vicinity of OMAHA and eight arty btys, eighty-five MG nests & eighteen a/tk positions covering the beach and its exits.
11. Taken from CMH Pub 100-11, *Omaha Beachhead*, p. 22.
12. Feuchtinger, MS # B-441.
13. Ziegelmann, MS # B-432.
14. Late in May, LXXXIV Corps received only forty-seven carloads of cement in a period of three days against a requirement of 249 loads – Seventh Army War Diary 23 May 44.
15. Richter, MS # B-621.
16. 2/192 Pz-Gren & 200 PzJg.
17. Feuchtinger, MS # B-441.
18. Zetterling, op.cit., pp. 370–7.
19. Richter, MS # B-621.

CHAPTER VI

Morale, Weapons and Tactics

Morale

Despite the risk of over-generalising, we must now consider the morale of the opposing armies.

Let us look first at the Allies. Inevitably this varied, not only between battalions and regiments but also between nationalities. The Americans displayed a cockiness and confidence that epitomised their 'New World' and irritated their comrades of the 'Old'. The fact that this cockiness was merely a natural part of the American psyche was not understood. However, as previously mentioned, it led to the 'Yanks' being unpopular with many of their British fellow servicemen who, often in an arrogant way, considered them amateurish and unprofessional. Supercilious remarks such as, 'where have you been for the last three years?' did little for Anglo-American relations! Even the way the Americans marched was different, as was the music to which they marched – neither was considered particularly 'military' by the British. Many British officers privately echoed the sentiments expressed by General Sir Harold Alexander when he wrote from Tunisia about the Americans:

> They simply do not know their job as soldiers and this is the case from the highest to the lowest, from the general to the private soldier. Perhaps the weakest link of all is the junior leader, who just does not lead, with the result that their men don't really fight.[1]

Whatever the truth of that statement, it was certainly not true of the men of the 29th Division. The Americans were just as well trained as their comrades in the British 3rd Division and, as we shall see, in some respects better trained for their future role. Nevertheless, both Armies suffered from problems with incompetent officers (five US Divisional commanders were sacked in Normandy alone) and numerous senior British officers had been removed since the outbreak of war and more were to go in the forthcoming campaign.

In general the morale of the 29th and 3rd Divisions was high. That is not to say though that the men in the first waves of the landings were confident. They knew that their chances of surviving were anything but good and this inevitably affected morale. Casualty awareness was particularly strong in the case of the British. The vast majority of men in the 3rd Division came from families that had lost fathers or brothers in WWI and almost five years of war since 1939 had inevitably added to this awareness. Major General 'Bolo' Whistler, who was to succeed Tom Rennie in command of the Iron Division, wrote in his diary:

> Male human life to the British is very precious – we have not got unlimited supplies. On the other hand the Boche and the Yanks have no worries and take and give casualties freely. We certainly try hard to inflict casualties but with machines and not personally.

A further problem, which did not affect the Americans, was the worry in the minds of many men in the 3rd Division about their families. The threat of German air raids was still present and within a week of D-Day the first V-1 'Flying Bomb' landed in south-east England.[2]

In the case of the Germans, morale also varied from unit to unit and from formation to formation. Many of the ordinary soldiers who had been conscripted into static or low calibre infantry divisions, like the 716th, had only one real aim and that was to survive the war. More than a few of them had been medically downgraded anyway. Similarly, captured Russian and Polish soldiers who had subsequently 'volunteered' for service with the Germans could hardly be expected to want to die for the Third Reich.

On the other hand the 352nd Division, with many combat experienced officers and NCOs and enthusiastic 18- and 19-year-old Hanoverian soldiers, was a very powerful and well-motivated formation, and the men of the 12th SS Panzer Division who would figure in the 3rd Division's battle were in a class of their own – they still believed in their Führer and the destiny he had planned for them. Most of them were more than ready to die for him.

Furthermore there were two highly motivating factors affecting all German soldiers. First, the Allied demand for unconditional surrender gave them little choice other than to fight on – this was particularly true of the Waffen-SS who knew they could expect little mercy if Germany lost the war; and second, the 'Morgenthau Plan', named after the adviser to President Roosevelt who initiated it. This called for the division of Germany into a few de-industrialised, agrarian states, with the aim of preventing that country from ever again threatening world peace. The Germans learned of its existence in May 1944 and needless to say Goebbels used it to stiffen the nation's resolve.

Weapons

By D-Day the Germans had designed, developed and produced highly advanced equipment in quantity. In virtually all respects, other than artillery and aircraft, it was superior to that in use by the Allies. It is important therefore, but without going into too much technical detail, to look at the weaponry available to both sides.

We will deal with infantry weapons first. American infantrymen were equipped with semi-automatic M1 rifles that took clips of eight rounds and had an effective range of 600m. All that was needed to fire a round was a squeeze on the trigger. The British Lee Enfield rifles and German Mausers also took clips of ammunition and had a similar range but they were bolt-action weapons requiring the firer to pull back the bolt and then push it forward again in order to load the next round. But it was in the field of machine-guns that the Germans had a clear advantage. Each American squad had a Browning light machine-gun (BAR) and each British section a similar weapon known as a BREN gun. They used magazines of 20 and 28 rounds respectively and were usually fired in bursts of two or three rounds in order to conserve ammunition. The BAR dated back to WWI and had a violent recoil which made accurate aiming very difficult. The German squad was usually equipped with an MG-42[3] which was not only much more reliable than the BAR or BREN but could fire 1,200 rounds a minute – more than twice as fast as the Allied equivalents. Moreover, it used 50-round belts of ammunition that could be joined together to form much longer belts for sustained fire in defensive operations. Like the BREN, but unlike the BAR, over-heated barrels could be changed quickly with only a minimum delay in reopening fire. When used with a bipod or tripod, the MG-42 had ranges of 600m and 2,000m respectively. This weapon was to become the scourge of the Allied infantrymen who soon learned to dread its sound. It was the first true General Purpose Machine-Gun, capable of being used in the light, medium or heavy role. A German infantry company, with an official strength of 142 men, had thirteen bipod-mounted and two tripod-mounted MG-42s. An American infantry company, with anywhere between 193 and 242 men at full strength, had only nine light, two medium and one heavy Browning machine-guns, and a British company with only 125 men at full strength had just nine BREN guns. The German sub-machine-gun, the MP-40, of which there were twenty-eight in a company, was also much superior to the British Sten gun. American infantry companies officially had no sub-machine-guns.

German battalions also had an advantage in mortars. In addition to the six 81mm weapons standard in all three armies, they each had four 120mm mortars with a range of 6,000m. And, as mentioned in a previous chapter, the Regiments of the 352nd Division were also equipped with six towed 75mm infantry light guns, with a rate of fire of up to 12 rounds a minute and a range of 4,500m, and two 150mm howitzers which fired out to 5km so giving an infantry commander his own artillery. In the case of infantry anti-tank weapons, the German Panzerfaust could penetrate 200mm of armour at whatever range it hit but was only sighted out to 80m. The US 2.36-inch Bazooka and British PIAT (Projector Infantry Anti-Tank) could both pierce up to 102mm of armour if the crew could get close enough – the frontal hull armour of a German Mark (Mk) IV tank was 80mm – but the latter, although effective up to 100m, was heavy, cumbersome and difficult to fire. And finally there was the German 'potato-masher' grenade which, with its long wooden handle, could be thrown much farther than the American or British hand grenades – to the Allied infantryman it seemed that the lessons of World War I had been forgotten.

Turning now to artillery, it has to be said that this was the outstanding and most effective arm possessed by the Allies. British massed-fire techniques developed in the Western Desert and for the most part imitated by the US Army, were used with devastating effect. The British 25 pounder (pdr) and American 105mm guns may have lacked killing power but they produced excellent suppressive fire; and although the majority of their guns were towed, they possessed medium and heavy guns in profusion in calibres from 90mm, through 155mm, up to 8-inch. The Germans had self-propelled and towed 105mm and 150mm guns and of course their renowned, very high velocity, towed 88mm which was highly effective as an anti-aircraft, anti-tank or conventional artillery piece. Their 100mm Kanone had a range of nearly 25km. And in one field they had a unique and terrifying monopoly – multi-barrelled rocket projectors know as Nebelwerfers. They came in three sizes, 150mm, 210mm and 300mm, firing out to 7,500m, 9,000m and 5,500m respectively. Dust and back-blast, however, made them relatively easy to spot for counter-battery fire and demanded frequent relocation.

In the assault gun and armoured anti-tank gun sphere the Germans enjoyed yet another advantage. The very effective StuG III (Sturm-geschütz) assault gun, with which the 21st Panzer Division was equipped, was really a turretless tank with a limited traverse, high velocity 75mm gun. Less than a third of the US anti-tank units were equipped with the inferior American equivalent – the thinly armoured and open-topped M-10 with a 3-inch gun. The majority of the Allied anti-tank guns, or Tank Destroyers (TDs) as the Americans called them, were towed 57mm, 75mm or 3-inch anti-tank guns which, as well as being quite unsuitable for the offensive operations planned for Normandy, were largely ineffective against German tanks. Only the British with the new discarding sabot (APDS) ammunition for their 6-pdrs had anything comparable to the Germans.[4]

In the case of tanks there is no doubt that the Germans were superior in every category. The low silhouette Mk IV was numerically the most important German tank in WWII. It weighed 25 tons and mounted a high velocity 75mm gun and two or three 7.92mm machine-guns. In terms of armament even this relatively 'light' tank was superior to the American Sherman and British Cromwell it met in Normandy. The Panther was almost certainly the best tank produced by any Western nation in WWII. With up to three 7.92mm machine-guns and a very high velocity 75mm gun, it weighed 45 tons. There is no point in mentioning Tiger tanks since none was deployed against either the 29th or 3rd Divisions. All German tanks used petrol rather than diesel (which was reserved mainly for submarines), and had a crew of five: commander, driver, gunner, loader and radio operator, and an average range of about 200km. All types carried about 80 rounds of main armament ammunition.

Facing this impressive array of German tanks, the Allies had Shermans, Cromwells, Churchills and Stuarts. They were provided on a lavish scale but had little to recommend them. The M4 Sherman was the standard medium tank of the American, Canadian, Polish and two-thirds of the British armoured units in Normandy. With its crew of five, it mounted a medium velocity, short-barrelled 75mm gun, had only 50mm of frontal armour and weighed just over 30 tons. It was highly vulnerable to all German tanks and the infantry Panzerfaust, and soon earned for itself the dreadful nicknames of 'The Ronson Lighter' or 'Tommy Cooker', due to its habit of catching fire after being hit. It was, however, superbly reliable and had a high rate of fire. The British mounted their high velocity 17-pdr gun on the Sherman chassis and called it the Firefly; this was much more effective than the 75mm Sherman but only four tanks in each squadron (company) were so equipped. Needless to say they soon became prime targets for German tank and anti-tank guns. The British Cromwells and Churchills were also under-armed with medium velocity 75mm guns[5]; the Cromwell was reliable and fast, with a top speed of 60kph in contrast to the heavy, well armoured but pedantic, 20kph Churchill. The American M3 Stuart light tank, with only a 37mm gun, was virtually useless other than for liaison, light reconnaissance and escort duties.

It is a sad fact that all Allied tanks could easily be knocked out by any German tank at any range out to 1,000m, and often more, whilst it took a lucky hit on the tracks, optics or gun for Allied gunners to disable a German tank. Blame for this scandalous under-gunning of Allied tanks must lie with the generals and others responsible for armaments who either did not understand or were not sufficiently interested in the technology of tank design and weaponry.

Although communications equipment does not strictly fall under the heading of weaponry, it is nevertheless vital for the success of military operations and in this field the Americans held the advantage. Within infantry companies their excellent amplitude modulated (AM) sets, known as handie-talkies, were supplemented by sound-powered telephones that allowed communication down to as low as squad level. In addition, unlike the British and Germans, who had only AM sets that were subject to interference, they had frequency modulated (FM) sets, known as walkie-talkies, at company and battalion level. These were virtually free from interference.

Lastly we come to aircraft, and here the Allies enjoyed clear advantages. Although the Germans led the field in the development of jet propulsion, very few operational Messerschmitt 262s had been produced and by June 1944 the Allies had achieved almost total air superiority. They were able therefore to cripple German supply lines and movements in daylight. Moreover, they had tank-busting Typhoons and P-47 Thunderbolts which were to do so much damage to the Panzer divisions – the Germans had no equivalent.

These then were the tools possessed by each side. The important difference was that the Germans had great confidence in theirs, whereas many personnel in the Allied armies, particularly infantrymen and tank crews, did not.

Tactics

American and British tactics in WWII were based on the principle of fire and manoeuvre – fire and movement as the British called it. In any attack, the objective was designated and if it was thought to be occupied by the enemy the attacker would attempt to pin down that enemy, and any others who might interfere with the attack, with long-range weapons such as mortars and artillery. As the US Army manual put it: 'Fire superiority is gained by subjecting the enemy to fire of such accuracy and intensity that his fire becomes so inaccurate and reduced in volume as to be ineffective.' This tactic would hopefully enable the attacker to advance, either with infantry supported by tanks or vice versa. Infantry would normally be expected to lead in close country or built-up areas and tanks in open country. In either case tanks were trained to stop short of the objective and 'shoot in' the infantry who had the unhappy job of closing with the enemy, killing or capturing him and occupying the objective. In theory the infantry and tanks were expected to use the same principle of fire and movement during their advance, with part of each sub-unit, platoon or company providing covering fire whilst the other part moved. In practice, where the ground allowed, the infantry and tanks usually advanced at a steady pace behind a 'wall' of artillery fire in exactly the same way as they had in WWI. This was because the Americans and British continued to place a heavy reliance on artillery support in both attack and defence. Individual Allied infantrymen were trained to conserve ammunition through tight fire control and to dig-in as soon as an objective was taken in case of hostile fire or immediate counter-attack.

Although the Germans had shown as early as 1939 how integrated battlegroups of tanks, infantry and engineers, closely supported by artillery and aircraft, could dramatically change the modern battlefield (Blitzkrieg), the infantrymen of the 29th and 3rd Divisions were untrained in such tactics. They were soon to learn that tanks, if they appeared at all, usually left them behind during an advance, nearly always disappeared to the safety of the rear as darkness fell and had crews with whom they could not communicate. It was only in armoured divisions that infantry–tank cooperation and battle procedures were properly practised and where the necessary radio communications were provided. But even in experienced armoured divisions such as the famous 'Desert Rats', where a relatively high level of infantry–tank cooperation had been achieved during the fighting in North Africa and Italy, the tanks and infantry stayed in their 'compartments' during the short period they had for re-training between arriving home in January 1944 and D-Day. They had only one Divisional exercise and, as one officer in the infantry brigade told the author, 'We never even expected to *see* [author's emphasis] tanks in our training.' It is a sad fact that, other than for the D-Day landings themselves, the infantrymen of the Blue and Gray and Iron Divisions were almost totally untrained in joint operations involving infantry, tanks and engineers.

There was also a basic difference in outlook between the American and British soldier that affected tactics. The pioneering spirit and traditions of the 'Wild West' with its lack of respect for authority were inherent in every GI and American officer – even if he was brought up in the Bronx district of New York. He had seen it around him in his daily life in the States and on his cinema screen once or twice a week. He was naturally more adventurous than his British cousin who, mainly as a result of the horrendous casualties suffered by his nation in WWI, had been brought up to respect authority and never to 'step out of line'. Whereas an officer, or even a wisecracking GI of the 29th Division, was quite likely to question an order or perhaps ask for some further explanation, the junior officer and Tommy Atkins of the 3rd Division would rarely think of doing so. The latter had both been taught, through indoctrination and endless drill parades, to react instantly and automatically to orders. This is not to say that they lacked initiative, but they were only likely to act for themselves if they found themselves without their immediate superiors. Finally, it has to be said that the British regimental system, which divides men into relatively small compartments and emphasises a regimental (battalion), as opposed to an army way of doing things, militated against the strong divisional spirit which was a major strength of both the US and German systems. On the other hand, the emphasis on regimental loyalty and long, glorious histories – even if sometimes a little exaggerated – gave British regiments an inner strength, which made them steadfast in adversity and dangerous adversaries, particularly in defence.

It has already been pointed out that many of the German officers and NCOs the Allies would encounter in the first few weeks of the Normandy campaign were experienced and battle-hardened, and that most German soldiers had a natural respect for authority and their superiors. On top of this the German military machine had managed to develop a belligerent attitude in its young, untested recruits without eroding that respect for authority. To some extent this was the result of their training in the Hitler Youth organisation, but when coupled with the morale factors and fine weaponry mentioned earlier, it resulted in generally excellent soldiers.

German tactics were quite different from those of the Allies. Blitzkrieg or 'lightning war' had proved highly successful in the early days of the war but by 1944, the Germans were on the defensive everywhere. Nevertheless, as a result of their experiences in WWI, the German generals had developed new tactics for this phase of war as well. Every officer and NCO was taught the vital importance of selecting the right ground for fighting a defensive battle, the necessity for depth and for constantly changing from one prepared position to another. He was taught the principles of 'mobile defence'. This predicated the need for outpost lines which identified and channelled enemy advances before they ran on to the main defensive positions and mobile reserves capable of launching immediate counter-attacks against any penetrations. Unlike the Allies, the Germans were prepared to lead with tanks in almost any conditions, relying on the shock effects of armour to win the day. In most cases, however, the tanks were closely accompanied by Panzer-Grenadiers.

NOTES

1. Nicolson, *Alex*, p. 211.
2. Of the 9,521 V-1s launched nearly 5,000 landed in southern England, causing 6,184 deaths.
3. Some units were equipped with the MG-34 which had a slightly slower rate of fire – 850 rounds per minute.
4. APDS ammunition for the 17-pdr did not enter service until after the Normandy campaign.
5. A few had 6-pdrs that were retained when the poor performance of the 75mm guns became evident.

CHAPTER VII

Plans for D-Day

The Blue and Gray on OMAHA

(Map 5)

It will be recalled that one Regiment of the 29th Division was to land on the western half of OMAHA and another from the 1st Division on the eastern half[1]; but whilst it clearly made sense to have a single officer in overall command of the landing force, the V Corps commander, Major General Gerow, instituted a surprisingly complicated command and control system to achieve this. He decided that the 116th Regiment of the 29th Division was to come under the direct command of Major General Clarence Huebner, the commander of the 1st Division and that the second and third Regiments of the 29th, the 115th and the 175th, were not to be deployed ashore without his personal authority. Brigadier General 'Dutch' Cota, the assistant Divisional commander of the 29th, with a small staff known as the '29th Division Advance Headquarters', was to supervise the movement of the 116th Regiment, and hopefully the 115th, from the beach to inland assembly areas and only on the morning of D+1 would Major General Gerhardt reassume command of his Division.

H-Hour for OMAHA was to be one hour after low tide and half an hour after sunrise – between about 0615 and 0645 hours depending on which of the three possible dates (5, 6 or 7 June) was chosen for the landings. The Allied naval bombardment against the German coastal defences and infrastructure would begin just after 0500 hours and by 0620 hours the Allied air forces would complete their missions.[2] In relation to the actual beaches, Omar Bradley said:

We're going to soften up each of the beaches with an 800-ton carpet-bombing. Ten minutes before the first wave touches down, we'll drench Omaha with 8,000 rockets . . . These rockets should tear his wire, detonate his mines, and drive him under cover the instant before we land. Then promptly at H-Hour we'll swim 64 tanks ashore.[3]

American commanders hoped to put 59,259 men and some 7,735 vehicles[4] ashore on OMAHA on D-Day, with the leading troops reaching the lateral road linking Vierville-sur-Mer with St Laurent-sur-Mer and Colleville-sur-Mer within two hours, followed by tanks and trucks driving off the beach and up through the draws leading to the villages an hour later. The plan envisaged a bridgehead 8km deep and 20km wide by the end of the day. Thirty-three minesweepers would clear the way to OMAHA beach and the difficulties and complexity of putting just the initial assault force of 34,142 men and 3,306 vehicles ashore can be gauged by the fact that it would involve the use of seven transport ships, thirty-six landing ships and 278 landing craft of various types.[5]

The plans for the landings of the leading reinforced Regiments of the 1st and 29th Divisions were almost identical, but for obvious reasons we will concentrate on those of the Blue and Gray.

The 116th Regiment was to be led ashore by thirty-two amphibious or Duplex Drive (DD) Shermans of B and C Companies of the 743rd Tank Battalion. These tanks were to enter the water some 6,000m offshore and 'swim' to the beach opposite the Vierville draw, making landfall five minutes before H-Hour. Their task was not to act as an armoured force but rather to provide fire support from the water's edge and some protection for the infantry.

Armor's characteristics of shock and mobility were to be disregarded, and no plans were to be made to use the tanks in exploitation from the beaches. . . It was expected that the majority of the tanks would fire from hull down in the water and would not leave the beach at all during the assault phase.[6]

So much for Monty's demand that 'Armoured columns must penetrate deep inland, and quickly, on D-Day'!

The leading tank Companies were to be followed at H-Hour by eight Landing Craft Tank (LCT)[7] carrying twenty-four Shermans of A Company of the 743rd, eight of them fitted with dozer blades and towing trailers loaded with explosives. These tanks were to make 'dry' landings astride les Moulins directly from the LCTs. Almost immediately afterwards, twenty-four landing craft would put four Companies of the 116th Regiment (over 700 Stonewallers) on to the beach across the whole of the 116th Regiment frontage. These landing craft would have travelled some

17km from their mother ships. A Company of the 116th was to land in the sector immediately east of the Vierville draw, G Company half way between the Vierville and les Moulins draws and E and F Companies astride les Moulins. Each Company was to be organised into six boat teams, known as sections, each with its own landing craft normally containing one officer and thirty men. These boat sections were further organised into rifle, wire-cutting, BAR, bazooka, 60mm mortar, flame-thrower and demolition teams.

Shortly after the Stonewallers, men of the 146th Engineer Combat Battalion were to come ashore from thirteen Landing Craft Vehicle/Personnel (LCVP). Assisted by the eight dozer Shermans of A Company of the 743rd, they were to go to work on the beach obstacles and clear and mark eight 50m-wide gaps. The DD Shermans already ashore would give them some protection but they had only thirty minutes in which to achieve their mission before the incoming tide would cover the obstacles. A diagram of the beach defences in the les Moulins sector is shown at Appendix G. Then, between H-Hour plus 30 minutes (H+30) and H+60, ninety-seven landing craft would bring in the remaining combat elements of the 116th Infantry, more engineers, some AA sub-units and two Companies of the 81st Chemical Weapons (Smoke) Battalion, followed between H+60 and H+120 by the rest of the Infantry Regiment, part of the Corps 58th Armored Field Artillery (FA) Battalion, the 111th Artillery Battalion in DUKWs[8] and the rest of the 467th AA Battalion. The 58th FA Battalion would already have taken part in the preparatory bombardment from its LCTs.

The authorised strength of the 29th Division and its attached units on D-Day was 15,686.[9]

Also due to land in the western sector of OMAHA on D-Day were twelve Companies of the 2nd and 5th Ranger Battalions. These had special missions on the right flank of the 116th Regiment. Three Companies of the 2nd Battalion were to scale the cliffs at the Pointe du Hoc (shown on maps and known in 1944 as the Pointe du Hoe), 8km west of Vierville-sur-Mer, and destroy what was believed to be the fortified battery of heavy guns located there. Another Company was to land opposite the Vierville draw just after H-Hour and attack enemy positions on the cliff at the Pointe et Raz de la Percée, 2km to the west. If the assault on the Pointe du Hoc was successful, the 5th Battalion and remaining Companies of the 2nd would land there; but if not, they would land opposite the Vierville draw between H+60 and H+80 and move overland to take on the Pointe du Hoc battery.

The plan outlined above was finalised[10] on 11 May in time for Monty's 'Final Presentation of Plans' before all the senior Allied commanders, Churchill and King George VI, at St Paul's School in London four days later. Among those present were Eisenhower, Bradley (US First Army),

Dempsey (British Second Army), Gerow (V US Corps) and Crocker (I British Corps). As the King left, Eisenhower said: 'Your Majesty, there will be eleven thousand planes overhead on D-Day and OVERLORD is backed by the greatest armada in history. It will not fail.'[11]

Needless to say, the reality of D-Day was tragically different from that envisaged in the plan.

The Iron Division on SWORD

(Map 7)

British plans for the landing on SWORD, including the naval and aerial bombardments, were very much the same in structure as those for OMAHA but even more complex and ambitious. Twenty-nine landing ships and 263 landing craft of various types were to be involved and the only additional element was a smoke screen to be laid by aircraft to give cover to the landing force from German 280mm artillery batteries and fast torpedo boats at Le Havre (Map 1). H-Hour, because of the tides, would be up to an hour later.

The overall plan required 8 Infantry Brigade, with an armoured Regiment (tank battalion), three medium machine-gun Platoons and specialist engineers in support, to secure and consolidate an initial beachhead roughly 5km wide and 4km deep. This was to include 'the high ground north of Périers-sur-le-Dan–St Aubin-d'Arquenay.'[12] The South Lancs with a Squadron of 13/18 H were tasked with securing a beachhead on the western half of QUEEN beach, capturing the inland village of Hermanville-sur-Mer and clearing the resort of Lion-sur-Mer. The East Yorks with another Squadron of the 13/18 H were to secure the eastern half of QUEEN, capture strongpoints SOLE and DAIMLER and then, after sending one Company and the tanks to relieve Commandos on the Caen canal and Orne river bridges at Bénouville, they were to move south and consolidate in the area of St Aubin-d'Arquenay. The Suffolks, initially in reserve with the third tank Squadron, were to capture strongpoints MORRIS and HILLMAN, and then to consolidate and 'form the centre of the Brigade beachhead'[13] on the Périers ridge. It is perhaps significant that, although the Divisional Operation Order specified that 8 Brigade was to establish this firm base on the Périers ridge quickly, the 8 Brigade orders did not stress the need for speed.

Approximately one and a half hours after H-Hour, the three infantry Battalions of 185 Infantry Brigade, with another armoured Regiment, a Troop (platoon) of self-propelled anti-tank guns, two Troops (platoons) of flail tanks, five medium machine-gun Platoons and a 4.2-inch mortar Company in support, were to land and drive straight for Caen, 14km inland, where they were to establish a bridgehead across the Orne. One of the infantry Battalions was to be carried on the tanks of the armoured Regiment and the other two each had one company mounted on bicycles to give greater mobility.

9 Infantry Brigade with its attached armoured Regiment was to be held in reserve. It was to move initially to a concentration area around Plumetot and Cresserons and then to St Contest and Mâlon in order to protect the right flank of 185 Brigade and prevent infiltration between it and the Canadians moving south from JUNO beach (Map 3). In the event of 185 Brigade failing to take Caen, 9 Brigade was to attack the city from the west. All three Brigades would be able to call on naval gunfire, the guns of the Divisional artillery and close air support; and the plans specified that the three armoured Regiments (battalions) of the 27th Armoured Brigade were to concentrate as soon as possible after they had completed their initial tasks with the three Infantry Brigades.

Lord Lovat's 1st Special Service (Commando) Brigade was placed under Major General Rennie's command for the landings and given two vital tasks: No. 4 Commando, with Nos 1 and 8 Free French Troops, was to secure the Iron Division's left flank by neutralising the strongpoint at Riva Bella and clearing Ouistreham; at the same time Lovat himself with No. 6 Commando was to advance to Bénouville, relieve the troops of the 6th Airborne Division who were expected to have captured the bridges across the Caen canal and Orne river leading to Ranville and then move north-east and secure the high ground east of the Orne. A Royal Marine (RM) Commando, No. 41, part of the 4th Special Service Brigade, was also to operate initially under Rennie's command and was to secure Lion-sur-Mer on the Division's right flank, neutralise strongpoint TROUT and then link up with No. 48 RM Commando in the area of Luc-sur-Mer. The latter was to land on the eastern flank of JUNO beach in the Canadian sector.

How were the landings on SWORD to be executed? As in the case of the Americans the way was to be led by the DD tanks of A and B Squadrons of the 13/18 H. These were to beach five minutes before H-Hour to provide fire support and protection for the infantry and engineers following them. They were to be launched 7,000m from the shore. Following these would be ten LCTs carrying the specialist engineer vehicles known as Armoured Vehicles Royal Engineers (AVREs) of 5 ARRE and the mine-clearing flail tanks (known as Crabs) of A Squadron 22nd Dragoons.[14] The AVREs included Churchill tanks with projectors, known as Petards, capable of throwing 40lb charges against the sea walls, flame-throwing Churchills (known as Crocodiles), armoured bulldozers to improve gaps, and other tanks carrying bridges, bangalore torpedoes to breach wire obstacles and fascines to fill ditches.[15] On either flank of these LCTs were to be RM LCTs, carrying sixteen Centaurs[16] with 95mm howitzers for fire support and following them the infantry of A and B Companies of the East Yorks and A and C Companies of the South Lancs in sixteen Landing Craft Assault (LCA) formed into four columns. More LCTs equipped with rocket projectiles were due to open fire at H–10, and at H-Hour eighteen LCTs with seventy-two 105mm howitzers of the Division's three Field Artillery (FA) Regiments would set off from their mother ships. These were to be followed five minutes later by the balance of the infantry Battalions, beach clearance engineers, fourteen LCTs carrying the Commandos, another twelve carrying the priority vehicles of 8 Brigade and C Squadron of the 13/18 H whose tanks were to wade ashore.

Before leaving the British plan it is important to draw the reader's attention to certain statements in the Operation Instruction issued by Lieutenant General John Crocker's I British Corps concerning the capture of Caen. Whilst it stated that: 'The task of 3 British Division is to capture Caen and secure a bridgehead over R Orne at that place', it went on to consider how the enemy might develop his counter-attacks through, or on either side of, the city:

(c) To counter these enemy measures 3 Brit Inf Div should, before dark on D Day have captured or effectively masked Caen and be disposed in depth with brigade localities firmly established: -
    (i) North West of Bénouville, in support of 6 Airborne Div operating east of R Orne (having relieved the Airborne troops and taken over the defence of the Bénouville–Ranville crossings).
    (ii) North West of Caen tied up with the left forward brigade locality of 3 Canadian Inf Div.
(d) Should the enemy forestall us at Caen and the defences prove to be strongly organised thus causing us to fail to capture it on D-Day, further direct frontal assaults which may prove costly, will not be undertaken without reference to I Corps. In such an event **3 Brit Inf Div will contain the enemy in Caen** [author's emphasis] and retain the bulk of its forces for mobile operations inside the covering position. Caen will be subjected to heavy air bombardment to limit its usefulness to the enemy and to make its retention a costly business.

As events were to turn out sub-paragraph (d) proved to be a prophetic statement!

NOTES
1. 116 Regt/29 Div & 16 Regt/1 Div.
2. According to the Official British History, the Allies flew 14,000 sorties on 5/6 Jun 44; 127 aircraft were lost.
3. Bradley, *A Soldier's Story*, p. 255.
4. CMH Pub 100-11, *Omaha Beachhead*, p. 8.

5. Battle Summary – No. 39, Operation Neptune, Landings in Normandy June 1944, Historical Section, Naval Staff, Admiralty, Jun 47, p. 37.
6. Assault Training Center, Training Memos 15 Jan & 1 Mar 44.
7. There were five types of Landing Ship and twenty-four types of Landing Craft. The largest ocean-going ships carried up to twenty Shermans and 200 troops and the smallest, known as Landing Craft Assault (LCA) and Landing Craft Vehicle/Personnel (LCVP) up to thirty-six men or a small vehicle. A Landing Craft Tank (LCT) could carry up to four Shermans.
8. DD amphibious truck.
9. HQ 29 Inf Div G-1 Periodic Reports dated 11 Jun 44.
10. Details have been taken from CMH Pub 100-11, *Omaha Beachhead (6 June–13 June 1944)*.
11. Eisenhower, *Eisenhower at War 1943–1945*, p. 234.
12. 8 Inf Bde Op Order No.2 dated 22 May 44.
13. Ibid.
14. A Sqn was equipped with four tps of five flails each & a roller tk tp. Its HQ comprised three standard Sherman tks.
15. These specialist vehicles were the work of Maj Gen Sir Percy Hobart and his staff who, as a result of the Dieppe disaster, had been ordered by the Chief of the Imperial General Staff, Gen Sir Alan Brooke, to convert 79Armd Div into an experimental formation for the development of specialised armour for the cross-Channel invasion. The Americans were offered all of these vehicles but although Eisenhower wanted them, Bradley accepted only Sherman DD tanks on the grounds that there was insufficient time to train American crews to handle the Churchill tanks in which most of the specialised equipment was installed.
16. An early version of the Cromwell tank but fitted with a 95mm howitzer.

CHAPTER VIII

D-Day on OMAHA– the Reality

The First Landings

(Map 6)

Shortly after 0415 hours on 4 June, Eisenhower reluctantly postponed D-Day for at least twenty-four hours. The previous two months had seen almost unbroken sunshine, culminating in sweltering heat in late May, but June had dawned dull and grey and the adverse weather forecasts gave him no other option. For the men of the Blue and Gray this was bad news indeed. They had already been embarked for over twenty-four hours and the cramped conditions aboard the ships did little for their morale as they heard and felt the worsening conditions.

At about the same time the following day, Eisenhower was faced with the choice of going ahead on 6 June in unfavourable weather, or postponing OVERLORD for at least two weeks. After consulting Montgomery, Admiral Sir Bertram Ramsay (CinC Allied Naval Forces) and Air Chief Marshal Sir Trafford Leigh-Mallory (CinC Allied Air Forces), he decided to launch the invasion fleet. It was a wise decision for as it turned out a violent storm broke out in the Channel in the early hours of 19 June and lasted for three days. This would have necessitated a further delay until early July. Omar Bradley surmised later that this could have had serious implications for the Allies: 'Instead of wintering on the Siegfried Line, we would have been lucky to reach the Seine.'[1]

H-Hour for OMAHA was set for 0630 hours on 6 June[2] and at 0400 the transports carrying the men of the 116th Infantry Regiment stopped engines 20km offshore – well out of range of the German shore batteries. The men began clambering over the iron rails in pitch darkness into the landing craft which hung from the sides of the ships. With an 18-knot wind and heavy swell, this proved a difficult transfer and a number were injured as they mistimed their jumps – some even fell overboard to their deaths. The average man was carrying over sixty pounds of equipment, including an assault jacket instead of his normal pack, combat rations, nine grenades, a half-pound block of TNT, rifle ammunition clips, an entrenching tool, a bayonet, gas mask and a poncho, and in some cases extra ammunition belts for BAR machine-guns, as well as his personal weapon.

The Stonewallers had been told that to ease their passage across the beach the battleships *Texas* and *Arkansas*, steaming within 12,000m of the shore, would shortly be opening fire with 14-inch guns and that in addition three cruisers and fifteen destroyers[3] would drench the enemy defences with pinpoint, rapid fire. Also that an air bombardment would blast the Nazi gun emplacements, that British Spitfires and four squadrons of American P-47s would be overhead at all times and that during the night paratroopers had already landed behind enemy lines to cut off reinforcements. Whilst this may have given them some encouragement, seasickness and the freezing spray from the rough sea was of more immediate concern and before long, as the landing craft circled in a holding pattern, they were being swamped and the men had to help the crafts' pumps by bailing with their helmets.

At least ten of the ferrying craft were swamped on their way in. More serious for the operation was the sinking of much of the artillery. The attempt to ferry guns ashore in DUKWs through the heavy sea proved disastrous. All but one of the 105mm howitzers of the 29th Division's 111th Field Artillery Battalion[4] were sunk. . . In addition . . . the 58th Armored FA Battalion . . . lost three of its pieces when the craft carrying them hit mines. In short, the artillery that was planned to support the infantry attack, particularly in the advance inland, did not reach the shore.[5]

It is hardly surprising that so many of the 111th's DUKWs sank. They had driven off their LCT at 0200 hours but were not due to beach until 0820 hours. They had little chance of surviving six hours in the water in such weather conditions. Three of the four that did were then sunk by shellfire.

As dawn lightened the infantry began their nightmare journey towards the beach. They could hear the drone of heavy and medium bombers overhead and at 0550 hours precisely the naval guns crashed out the first of over 3,000 rounds, and rockets began to scream towards the beach. For some seasickness and fear began to give way to excitement.

During the night General Omar Bradley, aboard the cruiser *Augusta*, the flagship of Rear Admiral Alan G Kirk, the commander of the Western (American) Task Force, had also heard the drone of 'more than 1,300 RAF bombers'[6] as they 'swarmed over the French coastline from the Seine to Cherbourg' and watched as a 'stricken bomber plunged toward the *Augusta*.'[7] He was already concerned about OMAHA:

> Just before boarding the *Augusta* in Plymouth harbour, Dickson [his Chief Intelligence Officer] had learned that the 352nd [German Infantry Division] had been moved from St Lô to the assault beaches for a defence exercise. He promptly forwarded this information to V Corps . . . but was unable to give it to the troops already 'sealed' aboard their craft.[8]

But even if Major General Gerhardt and officers of the 29th Division had been told about the 352nd, there was nothing they could have done about it. This failure of both the American and British intelligence agencies was particularly serious for, as readers already know, the 352nd was not on a defence exercise – it had taken up its positions eleven weeks before D-Day! A British intelligence reporter working at Bletchley Park[9] said later:

> We didn't get exactly what one panzer division was going to do, which was to attack the left-hand [eastern] section of the British landing, and we didn't get the positioning of 352 division, which was the one that held OMAHA beach. We didn't get the detail that it was going to be so close up and if we had we would have warned the American First Army that they were going to have a rather sticky time.[10]

Bradley continued his reminiscences of the early hours of D-Day:

> At 0615 smoke thickened the mist on the coastline as heavy bombers of

the US Eighth Air Force rumbled overhead. [But] not until later did we learn that most of the 13,000 bombs dropped by these heavies had cascaded harmlessly into the hedgerows three miles behind the coast. In bombing through the overcast, [the] air [force] had deliberately delayed the drop to lessen the danger of spillover on craft approaching the shore. The margin of safety had undermined the effectiveness of the heavy air mission.[11]

And there was more bad news for the Stonewallers. The low cloud, mist, dust and smoke caused by grass fires set alight on the bluffs by the naval bombardment soon obscured most of their targets and reference points and to compound the problem many of the British five-inch rocket-firing ships loosed off their salvoes when they were still well out of range. Most of the rockets fell well short of the sea wall. In fact, few of the German strongpoints were seriously damaged by the air and naval bombardments. The After Action Report of the 116th Infantry Regiment has the following statement:

> It was the consensus of all officers and men questioned that prior to H-Hour there was positively no evidence of friendly aerial bombardment of the beaches. There were no craters along the water's edge, no demolition of beach installations and also very little evidence of naval gunfire.

Whilst this may have been true of the immediate beach areas, the Telephone Log of the 352nd Infantry Division has the following entries:

> 0545 hours: between 0500 and 0510, Defence Works 44, 47 and 48 were heavily bombed.
> 0652 hours: The region of Maisy [11km west of OMAHA] is kept under fire from heavy naval artillery.
> 0704 hours: The coastal defences are subjected to heavy naval fire.
> 0715 hours: The Defence Work 60 [OMAHA Beach eastern draw] is subjected to particularly heavy artillery [naval] fire.
> 0726 hours: The coast between the Defence Works 59 and 60 [eastern end of OMAHA] is held under the heaviest artillery [naval] fire. Heavy bombing attacks on the emplacements of Battery 1716 [four Czech 100m howitzers]. Some guns buried by rubble, three of them have been . . . emplaced anew.

The sheer horror of what happened on OMAHA beach on the morning of 6 June has been vividly described in many of the books written about the Normandy invasion and realistically portrayed in the first few minutes of Steven Spielberg's film *Saving Private Ryan*. Most literary descriptions include personal accounts by survivors but this author will restrict himself to basic facts – they speak for themselves.

It will be remembered that DD Sherman tanks were to lead the assault, landing at H–5 (0625 hours). In the event the rough seas caused the naval officer in charge of the eight LCTs to give up any idea of launching the 743rd tanks 6,000m offshore. Knowing they would have little chance of reaching the beach before they were swamped, he decided to run his craft right onto the shore and let the Shermans drive off. It was a wise decision – the 741st Tank Battalion supporting the 1st Division on the eastern part of OMAHA lost twenty-seven of its thirty-two Shermans in its attempt to 'swim' them.[12] Even so, things did not go as well for the 743rd as had been hoped. Two of A Company's tanks were 'drowned' and B Company, landing opposite the Vierville draw, came under immediate artillery, cannon and anti-tank fire and lost seven of its sixteen tanks. The Company commander's LCT was sunk just offshore and four other officers were killed or wounded, leaving a single lieutenant in command.[13] Nevertheless, the nine remaining Shermans began engaging enemy positions from the water's edge. C Company touched down successfully to the east but soon attracted fire. The famous novelist Ernest Hemingway, who accompanied the invasion force but did not go ashore because of an injured leg, wrote later that he saw five tanks hit and set on fire – three of these were from the 741st Tank Battalion supporting the 1st Division. He described the Shermans as 'crouched like big yellow toads along the high water mark'.

Owing to the ineffectiveness of both the naval and air bombardments, many of the infantrymen in the first waves of the 116th Regiment found themselves under direct fire even before leaving their assault craft. The Companies landed more or less simultaneously: A Company of the 1st Battalion, coming ashore just to the east of the Vierville draw, suffered the worst, losing an estimated 65% of its strength within ten minutes. One LCA foundered a kilometre offshore on a sand bar and most of its complement drowned under the weight of their personal loads; another completely disintegrated after being hit by mortar bombs, and in a third all thirty-two men including the Company commander, Captain Taylor Fellers, were killed. The following account, prepared by the US War Department's Historical Division after interviewing survivors, paints a horrific picture of what it was like for the hapless soldiers of A Company:

All boats came under criss-cross machine-gun fire. . . As the first men jumped, they crumpled and flopped into the water. Then order was lost. It seemed to the men that the only way to get ashore was to dive head first in and swim clear of the fire that was striking the boats. But, as they hit the water, their heavy equipment dragged them down and soon they were struggling to keep afloat. Some were hit in the water and wounded. Some drowned then and there. . . But some moved safely through the bullet fire to the sand and then, finding they could not hold there, went back into the water and used it as cover, only their heads sticking out. Those who survived kept moving forward with the tide, sheltering at times behind under-water obstacles and in this way finally made their landings. Within minutes of the ramps being lowered, A Company had become inert, leaderless and almost incapable of action. Every officer and sergeant had been killed or wounded. . . It had become a struggle for survival and rescue. The men in the water pushed wounded men ahead of them, and those who had reached the sands crawled back into the water pulling others to land to save them from drowning, in many cases to see the rescued men wounded again or to be hit themselves. Within twenty minutes of striking the beach A Company had ceased to be an assault company and had become a forlorn little rescue party bent on survival and the saving of lives.

And so it was to be for many others on D-Day. C Company of the 2nd Rangers, coming in just to the west of the Vierville draw shortly after A Company, lost thirty-five out of sixty-four men. G Company of the 2nd Battalion 116th Regiment, which should have landed between the Vierville and les Moulins draws, ended up in scattered groups just to the east of les Moulins. Half the groups gained some protection from the smoke of brush fires set alight by explosions on the bluffs but those landing farther to the east ran into heavy machine-gun fire and one boat team lost fourteen of its complement of thirty-one. F Company of the 2nd Battalion came ashore just to the east of its planned sector, directly in front of les Moulins; half the Company, unprotected by smoke, came under heavy fire and took forty-five minutes to cross the exposed beach, many of the men using the beach obstacles for some sort of protection. 50% were cut down. The other half of the Company managed to reach the protection of the shingle bank[14], but by then they had lost all their officers and were largely disorganised. E Company of the same Battalion, meant to land on their left flank, veered over a kilometre to the east and ended up in scattered groups in the 1st Division's sector. Two of its boats made good landings with only two casualties, but a third was hit by an artillery shell and the others came under heavy machine-gun fire. The Company commander, Captain Lawrence Madill, was killed.

There were two reasons for so many of the assault boats landing well to the east of their designated positions: the strong current running laterally eastwards and the difficulties of navigating through the smoke and beach obstacles.

By 0700 hours A Company had been cut to pieces at the water's edge, F Company was disorganised with heavy losses, G Company was scattered but had some groups preparing to move west along the beach to find their assigned objective and E Company was nowhere to be found in the Blue and Gray sector.

Recall that the Special Engineer Task Force, which in the Blue and Gray sector comprised the 146th Engineer Combat Battalion and a number of Naval Combat Demolition Units, had the mission of preparing eight 50m gaps through the German obstacle belt in just thirty minutes. It ran into trouble even before coming ashore. Delays in loading and navigational problems resulted in four of the assault teams arriving ten or more minutes late and only three finding their designated disembarkation points. Most were swept to the east and a number landed where there were no infantry or tanks to give them covering fire. The conditions under which the teams had to work could not have been worse. Apart from enemy fire, friendly infantry sheltering behind the obstacles due for destruction and others passing through them towards the sea wall caused severe delays. In addition, only six of the Sherman dozer tanks assisting the engineer Task Force reached the beach in working order and three of these were soon disabled by artillery fire. Nevertheless, despite appalling casualties[15] two gaps had been cleared in the 116th's sector by 0700 hours. Sadly, the equipment for marking these gaps had been lost and so they were invisible in high water conditions.

Farther east in the 1st Division's half of OMAHA, 'the picture differed only in detail'.[16] There is no need to go into that detail except to say that the situation was just as harrowing and chaotic. Indeed, at 0641 hours the Division's G-3 duty officer aboard the USS *Ancon* wrote in his Operations Journal: 'entire first wave foundered.'

The Second Wave

At 0700 hours the second assault wave began touching down in a series of landings that lasted forty minutes. The US War Department's official narrative has this description:

> The later waves did not come in under the conditions planned for their arrival. The tide, flowing into the obstacle belt by 0700, was through it an hour later, rising eight feet in that period; but the obstacles were gapped at only a few places. The enemy fire, which had decimated the first waves, was not neutralized when the larger landings commenced. No advances had been made beyond the shingle, and neither tanks nor the scattered pockets of infantry already ashore were able to give much covering fire. . . Mislandings continued to be a disrupting factor, not merely in scattering the infantry units but also in preventing engineers from carrying out special assignments and in separating headquarters elements from their units, thus hindering reorganization.[17]

The follow-up infantry Companies were organised differently from those in the first wave. Two of the six sections were designated 'assault' and carried the same equipment and weapons as those in the first wave; however, the other four sections carried normal rifle company weaponry. It had been assumed that the beach defences would already have been penetrated and that the next wave would be able to move quickly inland towards the various battalion assembly areas without special 'assault' equipment. This was now clearly impossible.

The other three Companies of the 1st Battalion were scheduled to land on a 1,000m frontage to the east of the Vierville draw at 0700 hours in support of its now decimated A Company. In the event only two or three sections did so. B Company's assault craft failed to recognise the essential landmarks and the Company ended up being scattered a kilometre on each side of the A Company survivors. Those who did land in the right place suffered the same fate as their comrades and the Company commander, Captain Ettore Zappacosta, was killed. C Company landed ten minutes later in relatively good shape but a kilometre to the east of the Vierville draw. Drifting smoke gave it protection from direct fire and it suffered only five or six casualties, but the Company lost all its flame-throwers, 60mm mortars, bangalore torpedoes and demolition charges when the boat carrying them overturned in the surf. The Company found itself on its own but sheltered by a metre-high wooden sea wall. D (Heavy Weapons) Company was less fortunate. One boat was swamped and had to be abandoned, another was sunk by a mine or artillery round and a third stopped 100m offshore. The Company commander, Captain Walter Schilling, was killed – the third in the same Battalion that morning – and only three of its six medium mortars, three of its eleven machine-guns and a very limited amount of ammunition was brought ashore. To complete the misfortune of the Battalion:

> the three craft carrying the Headquarters Company, the command group and the Beachmaster's party . . . were brought in several hundred yards west of that sector and under the cliffs. . . The crossing of the tidal flat to the cliff against concentrated small arms fire cost one half to two thirds of the [Headquarters] group [including the commanding officer of the 58th FA Battalion]. The survivors, reaching the base of the cliffs, took refuge in the niches in the rock.[18] Not only was the command group [Lieutenant Colonel John Metcalfe] separated from all other Battalion units, but also the members of the group were so scattered that they had to use radio for inter-communication.[19]

It will be remembered that three rifle Companies of the 2nd Battalion of the 116th had landed in the first wave. Its Headquarters and Headquarters Company came in near the les Moulins draw just after 0700 hours:

When the ramps went down, fire was so heavy that many men took refuge behind some tanks at the water's edge, only to find them favorite targets for artillery fire. Major Sidney V Bingham Jr, Battalion commander, was among the first to reach the shingle, where he set to work trying to revive leaderless sections of F Company. For nearly an hour he had no radio[20] working to contact the widely scattered elements of his Battalion. During this period, the only part of the 2nd Battalion which had arrived at the embankment in good condition, four sections of G Company, set out to reach their planned assault sector [between the Vierville and les Moulin draws]. To do so meant a lateral movement of several hundred yards behind the now crowded shingle bank and under small arms fire. . . The four sections gradually lost all cohesion. . . Major Bingham's attempts to organise an assault at les Moulins was unsuccessful. He managed to get about fifty men across the shingle near the prominent three-storey house[21] at the mouth of the draw . . . [and] although Bingham led a group of ten men nearly to the top of the bluff east of the draw, they were unable to knock out an enemy machine-gun nest and had to return to the house.[22]

The last Company of the 2nd Battalion, the Heavy Weapons Company, became dispersed during the run-in to the beach. The machine-gun Platoon and two mortar sections ended up in the 1st Division's sector and the remainder, after suffering heavy casualties, found themselves around les Moulins.

At approximately 0715 hours, Lieutenant Colonel Max Schneider's Ranger Force[23] of eight, sixty-five man, Companies approached the Vierville draw in eighteen LCAs. Three other Companies, under Lieutenant Colonel James Rudder, were at this time assaulting the German strongpoint at Pointe du Hoc (Map 2) but nothing had been heard from them and it was wrongly assumed that the assault had failed. Schneider soon assessed the situation in front of him and ordered his force to swing east. Even so, A and B Companies of the 2nd Rangers landed where A Company of the 116th had been decimated and suffered the same fate. Only just over 50% reached the sea wall. Fortunately, the 450 men of the 5th Rangers came ashore halfway between the Vierville and les Moulins draws with 'only five or six' casualties.

Lieutenant Colonel Lawrence Meeks' 3rd Battalion of the 116th should have followed the 2nd Battalion onto the 2km sector of beach astride the les Moulins draw between 0720 and 0730 hours. In fact, it came ashore a few minutes late, well to the east, with part of L Company and the whole of M Company in the 1st Division's zone. Fortunately there were only a few casualties and it is clear that the later assault waves had a much easier time than those landing on or just after H-Hour. Five of the eight Companies of the 116th Regiment came ashore with their sections more or less properly organised and with relatively light casualties. It has been said that this was not just because of the protection provided by the burning grass and brush, but because the remaining enemy positions quite simply had too many targets to engage.

By 0730 hours, just as their British comrades were coming ashore on SWORD beach, the exhausted and mainly terrified men of the 116th Infantry Regiment were lining the whole of the sea wall or shingle embankment in their sector of OMAHA beach:

> Many companies were so scattered that they could not be organized as tactical units. At some places, notably in front of the German strong-points guarding draws, losses in officers and NCOs were so high that remnants of units were practically leaderless. . . Engineers, navy personnel from wrecked craft, naval shore fire control parties, and elements of other support units were mixed in with the infantry. There was definitely a problem of morale. . . behind them, the tide was drowning wounded men who had been cut down on the sands and was carrying bodies ashore just below the shingle. . . Stunned and shaken by what they had experienced, men could easily find the sea wall and shingle bank all too welcome a cover. . . Ahead of them, with wire and minefields to go through, was the beach flat [area between sea wall and bluff], fully exposed to enemy fire; beyond that the bare and steep bluffs.[24]

It was into this desperate and seemingly hopeless situation that Brigadier General 'Dutch' Cota, the deputy commander of the Blue and Gray, and Colonel Charles Canham, the commander of the 116th, and their command groups disembarked at 0730 hours. Losing only one officer, they landed more or less half-way between the Vierville and les Moulins draws and found C Company of the 1st Battalion, some 2nd Battalion elements and 450 men of Max Schneider's Provisional Ranger Force to their left and right. In most places the men were crowded shoulder to shoulder, sometimes several rows deep. Fortunately they and the command group were masked by smoke and not under direct fire from the bluff immediately to their front.

From Beach to Bluffs

The outstanding fact about these first two hours of action is that despite heavy casualties, loss of equipment [and] disorganization . . . the assault troops . . . found the necessary drive to leave their cover and move out over the open beach flat toward the bluffs. . . They improvised assault methods to deal with what defenses they found before them. . . Some penetrations were made by units of company strength; some were made by intermingled sections of different companies; some were accomplished by groups of twenty or thirty men, unaware that any other assaults were underway. Various factors . . . played a part in the success of these advances. Chance was certainly one; some units happened to be at points where the enemy defenses were weak, where smoke from grass fires gave concealment, or where dangerous strongpoints had been neutralized by naval fire or by the tanks. . . But the decisive factor was leadership.[25]

That leadership was provided initially by Brigadier General Dutch Cota and Colonel Charles Canham. Realising that they had little or no chance of storming the enemy strongpoints defending the Vierville and les Moulins draws, they resolved to advance up the bluffs. This involved crossing the flat salt marsh, some 100m deep, devoid of cover and blocked by a double-apron wire fence and anti-personnel minefield. The bluffs themselves were up to 30m high, steep and bare but pockmarked with small folds and depressions that provided some cover and fortunately the main German defences were sited to cover the beach and the draws themselves rather than the ground in between. On the crest of the bluffs Cota and Canham knew there were machine-gun and rifle pits connected by trenches.

There were countless acts of bravery by young officers and NCOs as they started breaching the wire obstacles and leading their men off the beach and through the minefields. C Company of the 116th, under its commander Captain Berthier Hawks who had suffered a crushed foot in the landing, led the way at about 0750 hours. At about the same time the senior officer on the beach, Brigadier General Dutch Cota, took personal command of another group and after the first man was cut down as he tried to move through a gap blown in the wire, led the way himself in the dash to the foot of the bluff roughly halfway between the draws. Apparently this was the occasion, immortalised in the film *The Longest Day*, when he bellowed: 'There are two kinds of soldiers on this beach – those who are dead and those who are going to die! So let's get the hell off the damned beach!'. Then at 0810 hours Max Schneider gave the codeword 'Tallyho'. It was the order for each platoon of Rangers to make their own way up the bluff and on to their designated assembly area south of Vierville. According to the memorial plaque to the Rangers in the Vierville draw, this happened after Cota gave the order, 'Rangers, lead the way!'. Colonel Canham, despite a severe wrist wound, led a mixed group of 2nd Battalion men up another part of the bluff nearer to les Moulins at about the same time.

Once on the hillside the various groups were protected from direct fire and by the smoke from the grass fires. In some places the smoke was so thick that men put on their gas masks. Cota tried to contact the 1st

Division during his move up the bluff to report his own actions and to find out what was happening on the other part of OMAHA, but without success.

The Move Inland

(Map 8)

By 0830 hours the last of more than 600 men were leaving the sea wall and by 0900 the crest of the bluff had been secured. No Germans were found in the trenches there and remarkably few casualties had been incurred. As well as C Company of the 116th, there were men from B, F, G and H Companies, the 121st Engineers, most of the 5th Rangers and of course Cota and Canham with his Regimental Headquarters. Tragically, most of the personnel of his Alternative HQ had been lost when a shell hit their craft shortly after landing. In the case of H Company, a machine-gun platoon had moved laterally all the way from the 1st Division's part of the beach. But the moves up the bluff had been uncoordinated with few of the men being aware of what was going on except in their immediate vicinity. On reaching the top of the bluff no one could see more than a couple of hundred metres because of the many hedgerows and most had no idea what to do next. When Cota arrived he found elements of the 116th and 5th Rangers scattered all over the fields beyond the crest with the farthermost groups near the coastal road. Some sporadic, long-range machine-gun fire was coming in from the direction of Vierville village[26] and the occasional artillery round landed in the general area, but there was no organised opposition. Even so it was another hour before Cota was able to bring some order into the mixed force and get units moving again. He personally organised some of the men into fire and manoeuvre teams and led the advance across the open fields. The small number of Germans in the area retreated and the Americans were soon able to advance along the track connecting les Moulins to Vierville.[27] Again C Company of the 116th was in the lead entering Vierville shortly before 1100 hours. Cota's group was not far behind. No Germans were found in the village but a platoon of B Company advancing towards the Château Vaumicel, just south of Vierville, had to overcome a small German resistance nest and then beat off a counter-attack. The Germans involved deployed from three trucks coming up from the south. Canham's group of 2nd Battalion men with some Rangers attached had been equally successful in their move from the beach and they too arrived in Vierville – again with very few casualties.

Just before midday C Company of the 116th and B Company of the 5th Rangers began a move down the coast road towards the Pointe du Hoc. 500m out of Vierville, however, they were halted by enemy machine-guns.[28] A full-scale attack by the main Ranger force to overcome this opposition was planned for the early evening but was later cancelled. The Rangers were now an essential part of the force defending the hard-won gains south and west of Vierville and Colonel Canham was not prepared to risk losing them. His force had few heavy weapons and no tanks or supporting artillery. Some guns of the 58th Armored FA Battalion had been landed on the beach but the crest of the bluff prevented them firing in close support. At 1830 hours John Metcalfe, commanding officer of the 1st Battalion, after finally managing to leave the cliff area to the west of the Vierville draw, reported to Colonel Canham in Vierville. This was the first time that the Regimental commander became aware of the true state of his 1st Battalion and it would be another five hours before he learned about his 2nd and 3rd Battalions at the head of the les Moulins draw near St Laurent.

By midday Cota and Canham had much of which to be proud, but the main task of clearing the two draws to enable tanks and vehicles to exit the beach was unfinished. At around 1300 hours a heavy naval bombardment, including fire from the battleship *Texas*, was directed at the strongpoints guarding the Vierville draw and it was not long before a destroyer reported Germans leaving the concrete emplacements to surrender. Shortly afterwards Dutch Cota, with his ADC and four men, calmly walked down the road to the beach to see why no vehicles were coming up. After receiving some scattered small arms fire and capturing five Germans, whom they made lead the way through a minefield, the Cota group reached the beach to find the sad remnants of A Company of the 1st Battalion and some Shermans of B Company of the 743rd Tank Battalion farther to the east. Cota found that despite their heavy casualties, the loss of some 75% of their equipment and isolated enemy snipers, Lieutenant Colonel Robert Ploger's 121st Engineers were about to start work on the obstacles in the draw. In the event, however, there were not enough infantry available for the systematic mopping-up of the Germans still in the area and the engineers themselves had to send out combat patrols to do the job, delaying their proper mission.

Dutch Cota continued his walk along the promenade to see what had happened at les Moulins. He was unaware that shortly before 1000 hours the commander of V Corps, General Gerow, had ordered Colonel Eugene Slappey's 115th Regiment of the Blue and Gray to land in support of the beleaguered 116th.

Slappey's men had been loaded in a dozen LCIs, each capable of carrying a company and putting them, dry-shod, straight on to the beach. The problem, however, was navigating these slow 246-ton LCIs through an uncleared obstacle belt in the face of continuing artillery fire. For the men of the 115th there was an additional problem – their vehicles were not due to come ashore on D-Day and so they were carrying abnormally heavy loads including extra ammunition.

The 115th was ordered to land near the les Moulins draw but it soon became clear to the LCI captains that in the absence of cleared and marked lanes through the beach obstacles a landing in that sector was out of the question. They asked for new orders and, despite the chaos there, were told to come ashore in the 1st Division's sector, about 1,500m east of les Moulins. Although the landing was difficult, with several LCIs colliding, it was effected with remarkably few casualties and Slappey soon received orders from the deputy commander of the 1st Division to attack and secure St Laurent, which was thought to be defended by about a company of Germans.[29] He in turn ordered his 1st Battalion to cut off the village from the rear while the other two Battalions attacked it frontally.

The 115th's advance to, and attack on, St Laurent did not go as planned. Although the 1st Division had marked a few lanes through the minefields below the bluffs, the men of the Blue and Gray did not trust them and progress was painfully slow. Lieutenant Colonel William Warfield's 2nd Battalion, which landed at 1030 hours, did not start its attack on the village until late afternoon. Even then naval gunfire fell short causing a number of casualties in the Battalion and the attack, despite the support of four Shermans of the 741st Tank Battalion from the 1st Division[30], ground to a halt. Slappey gave orders for the 2nd Battalion to break off the action and link up with the 1st Battalion. The latter had reached an area south of St Laurent near the Formigny road at about 1800 hours after running into snipers and mortar fire which killed its commanding officer, Lieutenant Colonel Richard Blatt. Major James Morris took command. Major Victor Gillespie's 3rd Battalion had still not reached the St Laurent–Colleville road (Map 2) when darkness fell shortly after 2200 hours.

> Elements of five Battalions had spent the afternoon and evening of D-Day fighting through an area of about a square mile which contained only scattered pockets of enemy resistance. The effectiveness of the attacking forces had been reduced by a number of factors, including lack of communications, difficulties of control, and the absence of artillery and armored support.[31]

On arrival in the les Moulins sector in the mid-afternoon Dutch Cota found the resistance there:

> still strong enough to block any movement . . . There and elsewhere, Germans made use of the maze of communications trenches and tunnels by emerging from dugouts to reoccupy emplacements believed neutralized. Snipers reappeared along the bluffs in areas where penetrations had been made. Above all, artillery from inland positions

kept up sporadic harassing fire on the beach flat. . . Hits were still occasionally made on landing craft, sinking or setting them on fire; vehicles were struck as they jammed the approaches to exits or tried to move laterally along the beach.[32]

By this time the beach had indeed become heavily congested with vehicles. Elements of the 81st Chemical Battalion, 112th, 146th and 149th Engineer Battalions, naval fire control parties, advance elements of artillery units, medical detachments, anti-aircraft units and even an RAF group[33] had all started to come ashore before 0800 hours, making it difficult if not impossible for the Shermans trying to support the infantry to manoeuvre:

Halftracks, jeeps and trucks . . . found themselves on a narrowing strip of sand without any exits opened through the impassable shingle embankment. . . [They] were caught in a hopeless traffic jam. Enemy artillery and mortars had easy targets. Losses in equipment ran high . . . affecting all types of material. Engineer supplies, necessary for clearing the beaches, were seriously reduced. The 397th AAA AW Battalion lost twenty-eight of its thirty-six machine-guns disembarking.[34]

Cota also found that although the 3rd Battalion of the 116th, less M Company pinned down on the beach in the 1st Division's sector, had reached the high ground east of the les Moulins draw by 1000 hours, its attempt to move south had been blocked by Germans in and near St Laurent. It made less than a kilometre's progress during the rest of the day, mainly because small enemy machine-gun detachments in well-prepared positions covered the mainly open ground over which it had to advance to its assigned assembly area west of the village. By midday most of L and K Companies and parts of I Company had reached the north-west edge of St Laurent where they were joined by Major Bingham from les Moulins with a handful of men from his 2nd Battalion. Unfortunately for the Americans, as we have already heard, the Germans were holding the village and the high ground around the crossroads where the road comes in from les Moulins and they were held there all afternoon. L Company suffered most of its D-Day casualties in this area. By last light the bulk of the 3rd Battalion and the command group and a few remnants of the 2nd Battalion were still at the head of the les Moulins draw. They were unaware of the presence of the units of their sister Regiment, the 115th, only a kilometre away to their south-east.

The Commanders

For Omar Bradley aboard the USS *Augusta*, the morning had been one of intense worry and frustration – frustration over an almost total lack of firm information about what was happening on OMAHA.

> When V Corps reported at noon that the situation was 'still critical' on all four beach exits, I reluctantly contemplated the diversion of OMAHA follow-up forces to UTAH and the British beaches... With the OMAHA landing falling hours and hours behind schedule, we faced an imminent crisis on the follow-up force... 25,000 troops and 4,400 more vehicles to be landed on the second tide... I was shaken to find that we had gone against OMAHA with so thin a margin of safety... Although the deadlock had been broken several hours sooner, it was almost 1:30 P.M. when V Corps relieved our fears aboard the *Augusta* with the terse message: 'troops formerly pinned down on beaches . . . advancing up heights behind beaches.'[35]

'Uncle Charlie' Gerhardt, commander of the 29th Division, came ashore during the mid-afternoon and set up his CP in an old quarry in the Vierville draw, but until Dutch Cota met him early that evening he had no real idea of the whereabouts of any of the units of his two Regiments ashore. Cota briefed him as best he could although he could not have been fully in the picture.

The Picture at the End of D-Day

By last light on 6 June (last light was officially 2248 hours), C Company of the 116th, the 5th Ranger Battalion and A, B and C Companies of the 2nd Ranger Battalion were defending the solid stone buildings on the western edge of Vierville, Colonel Canham's Regimental CP and elements of the 1st and 2nd Battalions were some 1,000m to the south-west of the centre of the village, and C Company of the 121st Combat Engineer Battalion was holding the Château Vaumicel. The 9th Squad of the 3rd Engineer Platoon had breached the concrete wall at the bottom of the Vierville draw at 1700 hours[36] and the rest of the Company had cleared enough of the remaining obstacles to allow vehicles to move up into the village by nightfall. The tanks of the 743rd Tank Battalion went into bivouac 100m west of the village at about midnight. Sixteen Shermans had been lost and one was disabled.[37]

In the St Laurent area, elements of the 2nd and 3rd Battalions of the 116th were at the head of the les Moulins draw which was still barred by enemy resistance in the old strongpoints. The 1st Battalion of the 115th Regiment was a kilometre south of St Laurent by the road to Formigny, the 2nd Battalion a kilometre south-east of the village and the 3rd Battalion 1,500m to the east.

In the case of artillery, all but one of the guns of the 111th Battalion supporting the 116th had been lost and none of those of the 110th, due to support the 115th, had been landed. The commanding officer of the 111th, Lieutenant Colonel Thornton Mullins, was wounded soon after leading his advance party ashore and died a few hours later. Of the self-propelled guns of the 58th Armored FA Battalion, five had been lost in the morning[38] but the rest of the Battalion had come ashore during the afternoon and one Battery had moved inland at 1800 hours to support the 115th Regiment near St Laurent.

(Map 5)

The situation in the eastern half of OMAHA, where the Regiments of the 1st Division were operating, was very similar and again need not be described in detail. Suffice to say that by nightfall they had advanced to a line just south of the road running from St Laurent to Colleville but the latter village, although virtually surrounded, was still in German hands. Farther east, the Americans had captured le Grand-Hameau.

7km to the west of OMAHA James Rudder's 2nd Rangers had success-fully stormed the German battery position at the Pointe du Hoc by 0800 hours only to find the casements empty. Five French 150mm guns[39] were found an hour later in an orchard, unmanned and unguarded; however, soon after disabling the guns, the Rangers found themselves cut off by a German counter-attack. By nightfall they were in a state of siege.

The American losses on D-Day were horrendous: fifty landing craft and ten larger vessels[40], and of roughly 35,000 men put ashore in the V Corps sector, 3,000 had been killed, wounded or were missing. On OMAHA the 116th Regiment alone suffered 1,007 casualties – 247 killed, 576 wounded and 184 missing[41]; twenty-six artillery pieces and fifty tanks had been lost. Sadly, the peacetime system of recruiting complete companies from specific towns and areas, as in the case of the British 'Pals' battalions in WWI, led to some tragic consequences. Bedford in Virginia, a village of only some 3,000 people, lost twenty-three men on D-Day – twenty-two of them, including three sets of brothers, in A Company of the 1st Battalion of the 116th Infantry!

A number of historians have criticised the American plan for the OMAHA landings. They say that the assault craft were launched much too far out to sea and that the initial attacks were directed head-on against the German strongpoints rather than at the more weakly held areas between these strongpoints. Whilst it is certainly true that the longer than strictly necessary run-in to the beach caused difficulties with navigation and led many units to land much farther to the east than planned, the second accusation is quite simply wrong. No companies were directed head-on at the strongpoints; but, as already pointed out, OMAHA was the most strongly defended beach on the Normandy coast and the interlocking structure of the German defences ensured that *wherever* the Americans landed they would come under both direct and indirect fire. Suggestions that the Americans should not have landed on OMAHA at all ignore several basic facts: one, their mission at this stage of the campaign was to clear the Cotentin peninsula and capture Cherbourg; two, it was militarily unacceptable to leave a gap of over 40km between UTAH and the British beaches (Map 1), and three, it was the only possible landing site between UTAH and the British beaches.

In summary it has to be said that the performance of the majority of the untried and unbloodied American soldiers on OMAHA on D-Day was exceptional and in the case of some of the leaders of the Blue and Gray, notably Dutch Cota, Charles Canham, Sidney Bingham and Berthier Hawks, outstanding. Many junior officers and NCOs, like Captain Lawrence Madill of E Company, Lieutenants Anderson of L and Hendricks of G, and Sergeant William Norfleet of D Company, to mention but a few, displayed qualities of great leadership and bravery. It is not surprising that the Stonewallers won twenty-three Distinguished Service Crosses, ten Silver Stars and 100 Bronze Stars on this day – Brigadier General Cota, Colonel Canham and Major Bingham were amongst those who were awarded the Distinguished Service Cross.

The Enemy in the OMAHA Sector

(Maps 1 & 2)

The actions of the soldiers of the 726th Grenadier Regiment manning the coastal defences covering OMAHA need no elaboration, but what of the Corps and Divisional commanders in this sector and the men of the 352nd Infantry Division? The following picture, which readers can compare with the one already described, is drawn basically from the Telephone Log of the 352nd Infantry Division[42] and the account of the actions of that Division by its Chief of Staff, Lieutenant Colonel Ziegelmann.[43]

Just over an hour after the first British airborne troops landed north-east of Caen on 6 June, Headquarters LXXXIV Corps in St Lô issued a warning order to its subordinate formations and by 0215 hours on D-Day all 352nd Division units, including the 726th Grenadier Regiment, had been alerted. Reports of enemy parachute landings in battalion strength near the Carentan canal followed at 0313 hours and a minute later the navy reported 'sea targets 11km north of Grandcamp'.

At 0410 hours Major General Kraiss' 352nd Divisional reserve, the 915th Regimental group under the command of a Colonel Meyer, became the LXXXIV Corps reserve and was ordered to move from the Bricqueville–Colombières area to engage the enemy paratrooper force known to have landed in the Isigny-sur-Mer–Carentan sector. Kampfgruppe (KG) Meyer, which took over an hour to get moving, comprised the two Battalions of the 915th Infantry Regiment, the 352nd Fusilier Battalion and an assault gun Company of ten StuGs.

At 0622 hours the German Naval Commandant Normandy reported 'fifty landing craft together with four bigger naval units, probably destroyers, lying off Port-en-Bessin' and ten minutes later Colonel Goth's 916th Grenadier Regiment reported landing craft nearing the beach in the Vierville–Colleville sector. At this point Kraiss began to realise that the threat from the sea was much more serious than that posed by the paratroopers around Carentan and at 0650 hours he suggested to his Corps commander that KG Meyer be halted in its move to the west. Marcks agreed. Two minutes later sixty to eighty landing craft were reported approaching the coast near Colleville.

At 0704 hours the 916th Regiment confirmed that '140 ships were assembled in the Bay of Vierville' and that its coastal defences were being subjected to heavy naval bombardment. Half an hour later the 726th Grenadier Regiment was reporting enemy forces on the beach in front of its strongpoints covering the Colleville draw (Map 5); and at 0825 hours the same Regiment said that one of those strongpoints had been pene-trated and another was being attacked from the rear. Ten minutes later Kraiss asked permission for one battalion of KG Meyer to be detached for a counter-attack to restore the situation in that area. Again Marcks agreed but both commanders knew that due to the distance involved it would be the best part of two hours before this attack could be launched.

At 0905 hours Goth's 916th Headquarters reported enemy penetrations into the Pointe du Hoc battery position and said that a platoon of the 9th Company of the 726th Grenadier Regiment would be making an immedi-ate counter-attack. Fourteen minutes later it confirmed that a Battalion of KG Meyer had been committed in the Colleville sector.

By 0935 hours the situation in the British sector, south of GOLD beach, was causing the German commanders much more concern than that at OMAHA, where they believed the sea-borne assault had been halted on the beaches. Reports such as that from the commander of the strongpoint at the Pointe et Raz de la Percée, saying that he could see a great many vehicles burning, including ten tanks, dead and wounded lying on the sand and that debarkation from the landing craft had ceased, only reinforced this impression. Farther to the east, however, they knew the enemy had broken through an Ost Battalion[44], leaving the road to Bayeux wide open and that at 0912 hours thirty-five enemy tanks (part of the British 50th Infantry Division) had been reported advancing towards Arromanches. Twenty minutes later they heard that Meuvaines was in British hands and Kraiss began to worry that his Division would be rolled up from the east. He therefore proposed to General Marcks that KG Meyer, less the 2nd Battalion already committed at Colleville, but with most of the

Panzerjäger (Anti-Tank) Battalion[45], should 'throw back to the coast and into the sea the enemy infantry and tanks penetrating our right wing'. Marcks had little choice but to agree; but an hour and a half later Kraiss was still asking Meyer: 'When are you going to start? In what direction?'.

At 1015 hours the 916th Regiment reported enemy debarking from sixty to seventy assault craft just to the east of les Moulins, but even as late as 1210 the strongpoints covering that draw were still 'firmly' in friendly hands. Nevertheless, the troops in those covering the Vierville draw were said to be 'very weak'.

At 1335 hours General Marcks was told that the Colleville counter-attack had been successful and that the village was secure. Within an hour and a half, however, it had been lost again and at 1526 hours the 2nd Battalion of the 916th Regiment reported 'tenacious resistance offered by the enemy, resulting in heavy casualties'.

Headquarters LXXXIV Corps was told that St Laurent had fallen at 1710 hours and, after reporting 'further strong landings on the coast near Vierville' at 1821 hours, the 916th Regiment finally reported the loss of Vierville at 1850 hours.

KG Meyer's counter-attack towards Arromanches was finally launched at 1700 hours. The move to its jump-off position had been severely interdicted by Allied fighter aircraft. The attack failed and at 1830 hours the Headquarters of the 915th Regiment reported that it had lost contact with its 1st Battalion and that its Fusilier Battalion had been forced to withdraw with its commander, Colonel Meyer, 'presumably seriously wounded and taken prisoner'. Just before midnight the Fusilier Battalion said that its strength was down to just forty men, plus six assault guns, and fifty men picked up from the 1st Battalion. KG Meyer had virtually ceased to exist.

Twenty minutes after midnight Kraiss gave his Corps commander the following report on the overall situation:

> Tomorrow the Division will be able . . . to offer the same kind of hard resistance . . . as was the case today. Because of heavy casualties, however, new forces have to be brought up . . . The troops occupying the strongpoints have fought gallantly. The strongpoints [west of Vierville], despite the losses they have suffered are still in full readiness to defend themselves. At the moment, the 352nd's Pioneer Battalion, together with the 7th Company of the 916th Regiment, is attacking . . . from Formigny. The 6th Company regained the [strongpoint at les Moulins], but was then entirely covered by heavy enemy naval gunfire. The 2nd Battalion of the 915th Regiment [originally part of KG Meyer] . . . is now encircled near Colleville and needs more ammunition. . . On the left wing the counter-attack by the 1st Battalion of the 914th Regiment against the Pointe du Hoc is still progressing. The Field

Replacement Battalion[46] . . . has been moved forward in order to defend Formigny . . . Almost all of the radio stations of the advanced [artillery] observation posts have been put out of action.

Marcks replied: 'All reserves available to me have already been moved up. Every inch of ground has to be defended to the utmost capacity until new reinforcements can be brought up.'

The Chief of Staff of the 352nd Division reported later that his Division, which included of course the 726th Grenadier Regiment of the 716th Division manning the coastal defences in the OMAHA sector, lost 200 killed, 500 wounded and 500 missing on D-Day.[47] These figures are supported by other wartime documents that show the Division suffered losses exceeding 1,000 men.[48]

St Lô on D-Day[49]

For the citizens of St Lô, 33km south of OMAHA, D-Day brought confusion and horror. During the early hours the sounds of many more aircraft than usual[50] and vague rumblings from the north alerted most people to the possibility of an Allied landing, but BBC radio broadcasts at 0630, 0730 and 0830 hours gave no news of an invasion and merely stated that towns and villages within 35km of the coast should be evacuated. Then, at around 0900 hours, captured Americans paratroopers were seen being brought into the city and half an hour later a BBC broadcast confirmed that the invasion had started and that liberation was at hand. This coincided with the appearance of notices, signed by the German Town Commandant, ordering everyone to stay indoors and keep off the roads. General Marcks' LXXXIV Corps Headquarters, which was located in the northern part of the city, moved out during the morning to a seminary at Agneaux, about 5km to the west.

The first air raid took place at about 0930 hours when the power station was attacked by American medium bombers, cutting electricity supplies and telephone communications. Many people decided, regardless of German instructions, that it was time to leave and started packing. The need to do so was stressed by another BBC broadcast at 1430 hours.

The rest of the afternoon passed peacefully, but at about 1730 hours a raid by up to fifteen Allied aircraft severely damaged the railway station, tearing up lines, setting fire to wagons and damaging a train. Surprisingly there were no casualties other than a man who had been hiding in one of the wagons. Mercifully the hospital, next to the station, survived unscathed and at 1800 hours the German Town Commandant gave permission for the building to be evacuated.

The main air raid on the city came at 2100 hours. This was followed by another at 2300 hours and a third between 0130 and 0200 hours on the 7th.

The Town Hall, Police Headquarters, Public Record Office, Banque de France, hospital, prison, electricity generating plant – all were hit and damaged to a greater or lesser extent. Whole streets were devastated and many people were trapped in the cellars where they had taken shelter. Fire added to the horror and before long the whole of the western sector of the city was ablaze. The flames were fanned by a strong wind from the south-west and the fire brigade found itself powerless to intervene since water supplies had been disrupted and their water tower destroyed. The worst single incident of the night occurred at the Police Headquarters where twenty-two people, policemen and members of their families, were killed or wounded.

It is estimated that 77% of St Lô had been destroyed by dawn on 7 June. It is impossible to determine the total number of civilian casualties resulting from the raids. The city memorial in the cemetery says 132; however, sometimes 'bones' or 'unknown', or a 'family' are listed, without specific numbers being given. It is also clear that the list is incomplete since some people were burned beyond recognition, some were totally pulverised and others may have been simply passing through the town at that time or had taken refuge there from seemingly more vulnerable places on the coast. The German casualties suffered by the garrison staff are unknown but were certainly insignificant.

Just four days before the invasion, the British Deputy Supreme Commander, Air Chief Marshal Sir Arthur Tedder, had expressed serious misgivings about the morality of air raids on French towns and cities. Without Eisenhower's authority, he told Leigh-Mallory, CinC Allied Air Forces, that he could not approve a programme that was certain to lead to many civilian casualties and the destruction of many historic buildings. The British War Cabinet had earlier expressed similar concerns in relation to the pre-invasion air offensive against the French railway system and Churchill had also appealed to Roosevelt against the bombing programme outlined by the Allied planners. Nevertheless, on 11 April 1944, Roosevelt had replied:

> I share fully with you your distress at the loss of life among the French population incident to our air preparations for OVERLORD. However regrettable the attendant loss of civilian lives is, I am not prepared to impose from this distance any restriction on military action by the responsible commanders that in their opinion might militate against the success of OVERLORD or cause additional loss of life to our Allied forces of invasion.

Churchill had no choice other than to acquiesce and Tedder's intervention was quickly rejected. The minutes of the Air Support Conference held on the afternoon of 4 June state:

The Supreme Commander very emphatically approved the planned bombing of French communications centres and strongly deprecated any suggestion that we should hold off from so vital a task from reluctance to cause civilian casualties.[51]

NOTES

1. Bradley, *A Soldier's Story*, p. 265.
2. Low tide was 0525 hrs, first light 0516 hours, sunrise 0558 hrs, the next high tide due at 1100 hrs, sunset at 2207 and last light at 2248 hrs.
3. Battle Summary – No. 39, Operation Neptune, Landings in Normandy June 1944, Historical Section, Naval Staff, Admiralty, Jun 47, p. 35.
4. The Bn providing dedicated close support for 116 Inf Regt.
5. Harrison, *Cross Channel Attack*, pp. 309–13.
6. According to RAF Bomber Command War Diaries, a total of 1,012 aircraft attacked the Normandy coastal batteries. Only three aircraft were lost.
7. Bradley, op. cit., p. 267.
8. Ibid., p. 271.
9. The British ENIGMA code-breaking centre.
10. Smith, *Action This Day*, p. 282.
11. Bradley, op. cit., p. 268. Of 446 Liberators despatched, 329 attacked between 0555 and 0615 hrs.
12. Remarkably only sixteen men were recorded as dead or missing.
13. 743 Tk Bn AAR dated 20 Jul 44.
14. Now disappeared and replaced with rocks.
15. The Special Engr Task Force as a whole suffered a total of 41% casualties. Fifteen officers & men received DSCs for their actions on this day.
16. CMH Pub 100-11, *Omaha Beachhead*, p. 47.
17. Ibid., p. 49.
18. Most of these niches have been filled by cliff erosion.
19. CMH Pub 100-11, pp. 50–1.
20. The AAR of the 116 Regt claims that three-quarters of its SCR 300 radios, upon which the bulk of its communications depended, were either destroyed by enemy fire or ruined by sea water.
21. Long since demolished.
22. CMH Pub 100-11, pp. 51–2.
23. Two coys 2 Ranger Bn & six coys 5 Ranger Bn.
24. CMH Pub 100-11, p. 57.
25. Ibid., p. 58.
26. Held by scattered elements of 916 Inf Regt.
27. Today this track is tarmac and easily driveable.
28. CMH Pub 100-11, p. 94.
29. Ibid., p. 97.
30. Ibid., p. 104.
31. Ibid., p. 98.
32. Ibid., p.101.
33. 158 RAF personnel were landed. They lost eight killed, thirty-five wounded & twenty-eight of their thirty-five vehicles – Hastings, *Overlord*, p. 113.
34. CMH Pub 100-11, p. 56.
35. Bradley, op. cit., pp. 271–2.
36. There is a memorial to the Squad at the location.

37. 743 Tk Bn AAR dated 20 Jul 44.
38. CMH Pub 100-11, p. 106 says five; Harrison, *Cross Channel Attack*, pp. 309–13 says three.
39. According to French & US sources.
40. CMH Pub 100-11, p. 109.
41. 29 Inf Div AAR dated 23 Jul 44. These figures are the best available but may well be slightly exaggerated since some of the missing were later found to be POWs and others reappeared with their units.
42. Extract from 352 Inf Div Telephone Diary – MS # B-388.
43. Ziegelmann. MS # B-432.
44. 441 Ost Bn.
45. The 1st Coy with fourteen Marder 38s was detached to 916 Regt in the Formigny area.
46. According to Zetterling, *Normandy 1944*, p. 278, the Bn had five companies with sixty-two MGs, six 80mm mors, two a/tk guns, two howitzers & two flame throwers.
47. Ziegelmann, MS # B-432.
48. Zetterling, op. cit., p. 280.
49. Details taken mainly from Maurice Lantier's *Saint-Lô au bûcher*, 1984.
50. According to RAF Bomber Command War Diaries, 1,065 aircraft dropped 3,488 tons of bombs on nine cities behind the invasion beaches, including St Lô and Caen, on 6/7 June. Eleven aircraft were lost.
51. Air 41/24: Air Historical Branch (AHB) Narrative: *The Liberation of Europe*, Vol. I., pp.183–4.

CHAPTER IX

D-Day on SWORD – the Reality

Author's Note

To assist the reader in following and understanding the complex sequence of events in the 3rd Division's sector on D-Day, a simple time chart is provided at Appendix K. Readers who may later visit the area should be aware that nearly all the villages have modern satellite housing estates on their outskirts. This often gives a false impression of their WWII size. Only stone-built houses are likely to be original.

The First Wave

The ships carrying the leading Assault Group of the Iron Division (8 Infantry Brigade Group) sailed at 0945 hours on 5 June from Spithead (between Portsmouth and the Isle of Wight). They bore the 3rd Division insignia of black and red triangles on their bows and funnels. As they passed HMS *Largs*, the Task Force Headquarters ship carrying Rear

Admiral Talbot, the Task Force commander and Major General Tom Rennie, the Divisional commander, she hoisted a signal spelling out the words: 'Good luck: Drive on!'. The Intermediate Group (185 Infantry Brigade Group) followed at 1215 hours from Newhaven and the Reserve Group (9 Infantry Brigade Group), from Spithead, at 1900 hours. In the case of the Assault Group, the Battalion Headquarters and two assault Companies of the South Lancs and the two follow-up Companies of the East Yorks were loaded on to the *Empire Battleaxe*. The Headquarters of the East Yorks with its two assault Companies and the two follow-up Companies of the South Lancs sailed in HMS *Glenearn*. This seemingly complicated arrangement ensured, however, that if one of the transports was sunk during the passage across the Channel, the other could still carry out the planned landings – the follow-up Companies having also been trained in the assault role.

For most of the soldiers the crossing was extremely unpleasant with winds varying from Force 3 to Force 5[1] and a sea swell of five to six feet. Despite the issue of sea-sickness pills many were ill and even the drone of friendly aircraft overhead, some carrying bombs and others the para-troopers who would secure their eastern flank[2], did little to quell their fear or raise their spirits. As the commander of A Squadron of the 13/18 H put it later: 'I think that all of us looked forward to being on dry land – wherever it might be!'. Another officer wrote: 'D-Day was our horizon and rightly or wrongly we didn't look much beyond it.' One of the soldiers' greatest worries was that their ship or landing craft might be hit and sunk. They knew that if this happened they had little chance of being picked up in the dark; they also knew that if their assault landing craft was hit and sunk as it made the final run-in to the shore no one was authorised to stop and pick up survivors. But at least they were now fully aware of their mission. Once the time and date of the landing had been confirmed, sealed orders were opened and everyone briefed on enemy dispositions, defences and beach obstacles. Maps with real rather than mock names were issued and for the first time all learned exactly where they were to land; in fact maps were in such abundance that it became a problem to know how to carry them.

The naval bombardment of SWORD beach by two battleships, a monitor, five cruisers and a gunboat[3], began at 0510 hours on D-Day and shortly afterwards aircraft laid a heavy smoke screen to shield the invasion force from the German coastal artillery batteries in Le Havre. Nevertheless, three enemy torpedo boats took advantage of this cover and carried out a daring attack beginning at 0515 hours during which the Norwegian destroyer, the *Svenner*, was hit and sunk. The men of the assault Battalions 'could see the bows . . . protruding almost vertically above the water' which did little for their morale. Fortunately, two other torpedoes passed between the battleships *Warspite* and *Ramilles* and another narrowly missed the Task Force Headquarters ship. The German boats were engaged but escaped through the smoke screen.

The tides affecting QUEEN beach dictated that H-Hour should be an hour later than for OMAHA – at 0725 hours. Even so this would still allow the engineers just sufficient time to clear the beach obstacles before they became submerged, whilst minimising the width of open sand to be crossed by the leading infantry Companies. At 0530 hours the men of those Companies, A and C of the South Lancs and A and B of the East Yorks, left the *Empire Battleaxe* and HMS *Glenearn* and began to clamber into their assault craft. They still had to suffer a further agonising wait whilst the LCAs went into a holding pattern before beginning their uncomfortable and, for many, terrifying 11km journey to the beach. The following account by the commanding officer of the East Yorks of these last moments before H-Hour would hardly have been echoed by many of his men:

> Battalion Headquarters' and each Company Headquarters' assault landing craft bore the black flag and white rose [of Yorkshire], the flags having been made for us by the ladies of Waterlooville Congregational Church . . . Battalion Headquarters' bugler sounded the 'Salute' as we bore away from the *Glenearn* and our own silver bugle [presented to the Captain of *Glenearn*] soon returned the compliment. The clear notes sounded very sweetly over the cool morning air. Our bugle sounded again as we passed our Divisional Headquarters ship and we saw senior officers on the bridge return the salute. Those were rather moving moments – the soldier's thank you to the sailor who had borne him faithfully to his goal.[4]

Whilst this was happening the LCTs carrying the DD tanks of A and B Squadrons of the 13/18 H and the thirty-four AVREs of the 5 ARRE continued their slow progress towards QUEEN beach. The forty DD tanks were due to be launched 7,000 yards from the shore but the waves were still running high and both the responsible naval commander and Brigadier Prior-Palmer, the commander of 27 Armoured Brigade, agreed that conditions were generally unsuitable for the tanks to swim. The order 'Floater 5000' was finally given for a launch at 5,000 yards and at 0615 hours, as thirteen destroyers joined in the naval bombardment, the DD tanks entered the water. The leading tank of B Squadron tore its canvas and was unable to launch and this blocked the way for the four tanks behind it. These five tanks came ashore directly on to the beach from their LCT when there was sufficient space at about 0810 hours. Another tank could not be launched because of a damaged ramp door and it was carried back to England. This left thirty-four; of these one from A Squadron failed to engage its propeller and was immediately overcome by the waves and sank, and two were rammed by overtaking LCTs carrying AVREs and also sank. As a corporal in command of one of the DD tanks, Pat Hennessey, wrote later: 'We were buffeted about unmercifully. . . Sea sickness was now forgotten. It took over an hour of hard work to reach the shore and it was a miracle that most of us did.'

At 0650 hours the seventy-two guns of the Division's artillery on eighteen LCTs opened fire at a range of about 10,000 yards in what was called a 'run-in-shoot'. Aimed at the foreshore and the buildings immediately behind it, some 6,500 rounds were fired in just over thirty minutes before the LCTs turned away to await their designated landing times. Following the artillery LCTs were five rocket-firing LCTs tasked with opening fire at 0715 hours. One officer in 8 Brigade wrote later:

> The comprehensive fire plan provided for battleships, cruisers and destroyers, together with heavy and medium bombers and fighter bombers (both RAF and USAAF), to attack known coast defence batteries[5], beach defences and headquarters and centres of communications before H-Hour and after. All these were adding to the deafening noise of the guns of the Division and its supporting craft. The coast disappeared under a cloud of smoke and explosions making it difficult to pick out landmarks until within a short distance of the beach.[6]

Not surprisingly the weight of fire landing in the beach area initially subdued and stunned the German defenders, but as the assault craft and DD tanks neared the shore and the bombardment lifted, the enemy began to react. As in the OMAHA sector the naval and air bombardments had in fact done little damage to the German concrete emplacements and soon, in addition to rifle and machine-gun fire, artillery and mortar rounds were falling amongst the invaders. Brigadier K P Smith of 185 Brigade wrote later that, 'The multi-rocket launching craft were a dismal failure, their rockets falling short of the shore and sinking some of our own craft'.[7]

The predicted speed of 4½ knots for the DD tanks was soon reduced to 3 by the heavy swell and the LCTs carrying the flail tanks, specialist engineer vehicles and assault teams quickly overtook them and landed first, just before 0725 hours (H-Hour). The thirty-one remaining DDs came in virtually with, rather than in front of, the infantry a few minutes later. They then sat, 'hull down' (only the turret above the water line) in the surf 'shooting with all their weapons at everything which caught the eye'.[8] The 13/18 H subsequently claimed to have destroyed 'three or four 75mm guns, four or five 50mm and numerous 20mm guns'.[9] According to the Official British History six DDs were knocked out by enemy fire in the surf and four a short time later.[10] According to the History of the 13/18 H :

> a number were subsequently overcome by the breakers and the rapidly

rising tide which swamped their engines. These tanks, however, remained in action with flooded turrets and the crews baled out when the guns themselves were almost awash. Their crews covered the remaining 200 or 300 yards of sea to the beach in their rubber dinghies.

And an assessment carried out soon after the landing by Captain Denny of A Squadron, whose own tank had been rammed and sunk by an LCT, concluded that nine Shermans in his Squadron had been swamped by waves. Despite the escape apparatus the rest of his crew were wearing they did not survive.

(Maps 9 and 10)

QUEEN beach was divided into two sectors codenamed QUEEN RED and QUEEN WHITE. Located in QUEEN RED but on the boundary with QUEEN WHITE was strongpoint COD.[11] This proved to be the biggest problem for Brigadier 'Copper' Cass's 8 Brigade in the first three hours of the landings and both assault Battalions were to be involved in its neutralisation. 300m wide and nearly 100m deep, COD was surrounded by wire and comprised twenty separate resistance nests with inter-connecting trenches. It contained one 75mm, one 37mm and two 50mm guns, three 80mm mortars and five posts each equipped with two or three machine-guns.

Arriving as they did a few minutes before the DD tanks and infantry, the flails and AVREs found themselves without the close support they needed for their task of clearing eight lanes through the beach obstacles and mines. Nine of the ten LCTs launched their charges, those of 79 Engineer Squadron on QUEEN RED and those of 77 Squadron on QUEEN WHITE. The tenth, carrying the commanding officer of 5 ARRE, Lieutenant Colonel Cocks, successfully launched the first flail tank but the second was hit by an anti-tank round which jammed the ramp door. The LCT was then hit by a mortar round that detonated its bangalore torpedoes. The two tanks behind were disabled and Cocks and two engineers killed; seven others were wounded. With one complete gapping team out of action the other seven, comprising thirteen flails of A and C Squadrons of the 22nd Dragoons and seventeen AVREs of 5 ARRE, went to work under fire from mortars, artillery and in some cases direct machine-gun fire from strongpoint COD. Three teams operated on QUEEN WHITE and four on QUEEN RED.

Some idea of what it was like for the officers and men of 5 ARRE can be gauged from the following extracts from *The Story of the 79th Armoured Division*:

On the right [QUEEN WHITE] No. 1 team beached correctly at a point surmounted by high sand dunes. Crabs flailed up the beach and over the dunes unaided, although in the face of fierce fire, especially from snipers. . . The first AVRE was hit repeatedly and drowned. . . The first Crab [of No. 2 team] (Sergeant Smyth) headed straight for a gun firing on the troop to his left and ran it over; the Crabs then flailed perfectly until one blew a track on mines. It was bypassed and a small box girder [SBG] bridge laid over the gun position by Sergeant Myhil who was later killed. . . No. 3 team's craft grounded on top of a drowned DD tank. The Crabs successfully completed a lane which was then carpeted [with logs]. . . An Assault crew under Sergeant Barclay did a fine job of work, disarming sixty-four Tellers [mines] and thirty-seven shells before last light. A good half of these were dealt with by Sapper [engineer] Glancy climbing each time to the top of 10-feet stakes.

[On QUEEN RED] No. 2 team landed on time and Crabs began their work but both were knocked out. The SBG bridge fell prematurely when the bomb release was hit. Captain Desanges dismounted and, with the aid of Sappers Price and Darington, placed charges against the dune. Small arms fire killed him but Lieutenant Nicholson just succeeded in lighting the fuse before he too was hit and wounded. By this time all the AVREs has been 'scuppered' and the bulldozer completed the gap. . . No. 3 team fared slightly better. The first Crab (Sergeant Wood, 22nd Dragoons) was disabled by gunfire but he silenced his opponent and shot the infantry into the enemy position. The second Crab started to flail but was knocked out and the lane completed by hand by dismounted assault Sappers. An SBG bridge was launched but soon blocked by a DD tank which fell off the side of it. A second gap was made by the bulldozer. A log carpet was laid but another DD tank struck a mine and the Squadron [79 Engineer Squadron] commander, Major Hanson, and another officer, Lieutenant Hutchinson, were compelled to clear a track round it by hand. No. 4 team beached to schedule and Crabs cleared up to the low dunes. Then one was hit four times by an 88mm gun and stopped. This gun was knocked out by a Crab of No. 1 team, Lieutenant Boal, 22nd Dragoons, and the second Crab was able to complete the lane.[12]

Exact casualty figures are difficult to establish but it is certain that in the first hours of D-Day the 22nd Dragoons lost eight flail tanks, two on QUEEN WHITE and six on QUEEN RED, and had twenty men killed or wounded.[13] 77 and 79 Engineer Squadrons lost nine AVREs and three of their eight bulldozers. Their share of the 117 casualties[14] suffered by 5 ARRE on SWORD and JUNO beaches on D-Day is unknown. Two Distinguished Service Orders (DSOs), four Military Crosses (MCs) and three Military Medals (MMs) were awarded to members of these two Engineer Squadrons for their actions on this day.

(Maps 7 & 9)

QUEEN RED

The East Yorks had the most extensive mission in 8 Brigade. They were to cooperate with the South Lancs in the capture of strongpoint COD, go on to capture strongpoints SOLE and DAIMLER, clear St Aubin-d'Arquenay and finally take over responsibility for the canal and river bridges between Bénouville and Ranville from troops of the 6th Airborne Division.[15] Its leading assault Companies, A and B, came under intense mortar and machine-gun fire as they approached the shore but their LCAs beached at full speed (4 knots) and although four were damaged by enemy fire, casualties were surprisingly light – just six infantrymen. They were supported by an assault demolition team from 16 Field Engineer Company and DD tanks of Major Rugge-Price's B Squadron of the 13/18 H.

Major 'Banger' King's A Company had the mission of subduing the eastern part of COD. Writing a month after the event, King[16] described how his Company, in spite of murderous fire, cleared a gap of about 200m wide in the German defences and mopped up various machine-gun nests and a 50mm gun. While his Company was doing this, his comrades in the South Lancs, as we shall hear shortly, were clearing the western part of this vital strongpoint and B Company under Major Sheath was clearing other defensive positions covering QUEEN RED.

The partial neutralisation of COD paved the way for Lieutenant Colonel Robert Dawson's No. 4 Commando and Nos. 1 and 8 Free French Commando Troops under Commandant Philippe Kieffer[17] to land at 0755 hours. Their fourteen LCAs were on time but unfortunately ahead of those of the East Yorks follow-up Companies and Lieutenant Colonel Hutchinson with his Tactical Headquarters – they came in fifteen minutes after their designated time, at 0805 hours. This caused some confusion in the battle plan but the Commandos, despite suffering some forty casualties while disembarking and crossing the beach, soon moved off to the east to clear the Casino strongpoint at Riva Bella and the port of Ouistreham (Map 10). Dawson was amongst the seriously wounded and he apparently asked Major Hanson, the commander of 79 Engineer Squadron, to take over.[18] D Company of the East Yorks lost some of its cohesion when a mortar round falling near its Headquarters group soon after landing killed the commander, Major Barber.

By now the tide was rising quickly and many of the wounded were struggling to reach the safety of the shoreline. Even so, descriptions of very heavy casualties in the East Yorks, with emotional phrases such as 'bodies stacked like cordwood' and 'a scene of utter destruction . . . dead comrades floating face down in the tide, others in grotesque positions'

EAGLES AND BULLDOGS IN NORMANDY, 1944

would seem to be exaggerated and have been discounted by others who landed at the same time. The commanding officer of the Battalion, Lieutenant Colonel Hutchinson, went out of his way to say that he saw no 'piles of dead'.

QUEEN WHITE

The infantrymen of A and C Companies of the South Lancs and an assault demolition team of 16 Field Engineer Company came ashore on QUEEN WHITE in knee-deep water only a few minutes behind the flails of Major Wallace's A Squadron 22nd Dragoons and the AVREs of 77 Engineer Squadron and virtually with the DD tanks of Major Wormald's A Squadron of the 13/18 H.

The South Lancs' mission was to assist in the reduction of strongpoint COD, secure the only major road leading south from the beachhead, capture Hermanville-sur-Mer and clear the enemy in Lion-sur-Mer. This latter task was to enable 41 Commando, due to land later, to neutralise strongpoint TROUT in the western part of the resort and then link up with No. 48 Commando operating under Canadian command from JUNO beach. The Battalion was fortunate in that it suffered no casualties during its actual disembarkation.

Major 'Spook' Harward's A Company, supported by the remaining six DD tanks of A Squadron 13/18 H, was given the responsibility of clearing the enemy on the right flank in Lion-sur-Mer. Two of his Platoons landed more or less in the right place, on the west side of QUEEN WHITE, although one of the Platoon commanders was killed whilst crossing the beach, but the other Platoon and Harward's Headquarters were swept to the east and landed practically under the western end of strongpoint COD. Harward himself was mortally wounded after igniting the fuse of three bangalore torpedoes being used to breach the 2.5m-high and 3.5m-wide wire fence covering the exit to the beach, and the Platoon with him only got through after an AVRE forced a breach, losing a track in the process. The Platoon commander, Lieutenant Eddie Jones, then led his men in an attack on a large house on the left of the exit. The garrison, mainly Russians and Poles, quickly surrendered and were locked up in a cellar. Jones then advanced to the coast road where he met up with Lieutenant Bob Pearce and his Platoon and the joint force then set off with the tanks to clear the buildings on the outskirts of Lion-sur-Mer.

Meanwhile Major Eric Johnson's C Company had crossed the beach with only light casualties and had begun its assault on the western part of strongpoint COD.

Some twenty-five minutes later the follow-up Companies, B and D, and Lieutenant Colonel Richard Burbury's Battalion Headquarters disembarked. They should have come ashore behind A Company but hit the

70

beach opposite the west end of COD and immediately suffered casualties. B Company set about helping C Company deal with COD, but its commander, Major Harrison, was killed whilst still on the beach and the commander of D Company, Major Eggeling, was wounded. The Battalion commander, who was carrying a Regimental flag in a way reminiscent of 18th-century warfare to indicate his position to his men, was killed soon afterwards by a sniper's bullet. His second-in-command, Major Jack Stone, took over. Lieutenant Bob Bell-Walker assumed command of B Company and a successful attack was launched against the western part of COD. As we have already heard, A Company of the East Yorks was attacking the eastern part of the strongpoint at about the same time. Lieutenant Bell-Walker was killed after lobbing a grenade through the gun port of one of the concrete pillboxes. One officer in the South Lancs said later:

> A good deal of confused fighting followed with platoons and sections taking on their own targets. There were many acts of individual heroism. The orders were that as soon as the beach task had been completed, the Battalion should rendezvous at Hermanville. The silencing of the concrete pillbox at the western end of COD by Bob Bell-Walker enabled Battalion Headquarters to work round to the right and begin the move towards Hermanville. The confused fighting on the beach lasted for a considerable time. The anti-tank platoon coming in at H+30 even had their share, with a corporal bringing one of the six-pounders into action on the sand to deal effectively with a machine-gun post.[19]

Nevertheless, at about 0830 hours, while A Company and the six tanks of A Squadron 13/18 H continued their move into Lion-sur-Mer, and B Company continued to deal with COD, the main body of the South Lancs headed inland to Hermanville-sur-Mer.

The Second Wave

(Maps 3 & 9)

Although four vehicle exits from QUEEN WHITE had been achieved by 0830 hours, the situation on QUEEN RED was very different. As we have heard, casualties amongst the flail tanks, five of which had been knocked out and a sixth damaged[20], meant that much of the mine clearance there had to be carried out by hand. The first vehicle gap was finally cleared using a bulldozer at about 0900 hours and two more by 0915. Before that, vehicles had been forced to move laterally along RED beach to the QUEEN WHITE exits and thence to the Hermanville-sur-Mer road which was the only way across the flooded and marshy ground behind the sand dunes. Although this saturated area was clearly shown on the official British maps, the fact that it was impassable for vehicles, including tanks, does not seem to have been fully taken into account by the planners.

At about 0805 hours thirteen more LCTs started to disembark their loads on QUEEN RED and WHITE. Three were carrying the tanks of C Squadron 13/18 H and the remainder the 6-pounder anti-tank guns and 3-inch mortars of the assault infantry Battalions, a medium machine-gun company of the Middlesex and the priority vehicles of 8 Infantry Brigade. This disembarkation took nearly an hour during which a mine damaged one LCT and several were hit by shell or mortar fire. The tanks moved off through an exit on QUEEN WHITE to an assembly area where they were to 'marry up' with Lieutenant Colonel Dick Goodwin's Suffolks. The latter had started coming ashore at 0820 hours astride the junction between QUEEN RED and QUEEN WHITE. Nine craft were damaged in the process and their naval crews suffered five killed and three wounded. The Suffolks were more fortunate losing only three men. A further naval casualty, however, was Captain Llewellyn, the Naval Forward Bombardment Officer attached to the Battalion. He and his entire party had been killed when a shell hit the LCA in which they were travelling. Goodwin wrote later: '[Llewellyn] controlled the fire of my naval support for the day – a 6-inch cruiser and a destroyer – so for that day's operations I was without that support.'[21]

The Suffolks moved quickly to an assembly area which they had expected to be in a wood about 800m from the beach; however, on arrival the wood was found to have been cut down to provide material for beach obstacles and the Battalion had to move on to a nearby apple orchard where, shortly after 0900 hours, it began 'marrying up' with its assigned tanks, a detachment of 246 Field Engineer Squadron and a machine-gun platoon of A Company of the Middlesex. The whole group then prepared for its multiple tasks of clearing Colleville-sur-Orne (now called Colleville-Montgomery[22]), strongpoints MORRIS and HILLMAN, and then consolidating on the Périers ridge. Goodwin held an 'Orders Group' in which he confirmed his previous orders and then moved off to meet the acting commanding officer of the South Lancs, Major Jack Stone, in Hermanville-sur-Mer. The village had been reported clear of enemy at 0900 hours. Stone's Battalion Headquarters was set up near the church and two of his Companies were dug in around the crossroads south of the village. The local population had welcomed them with flowers and calvados. A Company was continuing its move into Lion-sur-Mer and B Company was still involved in clearing up COD and other beach defences.

It was not in the plan for the South Lancs, who had already lost 107 officers and men killed or wounded in the beach-clearing operation, to move beyond Hermanville-sur-Mer. Their orders clearly stated that after capturing the village they were to 'consolidate and form the right flank of the Brigade beachhead'.[23] No attempt was made therefore to cross the Cresserons–Colleville-sur-Orne road and continue the advance to the Périers ridge which lay a mere 2km farther on to the south.

In the meantime, the self-propelled guns of 76 Field Artillery Regiment had disembarked on QUEEN RED at 0840 hours. Three of the twenty-four guns were lost when a shell hit one of the LCTs before beaching, but the Regiment deployed successfully on the beach and went into action in support of those ashore. At about the same time twelve more craft landed Lord Lovat's 1st Special Service Commando Brigade Headquarters and No. 6 Commando on QUEEN RED and No. 41 Commando a little farther to the west in front of COD. The latter suffered twenty-five killed and wounded to fire from elements of the strongpoint that were still holding out. It will be remembered that No. 6 Commando had the task of relieving the paratroopers holding the bridges across the Caen canal and Orne river[24] and No. 41 Commando, after linking up with A Company of the South Lancs in Lion-sur-Mer, had the mission of neutralising strongpoint TROUT on the western outskirts of that small resort.

The First Moves Inland

(Map 3)

At 0910 hours Nos. 3 and 45 Commandos landed and followed Lord Lovat's group to a forming up position farther inland. They were accompanied by another twenty-four self-propelled guns of 33 Field Artillery Regiment which immediately went into action beside those of 76 Field Regiment on the beach. The Commandos were complete in their assembly area by 0940 hours and Brigadier Lord Lovat immediately set off with the main group towards Colleville-sur-Orne, whilst No. 41 Commando headed for Lion-sur-Mer to meet up with A Company of the South Lancs. No. 4 Commando with the two Free French Commando Troops[25] moved east along the parallel roads leading to Ouistreham (Map 10). On the way one of the Free French Troops, with help by fire from one of the four Centaur tanks of the 5th RM (Independent) Battery[26] directed by Commandant Kieffer, took the strongpoint built on the foundations of the demolished casino at Riva Bella.[27] Two 20mm guns were knocked out in the process.[28] Later in the day, between 1530 and 1630 hours, No. 4 Commando, with ten AVREs of 79 Engineer Squadron, attacked the concrete bunkers defending the lock gates and Caen canal bridge farther east in Ouistreham. These were thought to contain four 155mm guns, but after fierce fighting during which fifty-seven prisoners were taken, the Commandos found only dummy guns made of old telegraph poles – the 155mm guns were in fact located near St Aubin-d'Arquenay. The

Germans had blown the eastern span of the canal bridge but the Royal Engineers successfully defused the demolition charges on the lock gates.

In the meantime, Brigadier Copper Cass[29], the commander of 8 Infantry Brigade, had come ashore just after 0945 hours and set up his Tactical Headquarters in Hermanville-sur-Mer. Fifteen minutes later C Company of the Suffolks under Major Charles Boycott and a Troop of C Squadron of the 13/18 H reported Colleville-sur-Orne clear of enemy. The way south-east was thus prepared for Lovat and his Commandos. The tank Troop leader, Lieutenant Eric Smith, later described the Colleville-sur-Orne clearing operation:

> Two tanks worked through the village, street by street, with the infantry in the approved manner, while two more tanks nosed through the surrounding orchards. . . We had no occasion to fire a shot. Much to our surprise the Boche had cleared out. I recall . . . the bewildered and haunted expressions of the inhabitants, who must have thought that their houses would be completely destroyed and probably doubted our ability to remain in Normandy for any length of time.[30]

Houses in the village had in fact been used as messes by German officers from strongpoint HILLMAN and the nearby 1716th Artillery Head-quarters at Point 61.

No. 6 Commando and five tanks from B Squadron 13/18 H reached Colleville-sur-Orne soon after the Suffolks but, just after 1030 hours as the Commandos continued their advance up the hill to the south-east, they came under fire from two pillboxes.[31] These were quickly cleared and Lovat and his Commandos were able to move on through St Aubin-d'Arquenay to the bridges across the Caen canal and the Orne river which they reached at 1330 hours. It is interesting to note that according to the History of the 13/18 H their tanks ended up with Lord Lovat by mistake:

> 1st Troop turned left [on reaching the coast road] and disappeared towards Ouistreham, where it became involved with the Commandos under Lord Lovat. All efforts to recall it failed. It eventually reached the bridge over the Orne and was not rallied till the evening [by which time two of the five tanks had been knocked out].[32]

While Lovat's Commandos moved on towards St Aubin-d'Arquenay, B Company of the Suffolks, with a breaching platoon from D Company, prepared to take on strongpoint MORRIS. This comprised four 100mm guns housed in three 2m-thick concrete bunkers (the fourth was still under construction), defended by one light anti-aircraft gun and two machine-guns. The strongpoint had been bombed in May and on 1 and 2 June, attacked by six US B-17s at H-Hour on D-Day and subjected to a bombardment by the six-inch guns of HMS *Dragon* during the morning. It was perhaps not altogether surprising therefore that at midday, when the B Company commander, Major McCaffrey, decided to blow the outer wire before calling for a planned artillery concentration, a white flag appeared and sixty-seven Germans emerged with their hands up. The way was thus cleared for the assault on strongpoint HILLMAN.

On the right flank of QUEEN beach things did not go so well for the Commandos. At 1000 hours, just as the East Yorks reported COD clear of enemy[33], part of the 3rd Battalion of the 736th Grenadier Regiment, with four 100mm howitzers of the 'Graf Waldersee' Battery of the 1716th Artillery Regiment, successfully counter-attacked from Cresserons towards Lion-sur-Mer. The attack reached the area of the church in Lion and two howitzers and some Grenadiers even got as far as the beach where it is said they were able to open fire on incoming landing craft. A quick counter-attack by A Company of the South Lancs soon forced them to withdraw, but a further move to clear the buildings on the south-west edge of the town resulted in a number of casualties, mainly from enemy mortars, including Lieutenant Pearce, the acting Company commander. While all this was going on two of the Commando Troops with three AVREs under command, had been directed against the elegant Château on the western edge of the town and the third Commando Troop had moved against strongpoint TROUT. Before the AVREs could get within range of TROUT to fire their petards, however, all three were knocked out. The Troop commander, Captain McLellan, was killed. By 1130 hours the situation had reached stalemate with the Commandos having exhausted all their mortar ammunition against TROUT. The German force that had carried out the counter-attack 'disengaged itself and remained in position south of Lion'[34] and the Commandos were left holding Lion-sur-Mer but were unable to advance any farther. At 1500 hours the Commandos were placed under Brigadier Cass's command and at 1600 hours A Company of the South Lancs, now under the command of Lieutenant Eddie Jones, was recalled to join its parent Battalion in Hermanville-sur-Mer.

The Third Wave

Just before 1000 hours Brigadier K P Smith's 185 Infantry Brigade started coming ashore on QUEEN beach. Recall that this was the Brigade tasked with driving hard for the city of Caen. By 1100 hours its three infantry Battalions, the Warwicks, Norfolks and KSLI, were complete in their assembly area astride Hermanville-sur-Mer, waiting for the tanks of Lieutenant Colonel Jim Eadie's Staffordshire Yeomanry to join them for the push inland. Two companies of the Warwicks came under fairly accurate machine-gun fire from the direction of Cresserons but otherwise all seemed well for the thrust south. At 1105 hours Brigadier 'Kipper'

Smith established his Tactical Headquarters beside the gates of the Hôtel de Ville in Hermanville-sur-Mer and called an 'Orders Group' for midday. The fact that everyone already knew what they were required to do and that the landing had gone better than expected made no difference – this was the time-honoured system in the British Army in 1944 and an hour was to be wasted. Smith, who was later described as 'a short, fierce little man who suffered from the inability of his liver to get into his stride before 1100 hours', had either forgotten the I Corps Operation Order No. 1 dated 5 May, or chose to ignore it. It read:

> The task of the assaulting divisions is to break through the coastal defences and advance some ten miles inland on D-Day. Great speed and boldness will be required to achieve this. . . As soon as the beach defences have been penetrated therefore, not a moment must be lost in beginning the advance inland.

While the leading assault units had been fighting their way off the beaches, the sea conditions behind them were making life extremely difficult for the men of 629 Field Engineer (Beach Clearance) Company and the Royal Navy's Landing Craft Obstruction Clearance Unit. They were tasked with clearing paths through the obstacles both above and below the water line.[35] Furthermore the delays in clearing the vehicle exits had caused serious congestion on a beach that was rapidly decreasing in size owing to the incoming tide and where, in addition to the vehicles waiting to move inland, there were nearly fifty self-propelled guns of 33 and 76 Field Artillery Regiments. High tide was due at midday and the strong wind had driven the water to within ten metres of the sand dunes. It was not long before the guns were standing in several feet of surf. Inevitably the congestion caused delays in unloading the tanks of the Staffordshire Yeomanry and to compound the problem just after 1100 hours, when it was estimated that it would take two hours to clear the backlog of vehicles, QUEEN RED was closed. The War Diary of the Yeomanry records that there seemed to be no proper organisation or traffic control, with the result that the majority of the tanks were stationary for the best part of an hour and that even after leaving the beach vehicles remained head to tail for long periods. Major Dunn of 7 Field Artillery Regiment, whose self-propelled guns were scheduled to land ten minutes after the tanks, described the LCTs on the beach as like 'a pack of hounds with their noses in a trough'; and Lieutenant Commander Mackie Miller of the Royal Navy, who commanded a Squadron of LCTs carrying part of 185 Brigade and who won a Distinguished Service Cross on D-Day, later remembered:

> Unfortunately, in our rehearsals, we had never had a couple of

destroyers dashing across our bows at the last moment, at full speed, with all guns firing and the shells from an enemy battery [le Havre – Map 1] falling all round them, nor had we encountered wrecked and burning landing craft in our path. . . We were doing fourteen knots and were less than 30 feet apart, so the slightest failure of nerve on the part of one would have meant an unholy crash for all. . . The next moment we were in among the mines and struggling to find a patch of bare sand on which to beach. Fortunately the mines were land mines tied to the top of underwater stakes and too small to stop a 300-ton landing craft. . . After dodging a few sunken tanks, we ground our way through the wreck of an assault craft onto the beach. . . The rising tide had brought the landing craft up the beach into range of a line of villas on the seafront and the enemy inside them had opened up on us. We . . . stood it as long as we could because the confused fighting ashore was milling around the houses and we were afraid of hitting our own men. Eventually someone lost his temper and opened up and, within seconds, thirty-six Oerlikons, three from each craft, had joined in and the line of villas folded up like a pack of cards.[36]

Major Dunn went on to say that as he walked along the beach and coast road he found tank crews brewing tea and not prepared to leave the road for fear of mines and of becoming bogged in the saturated area immediately behind the sand dunes. Then, with the congestion at its height, German artillery fire began hitting the beach with considerable accuracy and it soon became clear that they were using the sixty barrage balloons protecting the landing craft against possible low-level air attacks[37] to indicate their targets. At 1130 hours the balloons were cut free.

The 185 Brigade plan saw the infantrymen of the KSLI riding on the Staffordshire Yeomanry tanks. They were to be supported by B Troop of 41 Anti-Tank Battery with M-10s, four 22nd Dragoon flails, three tank-mounted box-girder bridges from the Westminster Dragoons and the 7th Field Artillery Regiment (battalion). The infantrymen of the Warwicks would protect the right flank of this thrust for Caen and those of the Norfolks the left. Frustrated by the non-appearance of the tanks, the commanding officer of the KSLI, Lieutenant Colonel Jack Maurice, took off on a bicycle to find out what was happening and came back to report to his Brigade commander that only half had got off the beach; nevertheless he was prepared to begin the advance. Brigadier Smith disagreed and although the Divisional commander, Major General Tom Rennie, who had landed at 1030 hours, appeared on the scene at about midday, the order to move was still not given. This inaction was completely at odds with Rennie's original orders to Smith issued before D-Day:

this advance will be carried out with speed and boldness so that the enemy's local reserves can be overcome quickly and the Brigade established on its objective ready to meet counter-attacks by reserve formations which may develop towards evening on D-Day.[38]

But worse was to follow. At about midday Smith received reports of heavy firing from Périers-sur-le-Dan and of the Canadians running into strong resistance on his western flank. He immediately changed the plan and gave orders that the Warwicks were to move on the left flank instead of the right. He had done a similar thing during the last major Divisional exercise in Scotland when he had attempted to move two battalions round a left flank in a wide turning movement whilst keeping his third battalion on his Brigade's original thrust line. The result had been chaos and General Rennie's reaction was to say wearily: 'You won't let this happen on the day, will you KP?'. With the benefit of hindsight, Smith later defended his decision as follows:

> I received information that 21st Panzer Division was advancing west of Caen but there were no signs of my Staffordshire Yeomanry having got through the congestion on the beach and remembering the case of a Brigade commander, one of whose battalions was decimated because he had sent them forward without anti-tank support, I was not going to send either KSLI or the Warwicks into a tank trap. I accordingly ordered Colonel Herdon [CO Warwicks] to move over to the other flank and to advance by the river Orne road. I had decided that, in any case, the Warwicks would be better placed on the left flank[39]

Despite Smith's statement that he was not prepared to send the KSLI 'into a tank trap' and without waiting for HILLMAN to be cleared, at approximately 1230 hours he ordered Jack Maurice's Battalion to set off on foot along the road from Hermanville-sur-Mer to Biéville. The column was led by Major Guy Thorneycroft's X Company.[40] The tanks and the Troop of 41 Anti-Tank Battery were told to catch up as soon as possible. Although the light infantrymen were not, as might have been expected, engaged by the Germans in HILLMAN, the leading platoon, under Lieutenant H Jones, came under rifle and machine-gun fire from the Périers ridge at 1315 hours; however, when it neared the crest the enemy[41] unexpectedly withdrew and drove off in lorries parked on the reverse slope. A bunker on the crest at Point 61 was found to be empty – it was that of a Major Hof, the commanding officer of the 1st Battalion of the 1716th Artillery Regiment. A German officer[42] later confirmed that the German retreat was hastened by the appearance of tanks. These were in fact the leading tanks of C Squadron of the Staffordshire Yeomanry that had 'galloped to Point 61 to find it clear of enemy'.[43] They quickly 'married up'

1. Ike visiting a unit of the 29th Infantry Division at Tregantle Fort, Torpoint, Plymouth, Devon, on 5 February 1944.

2. Winston Churchill examining a bazooka during a visit to the US 2nd Armored Division somewhere in England on 24 March 1944. The Divisional commander, Major General Edward Brooks on right and Lieutenant General Omar Bradley in background.

3. Lieutenant General Omar Bradley, commander First US Army and General Sir Bernard Montgomery, commander 21st Army Group.

4. Major General Charlie Gerhardt, commander 29th Infantry Division.

5. Brigadier General Norman 'Dutch' Cota, deputy commander 29th Infantry Division.

6. Major General Tom Rennie, commander 3rd Infantry Division 25 Dec '43 – 13 June '44. Taken in early 1945 when he was commanding the 51st (Highland) Division.

7. Field Marshal Erwin Rommel inspects beach defences – February 1944.

8. General Erich Marcks, commander LXXXIV Corps.

9. Major General Edgar Feuchtinger, commander 21st Panzer Division.

10. German strongpoint QUEEN beach.

11. Strongpoint on OMAHA beach with 75mm gun and protective walls. The left hand wall blocked the road to Vierville.

12. Men of the Blue and Gray approaching OMAHA on D-Day.

13. D-Day – wading ashore OMAHA beach.

14. D-Day – wounded and exhausted men of the Blue and Gray shelter under the cliffs.

15. The house at Les Moulins captured by members of F Company, 116th Infantry under Major Bingham on D-Day.

16. Members of the Blue and Gray interrogate a Frenchman – D-Day.

17. Members of the Engineer Special Brigade come ashore on OMAHA late on D-Day.

18. Members of
the 185 Infantry
Brigade wade
ashore on
D-Day (IWM).

19. QUEEN RED beach – 0730 hours D-Day (IWM).

20. QUEEN RED beach – 0845 hours D-Day (IWM).

21. QUEEN RED beach – 0845 hours D-Day (IWM).

22. DD Sherman of the 13th/18th Royal Hussars on SWORD beach.

23. Strongpoint COD on SWORD beach (IWM).

24. Men of 2 KSLI and an AVRE of 253 Squadron RE coming ashore at La Brèche (IWM).

25. Flail tank in action.

26. Churchill fascine.

27. Caen – afternoon 6 June.

28. Caen – end of the afternoon 6 June.

29. Lion-sur-Mer beach from German gun position, with DD tank and crashed 'Thunderbolt'.

30. Reinforcements coming ashore in the Les Moulin sector of OMAHA.

31. Men of the Blue and Gray under fire as they advance inland.

32. Advancing column halted while the way ahead is checked for mines.

33. Isigny liberated – 11 June.

with the KSLI and a short time later B Squadron of the Yeomanry and the flails were also ordered forward, but as they advanced they were engaged from their right flank by the three remaining 88mm guns of the 21st Panzer Division's Panzerjäger Battalion on the ridge north of Périers-sur-le-Dan. Three Shermans and two flails of the 22nd Dragoons were knocked out forcing the group to halt and deploy facing south-west. One 88mm gun was claimed by the Yeomanry and the others presumably escaped. Readers may recall that according to the commander of the 21st Panzer Division, Lieutenant General Fuechtinger, the twenty-four 88mm guns of his Panzerjäger Battalion had been positioned in the area Périers–Plumetot–Mathieu–Beuville before D-Day and placed under the command of General Richter. Fortunately for the Staffordshire Yeomanry the latter had ordered these guns to move west during the early morning to counter an advance by the reinforced 8th Canadian Brigade in the Bény-sur-Mer–Tailleville sector – an advance he considered more threatening. 'I remember that I issued this order to the Panzerjäger Battalion 200 in the early hours of the morning between 6 and 7 o'clock.'[44] It is not clear why three guns remained behind or exactly what happened to the main part of this powerful force. Richter claimed that the Battalion 'encountered the enemy towards 11 o'clock in the Seulles valley', and Feuchtinger said later that: 'a few Pak [anti-tank] platoons of Panzerjäger Battalion 200 were part of a force holding up the enemy in the Seulles valley that evening'. He added that 'the whole Panzerjäger Battalion with the exception of three guns had been lost through its subordination to the static Division [Richter's] on 6 June'.[45] As a footnote to this story it is interesting that the Canadians claimed to have captured at least one 88mm battery in the Bény-sur-Mer sector that afternoon.[46]

At 1425 hours, as the KSLI and C Squadron of the Staffordshire Yeomanry approached the outskirts of Beuville, they came under fire from a battery of four 122mm guns of the 1st Battalion of the 21st Panzer Division's 155th Artillery Regiment positioned on the reverse slope in the wooded area running south-east from Périers-sur-le-Dan. One Sherman was knocked out and an artillery forward observer, Captain Gower, killed. Ordering his main body to continue the advance, Lieutenant Colonel Maurice detached Major Wheelock's Z Company to deal with the problem. The Germans were soon driven from their guns but they maintained a stubborn defence in concrete shoulder-high emplacements and foxholes surrounded by wire. The position was finally taken with the help of a captured Polish soldier who showed the way into the position by a back entrance but by then it was 2000 hours and Z Company had lost six killed and twenty-three wounded.[47] It is of interest that had the Warwicks been following up on the western flank as originally planned, or if the South Lancs had been ordered to advance south from Hermanville-sur-Mer, they would have been ideally placed to deal with these guns. Sadly,

Smith's disastrous change of plan, Cass's methodical attitude and Rennie's reluctance to interfere and exercise personal command ensured that the only direct thrust towards Caen on D-Day would be made by a single depleted Battalion and a few tanks of the Staffordshire Yeomanry.

We will return to the KSLI's advance shortly, but it is time now to look at the attack on strongpoint HILLMAN by A Company of the Suffolks and the tanks of Major Philip Papillon's C Squadron of the 13/18 H. The early reduction of this strongpoint was a major requirement in the Divisional plan, since it not only presented a threat to the move of the KSLI and Staffordshire Yeomanry across the Périers ridge, but it also completely blocked the planned advance by the Norfolks on the eastern flank of 185 Brigade. It is surprising therefore that it took the Suffolks and their attached armour more than four and a half hours to launch their first attack against this important objective. Why was this? Principally because the advance by the Suffolk group had been planned in three distinct phases and each phase was carried out at a plodding pace. As we have heard the whole Battalion group was ready to move off shortly after 0900 hours and by 1000 hours C Company had cleared Colleville-sur-Orne. It was another two hours, however, before B Company took MORRIS, despite there being no opposition, and then another hour before A Company with a breaching platoon from D Company was ready to attack HILLMAN.

This first assault against HILLMAN is described in detail in the Suffolk's War Diary[48] and is repeated here in a simplified form. Captain Geoff Ryley, after moving A Company round the east side of Colleville-sur-Orne, was able to see the outer wire fence of the strongpoint and one of three steel cupolas which the attacking force would soon discover were impervious to all its weapons.[49] In fact the cupolas came as a complete surprise to the Suffolks since they had not been spotted on the pre-D-Day air photographs. Only trenches and bunkers covering an area approximately 600m by 400m and surrounded by a minefield within two 3m-wide belts of wire had been identified. With a garrison of about 150 men, seven machine-guns in steel cupolas and two infantry guns in 3.5m-thick concrete emplacements, the true strength of HILLMAN had been seriously underestimated.

The planned H-Hour air attack on the strongpoint by six US B-17s had failed to materialise because of low cloud cover and Ryley had no way of communicating with the supporting naval guns lying offshore. It will be remembered the naval Forward Bombardment Officer had been mortally wounded during the landing. Ryley therefore had to rely on the Battalion's mortars and the guns of 76 Field Artillery Regiment, both of which were virtually useless against the concrete emplacements and steel cupolas. At 1310 hours the codeword GRAB was given for a five-minute artillery and mortar bombardment supported by direct fire from the tanks of C Squadron of the 13/18 H. The breaching platoon of D Company led by Lieutenant Mike Russell then crawled through the half metre-high corn and pushed their bangalore torpedoes through the wire. With the outer wire blown the engineers cleared a metre-wide path through the minefield, suffering some casualties from heavy machine-gun fire in the process, and then a second bangalore party placed their charges under the inner fence. The initiating device failed to go off and Russell had to return through the minefield for a second one. This exploded successfully and the way was open for Lieutenant Sandy Powell's Platoon to assault the bunkers. Although the 13/18 H tanks provided covering fire, the Platoon immediately came under intense machine-gun fire and the leading section commander was killed. Powell fired three rounds from a PIAT (hand-held anti-tank weapon) at the cupola without effect. Even so his Platoon managed to advance into the trenches only to find the enemy had withdrawn into their concrete bunkers. A second attack by Lieutenant Trevor Tooley's platoon, led by the Company commander himself, took some prisoners but failed to penetrate into the position. Ryley was killed and Tooley badly wounded. A 17-pdr shot from a 13/18 H Firefly tank failed to deal with the cupola causing most of the trouble and the commanding officer, Lieutenant Colonel Dick Goodwin, decided to withdraw A Company before trying again with more tanks accompanying his infantry right into the position. It was to be over two hours before this second attack was mounted.

The Fourth Wave

At about midday the three Battalions of Brigadier J C Cunningham's 9 Infantry Brigade – the Lincolns, KOSB and Ulster Rifles – began disembarking from nine LCI (L)s on QUEEN WHITE beach. QUEEN RED was still too congested. This was the Reserve Brigade of Rennie's Iron Division and it had the mission of protecting the right flank of 185 Brigade's thrust for Caen and preventing infiltration between it and the Canadians moving south from JUNO beach. The Brigade orders issued before D-Day stated clearly that the Lincolns, with tanks of the East Riding Yeomanry attached, were to destroy the enemy in the Cresserons and Plumetot area and secure a suitable concentration area for the main advance by the KOSB to St Contest, the Ulster Rifles to Buron and finally the tanks of the East Riding Yeomanry to Couvrechef. In the event of 185 Brigade failing to take Caen, the Brigade was to attack the city from the west.

9 Brigade's disembarkation went well except that the tanks of the East Riding Yeomanry, due to land at 1255 hours, were delayed for an hour by continuing congestion on the beaches and it was 1440 hours before the Regiment reported that it was safely ashore and in its assembly area.

Brigadier Cunningham came ashore with his Tactical Headquarters at about 1300 hours and immediately moved to Hermanville to look for his counterpart in 8 Brigade, Brigadier Copper Cass. On the way he was astonished to meet not only his Divisional commander but also his Corps commander, Lieutenant General John Crocker. They were standing in the grounds of the Mairie (town hall) at Hermanville-sur-Mer where Rennie's Headquarters was being set up. Cunningham said later that he exclaimed to them: 'I've been in half a dozen campaigns but never before have I been beaten into the battlefield not only by my Divisional commander but by my Corps commander!'. The amusement was short lived. He was ordered to forget his previous orders and as soon as his armour joined him he was to move his Brigade to the eastern flank to help the 6th Airborne Division which was under attack by elements of the 21st Panzer Division in the area of the Caen canal and Orne bridges. His plea to be allowed to thrust for Carpiquet and then attack Caen from the west as planned, and as was expected by his whole Brigade, fell on deaf ears. Cunningham later described what happened next:

On the way back to the beach I did no more than warn the KOSB that we had to get across to assist 6th Airborne at Pegasus Bridge [over the Orne west of Ranville]. My armour was still trying to find a place to land when I viewed it from the shore, so I returned to my Brigade HQ. On arrival there, I left my carrier and went towards my armoured command vehicle. My anti-tank gunner and my intelligence staff moved to join me there. At that moment a stick of mortar bombs landed on us killing six and wounding six. I was wounded [both his arms were smashed] and unable to convey the new instructions to my staff. Colonel Dennis Orr . . . my second-in-command . . . had been ordered to go over to Pegasus Bridge to (I think) report on the situation. . . When I was wounded he was not present to take over, and in fact I was told it was a very long time before he managed to get back. The result was a long hiatus when the Brigade should have been moving and nothing happened.

The decision to divert 9 Brigade to the eastern flank ended any real hope of capturing Caen on D-Day and has been strongly criticised by a number of commentators. Seen from the Corps commander's standpoint, however, the beleaguered airborne bridgehead east of the Orne was already under serious threat and if the Pegasus Bridge was lost all his troops on that side of the river would be trapped. He therefore deemed it essential to secure the bridge and the nearby landing zone for the airborne reinforcements due to be flown in that evening.

With the exception of Lieutenant Colonel George Renny's KOSB, the units of 9 Brigade were of course unaware of their new mission. The

Lincolns, in accordance with their original orders, established a Brigade concentration area near Hermanville-sur-Mer but did not clear Cresserons and Plumetot or take on the German counter-attack force just south of Lion-sur-Mer. They remained in the concentration area with the Ulster Rifles and tanks of the East Riding Yeomanry, waiting for the order to advance south towards St Contest and Mâlon – an order that never came. At 1645 hours the commanding officer of the Ulster Rifles, Lieutenant Colonel Ian Harris, was told that he was in command of the Brigade but at that time he had no idea that its mission had been changed. Strangely, no one in the Divisional Headquarters seems to have passed on the new orders. The result of this appalling muddle was that only the KOSB moved to the east flank where some five hours later they occupied St Aubin-d'Arquenay and the high ground overlooking Bénouville with the aim of protecting the landing zone of 6 Airborne Division's Airlanding Brigade. 9 Brigade was thus fragmented and spread across the entire Divisional front; worse still, there was now a serious gap between the British and Canadian 3rd Divisions which, as we shall see, was about to be exploited by the Germans. To add to the overall confusion, the Canadian liaison officer at Cunningham's Headquarters was one of those killed in the mortar attack and the Canadians were unaware of this dangerous situation.

Let us return for a moment to 8 Brigade. Recall that after clearing QUEEN RED the East Yorks were tasked with the capture of strongpoints SOLE and DAIMLER and then establishing themselves on the high ground at St Aubin-d'Arquenay. SOLE was the underground Headquarters of the 1st Battalion of the 736th Grenadier Regiment and DAIMLER a gun position about a kilometre farther on containing four 155mm howitzers, two light anti-aircraft guns and two machine-guns. Both were emplaced in concrete and were believed to be well defended. C Company under Major de Symons Barrow, accompanied by a Troop of B Squadron 13/18 tanks, took SOLE without a fight at 1300 hours. The artillery Forward Observation Officer accompanying the Company, Captain Featherstone, established his group in the enemy position only to be: 'slightly embarrassed by the appearance of eighty Germans surrendering from a dug-out. . . A section of the East Yorks was asked to take the Germans in charge'.[50] A and B Companies, after finishing their tasks on the beach, arrived in time to help consolidate the area and the Battalion then prepared to take on DAIMLER. Unfortunately, while Lieutenant Colonel Hutchinson and some of his officers were carrying out a reconnaissance for this task at about 1430 hours, a salvo of enemy artillery fire landed amongst them and Hutchinson was wounded. Major Field took over but a serious delay ensued before the attack on DAIMLER took place.

Meanwhile, at 1400 hours Brigadier 'Kipper' Smith of 185 Brigade had moved his Tactical Headquarters forward to Colleville-sur-Orne. Lieutenant Colonel Nigel Tapp, whose 7 Field Artillery Regiment was supporting the Brigade, accompanied the Brigadier and he later described the scene in the village as one of great confusion. Two tanks were blocking the track leading up to HILLMAN after being immobilised on mines, the road leading in from the north was blocked by more tanks and by the vehicles of 8 Brigade, and there were three Battalions of infantry, the Norfolks, Warwicks and most of the Suffolks, crowded into the orchards and gardens of the village, waiting for HILLMAN to be cleared.

It was at about this time that Rennie, the Divisional commander, arrived in Colleville-sur-Orne. He found Dick Goodwin of the Suffolks and told him that he had to capture HILLMAN before dark and that he was then to dig-in 'as the enemy armour is about and they will probably counter-attack about first light [the next day]'. It is, at least to this author, surprising that Rennie gave Goodwin a further seven or eight hours to complete this clearly urgent task. The Divisional commander also found Brigadiers Smith of 185 Brigade and Cass of 8 Brigade in the village. Rennie told Smith to 'get on' as time was getting short – he was thinking particularly of the Norfolks who were required to protect the left flank of the KSLI in its advance towards Lébisey. However, in an unbelievable failure of intelligence and/or communication, the commanding officer of the Norfolks, Lieutenant Colonel Hugh Bellamy, was led to believe that St Aubin-d'Arquenay was still held by the enemy and that he should therefore stay well to the west of that village. Recall that Lovat's Commandos had passed through St Aubin roughly an hour earlier. A farm at Bellevue, 2km south-west of St Aubin-d'Arquenay was made Bellamy's new objective rather than Biéville, 5km away, as in the original orders. Unfortunately this new axis leading south from Colleville-sur-Orne would take his men within a few hundred metres of the eastern edge of HILLMAN. A and B Companies, under the Battalion second-in-command, Major Humphrey Wilson, were sent off with strict instructions that they were not under any circumstances to get mixed up with the Suffolks attacking HILLMAN.

By mid-afternoon the Iron Division's bridgehead was some 5km wide, stretching from Lion-sur-Mer to Ouistreham and some 4km deep to its farthest point – the old German artillery Headquarters at Point 61 on the Périers ridge. Into this area of approximately twenty square kilometres, with only one proper road leading away from the beachhead, were squeezed nine infantry Battalions, a machine-gun Battalion, two Commandos, three tank Regiments, three self-propelled artillery Regiments, an anti-tank Regiment, an Assault Regiment Royal Engineers, a Beach Group with its engineers, Pioneers, Provost and an extra infantry Battalion[51], plus of course the rest of the Divisional units such as

Engineers, Signals, and Medical – somewhere in the region of 1,000 vehicles. One could be forgiven for thinking that the Division was well set up for achieving its mission of capturing Caen but, as readers are already aware, many things were beginning to go wrong. We have heard about the chaotic situation pertaining in 9 Infantry Brigade – far from thrusting down the right flank towards Carpiquet and possibly attacking Caen from the west, it was spread across the Divisional front in a defensive posture. None of its infantry Battalions or its armoured Regiment had seen any significant action. 8 Brigade had two of its Battalions still involved in clearing up Lion-sur-Mer and strongpoint DAIMLER and the third doing nothing in Hermanville; and in the case of 185 Brigade, Brigadier Smith had caused confusion by switching the Warwicks from the right flank to the left and only the KSLI group was proceeding as planned towards Beuville.

Let us return now to this single remaining thrust towards Caen. At 1430 hours X Company of the KSLI was held up in Beuville by some accurate sniper fire and at 1450 hours Lieutenant Colonel Maurice ordered his W and Y Companies to bypass the village and get on to Biéville. They reached the northern outskirts of the village at 1545 hours. Major Steel's Y Company reported no opposition on the left flank, and so while Major Slatter's W Company mopped up in the area of the Château, Steel's men pressed on towards Lébisey. Slatter and another officer were wounded during the action near the Château and Captain Rylands took over W Company. Meanwhile, most of the Reconnaissance Troop and all except one Troop of C Squadron of the Staffordshire Yeomanry had moved forward on the right flank and at about 1615 hours the former spotted German tanks approaching from the west. It was the beginning of a counter-attack by the 21st Panzer Division designed to reach the sea between Lion-sur-Mer and Ouistreham. Most of C Squadron's tanks, the M-10s of 41 Anti-Tank Battery and the 6-pdrs of the KSLI Anti-tank Platoon immediately deployed to meet this attack and within a short time four or five Mk IVs had been knocked out[52] and the German attack brought to a halt. During this action Y Company and one Troop of tanks continued the advance towards the Lébisey wood.[53] One tank became bogged down in the natural anti-tank obstacle north of the wood formed by the soft ground in the valley between Biéville and Lébisey, but the other three and Y Company reached the northern outskirts of the wood at 1730 hours only to be met by heavy machine-gun fire. Panzer-Grenadiers were already defending the area in some strength and shortly afterwards a party of about forty Germans was seen moving round the right flank into the valley between Lébisey and Biéville. Lieutenant Colonel Maurice decided that any further advance that evening was out of the question and at 1800 hours he ordered his Battalion to form a firm base in and to the south of Biéville. With the Norfolks and Warwicks well to the rear instead of guarding his flanks, strong opposition to his front and a major German counter-attack in progress on his right flank, he had no other option. By 2000 hours the KSLI was dug in with its 6-pdrs and the M-10s providing a strong anti-tank defence on its right flank. One M-10 had been knocked out during the German counter-attack and a sergeant and gunner killed. As dusk approached the Staffordshire Yeomanry tanks moved back to a rear rally position at Beuville. Two of their tanks had been hit by enemy fire during the German counter-attack but none lost and the Regiment had suffered only seven killed, three wounded and six missing. Y Company, under the command of Captain Dane, withdrew at 2315 hours – Major Steel had been killed by a machine-gun bullet and the Company had suffered twenty-three casualties. The single thrust for Caen was at an end. It had cost the KSLI 113 officers and men killed and wounded. Maurice was awarded a DSO for his leadership and the performance of his Battalion on D-Day.

What of the Norfolks who had been tasked with advancing on the left flank of the KSLI? According to their Regimental History:

> A Company (Captain Adrian Kelly) and B Company (Major Eric Cooper-Key) suffered several casualties when they came under fire from our own tanks which mistook them for enemy troops escaping from the strongpoint [HILLMAN]. They were also engaged by machine-gun fire from HILLMAN and pinned down for two and a half hours. . . Lieutenant Toft and thirteen other ranks [were] killed and Captain Kelly, Lieutenant Ward and a number of other ranks wounded.

When it was finally discovered that there were no Germans in St Aubin-d'Arquenay, Lieutenant Colonel Bellamy was able to direct the remainder of his Battalion farther to the east and avoid the fire from HILLMAN. Bellevue was reached at 1800 hours, A and B Companies rejoined sometime afterwards and the Norfolks went firm. They were a long way from Biéville and had never been in a position to protect the left flank of their comrades in the KSLI. Ellis' official History *Victory in the West*, Chester Wilmot's *Struggle for Europe* and Norman Scarfe's *Assault Division* all claim the Norfolks suffered some 150 casualties during this action. On the other hand the Regimental History lists only twenty killed on D-Day and in his book, *Monty's Iron Sides*, Patrick Delaforce gives figures of 'about fifty casualties including six killed'. It is certainly a fact that if A and B Companies had indeed suffered 150 casualties they would have virtually ceased to exist. We know they did not.

And what about the Warwicks who had been brought over from the right flank with orders to relieve the Commandos on the Caen canal and Orne bridges? When General Rennie appeared again at Brigadier Smith's 185 Brigade Headquarters in Colleville at about 1700 hours he was incensed to find the Warwicks still there and getting ready to attack St Aubin-d'Arquenay – a village he had just driven through! He made his anger clear. The Battalion was ordered to move at once and within an hour and a half its A Company had, with help from men of the 6th Airborne Division's follow-up Airlanding Brigade, who literally landed on top of it, secured Bénouville. Responsibility for the Caen canal bridge passed to D Company of the Warwicks at 1830 hours. The rest of the Battalion then pushed on 'meeting opposition the whole way from a German Mobile Delaying Force armed with MGs and anti-tank guns'[54] to reach the outskirts of Blainville at midnight. The Warwicks had four killed and thirty-five wounded on D-Day, some incurred when two of their LCIs were hit on landing and others 'from accurate small arms and MG fire' in their initial assembly area south of Lion-sur-Mer from the direction of Cresserons and Plumetot.[55]

The East Yorks followed the Warwicks into St Aubin-d'Arquenay. Their A and C Companies, with support from a troop of B Squadron 13/18 H, had earlier surrounded strongpoint DAIMLER, but when a Canadian officer on loan to the British Army, Lieutenant James McGregor, had gone up to the entrance of the fortification and called on its garrison to surrender he had been cut down by machine-gun fire.[56] Fortunately DAIMLER surrendered shortly afterwards, at 1830 hours, with seventy Germans offering themselves as prisoners. The Battalion was then able to move on to St Aubin-d'Arquenay.

And finally, we must come back to the Suffolks' attack on HILLMAN. After the failure of the first assault, the commanding officer, Dick Goodwin, asked his Brigadier for two flails to speed up the mine clearing and for more tanks to join C Squadron of the 13/18 H. A Squadron of the Staffordshire Yeomanry was allocated, again depleting the main thrust by the KSLI group towards Caen, but at 1615 hours it had to be withdrawn from the operation in order to meet the tank attack by the 21st Panzer Division already mentioned. The flails eventually proved unnecessary, because by the time they arrived at about 1700 hours, Lieutenant Arthur Heal and a corporal of 246 Field Engineer Company had already cleared a gap through the mines using gelignite. The gap was wide enough for tanks to penetrate into the strongpoint and after a five-minute artillery bombardment they moved forward, quickly followed by A Company with an additional platoon from D Company under command. C Company continued to provide left flank protection. With some nine tanks inside the position, 'their commanders winkling Germans out of their trenches by throwing grenades from their turrets'[57] and the Suffolks dropping more grenades down the ventilation shafts, resistance soon began to crumble and the first prisoners were taken. Nevertheless, it still took over three hours, until 2000 hours, for resistance to cease. By then fifty prisoners had been taken; but unknown to the Suffolks, HILLMAN was by no means clear of the enemy. At 0645 hours the following day Colonel Krug, the commander of the 736th Regiment, appeared from his underground bunker, immaculately turned out and with his orderly carrying two suitcases. Two other officers and seventy soldiers surrendered with him!

After active resistance from HILLMAN ceased, Lieutenant Colonel Goodwin ordered his B and D Companies forward and by 2115 hours they were digging in south-west and south-east of Colleville-sur-Orne respectively. D Company cleared a farm some 300m forward of its position, capturing two officers and thirty-eight men in the process. C Squadron of the 13/18 H had been pulled back to a forward rally position near Goodwin's Headquarters at 1930 hours for replenishment. 'The countryside was very pleasant; the evening was fine and sunny and there was little shelling going on. Looking across the green fields dotted with flowers and the trees in blossom, it was hard to believe that a war was raging'.[58] Only one tank had been lost to enemy action and the total casualties numbered one man dead from wounds and seven others wounded. The Suffolks' casualties were surprisingly light – only six killed and eight wounded in the HILLMAN operation[59] and a total of seven killed, twenty-four wounded and four missing during the day.

The German Counter-Attack

It is time now to look in more detail at the counter-attack launched by the 21st Panzer Division. In an interview given to Milton Shulman in August 1945 its commander, Lieutenant General Edgar Feuchtinger, said:

I first knew that the invasion had begun with a report that parachutists had been dropped near Troarn a little after midnight on 6 June. Since I had been told that I was to make no move until I heard from Rommel's Headquarters, I could do nothing immediately but warn my men to be ready. I waited impatiently all that night for instructions. But not a single order from higher formation was received by me. Realizing that my armoured division was the closest to the scene of operations, I finally decided, at 0630 in the morning, that I had to take some action. I ordered my tanks to attack the English 6th Airborne Division which had entrenched itself in a bridgehead over the Orne. To me this constituted the most immediate threat to the German position.

Hardly had I made this decision, when at 0700 I received my first intimation that a higher command still existed. I was told by Army Group 'B' that I was now under the command of Seventh Army. But I received no further orders as to my role. At 0900 I was informed that I would receive any future orders from LXXXIV Infantry Corps [General Erich Marcks], and finally at 10 o'clock I was given my first operational instructions. I was ordered to stop the move of my tanks against the Allied airborne troops and to turn west and aid the forces protecting Caen [Richter's 716th Infantry Division]. Once over the Orne, I drove north toward the coast. By this time the enemy, consisting of 3rd British and 3rd Canadian Infantry Divisions, had made astonishing progress and had already occupied a strip of high ground about 10 km from the sea. From here the excellent anti-tank gun fire of the Allies knocked out eleven of my tanks before I had barely started. However, one battle-group did manage to by-pass these guns and actually reached the coast at Lion-sur-Mer at about 7 in the evening.

I now expected that some reinforcements would be forthcoming to help me hold my position, but nothing came. . . I retired to take up a line just north of Caen. By the end of that first day my Division had lost almost 25% of its tanks.[60]

Feuchtinger elaborated on this in his interrogation in February 1947.[61] After describing the difficulties of moving through Caen with only one bridge available and under fire from naval guns and attack from the air[62], he said his Division was ready to attack at 1600 hours with two Combat Teams or Kampfgruppen (KGs). The first, KG Oppeln, was based on the 22nd Panzer Regiment[63] and the second, KG Rauch, on the 192nd Panzer-Grenadier Regiment.[64] Suggestions that only three companies of tanks were available for this counter-attack are wrong. It is true that one Panzer Company[65] remained east of the Orne with KG von Luck in action against the British 6th Airborne Division, but the rest of the Panzer Regiment, over eighty Mk IVs[66], moved to the west side of the river. KG Oppeln formed up in the area west of Hérouville and was given as its objective the coast between the mouth of the Orne and the eastern outskirts of Lion-sur-Mer; KG Rauch, after forming up between St Contest and Cussy was tasked with reaching the coast around Lion-sur-Mer. The counter-attack was therefore being launched into the weakest part of the Allied bridgehead north of Caen – the gap between the Iron Division and the Canadians. Feuchtinger went on to say that the attack was launched at 1620 hours and that KG Oppeln 'threw the enemy out of Lébisey' and reached the heights north of there. It then continued its advance through Epron but when it reached the area of Mathieu and Cambes-en-Plaine it came under heavy fire from tanks and artillery on the Périers ridge and lost 'a number of Mk IV tanks'. He further claimed that KG Rauch reached the coast at Lion-sur-Mer but that:

a heavy tank attack together with an airborne landing had meanwhile engaged the left wing of the Combat Team and threatened to destroy it . . . we succeeded in keeping the Combat Team together but lost a large amount of men and material, in particular a number of self-propelled guns and the largest part of the 1st Company 192 Regiment which was cut off in a radio communications strongpoint near Douvres.

Feuchtinger concluded that under the cover of darkness his Division withdrew to positions running from St Contest, through Epron, to the heights north of Lébisey and the northern outskirts of Hérouville.

This account of KG Oppeln's actions fits in reasonably well with the British version of events. As we have heard, the Reconnaissance Troop of the Staffordshire Yeomanry spotted von Oppeln's tanks moving forward in the Lébisey area and A Squadron of the Staffordshire Yeomanry, after being withdrawn from the attack on HILLMAN, moved quickly to a position just to the west of Beuville where it could engage the tanks moving past the west end of the valley between there and Biéville. Two Mk IVs were claimed. Two troops of A Squadron then moved farther to the right flank where they claimed another four enemy tanks. Estimates of the total German tank losses vary from Feuchtinger's eleven to British reports of thirteen or fourteen. Certainly four Mark IVs were knocked out and another hit and damaged in the initial engagement with the Shermans, M-10s of 41 Anti-Tank Battery and 6-pdr anti-tank guns of the KSLI; and almost certainly another nine were knocked out, including six by A Squadron and three by the 17-pdrs of B Squadron's Fireflies on the high ground around Point 61.

It is when we come to Feuchtinger's account of KG Rauch's actions, however, that we find a major discrepancy. Whilst it is certainly true that at least one Battalion[67] of Panzer-Grenadiers reached the coast near Lion-sur-Mer at about 2000 hours and found part of the 3rd Battalion of Richter's 736th Regiment and the Battery of the 1716th Artillery Regiment still in position just to the south of the small resort, it is quite untrue that there was a heavy tank attack or that 'an airborne landing had meanwhile engaged the left wing of the Combat Team'. The reality is that the tanks of KG Oppeln failed to get past the British anti-tank defences between Beuville and Périers in their attempt to reinforce KG Rauch, and the sight of 250 tugs and 250 gliders of the 6th Airlanding Brigade escorted by a host of fighters flying over them on their way to land astride the Orne panicked the Germans into thinking that they were about to be cut off. This led to a hasty withdrawal carried out under heavy naval and artillery fire, initially to the Anguerny area and later back to St Contest.

Feuchtinger's counter-attack into the Iron Division's sector had failed but it caused great consternation in the British camp where the commanders realised that they now had to fight their way through a Panzer Division in order to reach their objective. At this stage though, they had no idea that the 12th SS Panzer Division Hitlerjugend (see Appendix J) was also on its way to confront them in their bid for Caen. The commander of its 25th SS Panzer-Grenadier Regiment, Kurt 'Panzer' Meyer, is reported to have said to Feuchtinger that evening: 'Little fish! We'll throw them back into the sea in the morning.'[68]

The Picture at the End of D-Day

(Map 11)

According to the Official British History[69], 28,845 troops were landed on SWORD beach[70] on D-Day and certainly by the time darkness fell the Iron Division had established a significant bridgehead. Nonetheless, far from being in a position to strike for Caen on D+1 it was clearly on the defensive with its armour dispersed – a far cry from Monty's demand that 'armoured columns must penetrate deep inland, and quickly, on D-Day' and certainly not in accordance with the original I Corps plan that required the three armoured Regiments to concentrate as quickly as possible after completing their tasks with the Infantry Brigades.

On the Division's right flank, No. 41 Royal Marine Commando was held up in front of strongpoint TROUT and on its left small pockets of enemy were still holding out in Ouistreham. In the 8 Brigade area, Hermanville was firmly held by the South Lancs while the East Yorks were re-organising in a cornfield to the west of the village after losing sixty-five killed and 141 wounded during the day – the highest losses suffered by any 3rd Division unit on D-Day. The Suffolks were concentrated within a kilometre of Colleville-sur-Orne. The tanks of the 13/18 H were still dispersed to their designated infantry battalions – A Squadron with the South Lancs was down to just six tanks, but B Squadron with the East Yorks still had ten and C Squadron with the Suffolks at Colleville-sur-Orne thirteen.

9 Brigade was widely dispersed with the Ulster Rifles around Point 61 on the high ground half way between Périers-sur-le-Dan and Colleville-sur-Orne and the KOSB in St Aubin-d'Arquenay. Neither unit had been involved in any offensive action after coming ashore. The Lincolns, who had suffered only thirteen casualties, were dug in half way between Hermanville-sur-Mer and the Commandos in Lion-sur-Mer. Colonel Dennis Orr[71], after returning from his reconnaissance of the Pegasus bridge area, had taken over command of the Brigade from Harris of the Ulster Rifles in the temporary rank of brigadier. The tanks of the East Riding Yeomanry were concentrated to the south-east of Colleville-sur-Orne. The Regiment had hardly fired a shot since landing.

In the 185 Brigade area, the Périers ridge was clear of enemy with the Norfolks at Bellevue overlooking Beuville. Just beyond them the KSLI was holding Biéville and looking across the valley towards Lébisey and its wood. The Staffordshire Yeomanry was leaguered to the west of Biéville.

Farther away to the south-east, D Company of the Warwicks was guarding the Caen canal and Orne bridges, and the rest of the Battalion was on the outskirts of Blainville.

The total number of casualties suffered by the Iron Division on D-Day is unknown. A British Army Operational Group study[72] gives a figure of 630 but for reasons that will be explained later, this author believes a minimum total of 752 would be more accurate.[73]

Readers will have noted that the centre of gravity of the Iron Division was clearly to the east of its planned centre line with virtually no troops west of a line drawn from Lion-sur-Mer, through Hermanville-sur-Mer to Périers-sur-le-Dan and Lébisey. Units of the Canadian 3rd Infantry Division were farther to the west at Villons-les-Buissons and Anguerny but the 3km to 6km gap between the two Divisions, already exploited by 21st Panzer, had still not been closed. Readers should also note that only some 60% of the infantry and tank units in Rennie's Division had seen serious action on D-Day.

A number of well-known historians and commentators, notably Chester Wilmot and David Belchem, have severely criticised the 3rd Division's performance on 6 June. Rather than follow in their footsteps, however, this author will leave the reader to draw his own conclusions from the facts presented. That said, it is clear with hindsight that had the 100 or more Shermans of the Staffordshire and East Riding Yeomanry, supported by infantry, engineers, artillery and on-call ground attack aircraft, been used during the first afternoon (they were both available at 1440 hours) in a single powerful thrust on the ideal armoured axis: Hermanville-sur-Mer–la Basse Campagne[74]–Périers-sur-le-Dan–la Londe–Epron, instead of being dispersed to 9 and 185 Infantry Brigades, the northern outskirts of Caen would almost certainly have been reached on D-Day. An advance on this axis, across open rolling country, would have had the added advantage of bypassing both HILLMAN and the Lébisey feature. Furthermore, it would have led inevitably to a head-on clash with the 21st Panzer Division – a clash that should have seen the destruction of the bulk of the German armour on the west side of the Orne. The way into Caen would then have been open for Rennie's infantry. Monty had demanded this type of strong armoured thrust but Dempsey and Rennie were both infantrymen who had apparently learned nothing from the tactics demonstrated by the Germans as early as 1939 and had either forgotten or were unaware of Clausewitz's dictum that a commander should 'point with the fist, not the finger'. The failure of Lieutenant General John Crocker, the Corps commander, to interfere is less understandable. He was a Royal Tank Corps officer who had previously commanded an armoured brigade and in his pre-D-Day orders he had demanded that 'Armour should be used boldly from the start'. It has to be said though, that in the British Army it was, and still is, unusual for a corps commander to interfere in the handling of one of his divisions in the early stages of an operation.

Caen on D-Day

According to the French authorities gas, water, electricity and telephones were cut off in Caen soon after 0800 hours and loudspeaker vans toured the city telling people to say at home in case of street fighting. At 1330 hours and again at 1625 hours the city was bombed. Allied Air Force records indicate that owing to cloudy weather the first wave of fifteen American bombers failed to find the aiming point and bombed beach defences instead.[75] Nevertheless, the fifty-eight US Eighth Air Force B-24 Liberators following up found their target and beginning at 1330 hours they dropped 141 tons of high explosive, severely damaging the districts of the rue St Jean, the Boulevard des Alliés, the rue Basse, rue des Chanoines and St Gilles square. Caen was of such importance that it was re-targeted – the only French town in the invasion area to be so on D-Day – and in further raids beginning at 1625 hours seventy-two out of 117 B-26 Marauder medium bombers dropped another 122 tons of explosive on the city causing damage in the rue de Caumont, rue de Carel, and the rue Gaillarde where the St Jean old people's home was destroyed.

For the citizens of Caen, as for those of St Lô, the first day of the promised liberation was inevitably both confusing and terrifying. They too listened to the BBC broadcasts but it was not until 0930 hours that they finally learned that the Allied invasion had begun and heard the warning: 'Please evacuate towns and villages within 35km of the coastline. As far as possible you will be warned of any air raids.' No one went to work, the schools were closed and during the morning people met excitedly in the streets to discuss events. The first British prisoners of war were seen arriving in the city at about 1030 hours. Needless to say, the afternoon and evening raids emptied the streets and forced everyone into whatever shelters they could find.

One of the most tragic events on D-Day was the summary execution of French prisoners in a part of the Caen prison guarded and managed by the Germans. 'Apparently obeying a general order, executions started in the first hours of the [Allied] landing. . . There were many Resistance fighters among the eighty-five victims'.[76]

NOTES

1. 19–24 mph on the Beaufort scale.
2. 3 & 5 Para Bdes of 6 Airborne Div.
3. Battle Summary – No. 39, Operation Neptune, Landings in Normandy June 1944, Historical Section, Naval Staff, Admiralty, Jun 47, p. 35.

4. Lt Col Hutchinson.
5. According to the Bomber Command War Diaries, the RAF attacked the Ouistreham coastal batteries during the night 5/6 Jun in clear weather.
6. Lummis, *From Sword to the Seine.*
7. Smith, *Adventures of an Ancient Warrior*, p. 104.
8. Miller, *History of the 13th/18th Royal Hussars 1922–1947*, p. 98.
9. Ibid. Almost certainly an exaggeration due to several tanks claiming the same target.
10. Ellis, *Victory in the West, Vol. I, The Battle of Normandy*, p. 184.
11. The small square on the sea front called 'Place de 3e D. I.' is the site of strongpoint COD.
12. *The Story of the 79th Armoured Division*, pp. 45–7, 49.
13. Ibid.
14. Ibid.
15. 2 East Yorkshire Op Order No. 1 dated 28 May 44. The capture of these bridges was the task of 6 Airborne Div.
16. King, who was awarded two DSOs during the war, was killed in Apr 45. He is well remembered for reciting an extract from Shakespeare's *Henry V* to his men through a loudhailer as they approached the beach.
17. Of No.10 (Inter-allied) Commando.
18. *The Story of the 79th Armoured Division*, p. 50.
19. Major Adrian Rouse, an acquaintance of the author in the 1960s.
20. *The Story of the 79th Armoured Division*, p. 49.
21. Delaforce, *Monty's Iron Sides*, p. 37.
22. On 30 Sep 44 the villagers of Colleville-sur-Orne, at the urging of their Mayor, Alphonse Lenauld, successfully petitioned for permission to add the *Montgomery* to the name of their Village rather than *Orne.*
23. 8 Inf Bde Op Order No. 2 dated 22 May 44.
24. 7 Para; a coup de main party of 2nd Bn Oxfordshire and Buckinghamshire Light Inf had seized these bridges some nine hours earlier.
25. A total of 177 men.
26. Part of the RM Armd Support Gp.
27. A modern casino has been built on the exact site.
28. Nos 1 and 8 French Cdo Tps suffered forty-one casualties on D-Day including Kieffer wounded.
29. Cass had won a DSO & an MC in France in WWI & had commanded 11 Inf Bde in the invasion of North Africa in Nov 42.
30. Miller, op. cit., p. 102.
31. It is possible that these two pillboxes were in fact the concrete gun emplace-ments of a bty of the 1st Bn, 155th Arty Regt located in this area.
32. Miller, op. cit., p. 101 and 13/18 H War Diary 6 Jun 44.
33. HQ 3 Inf Div War Diary 6 Jun 44.
34. Richter, MS # B-621.
35. The Naval teams were responsible for clearing obstacles from a depth of ten feet to four feet six inches and the Engrs for obstacles above that level.
36. Miller, *Combined Operations*, pp. 32–4.
37. The Luftwaffe flew only 319 sorties over France on 6 Jun 44 and all but a few of these were turned back or shot down.
38. Scarfe, *Assault Division*, p. 78.
39. Smith, op. cit., p. 106.
40. Most British battalions have companies labelled A, B, C & D. 2 KSLI had W, X, Y & Z. This labelling was adopted in WWI to avoid confusion when the Regt's 1st & 2nd Bns were serving side by side in France.

41. 7/192 Pz-Gren Regt of 21 Pz Div.
42. Lt Rudi Schaaf of the *Graf Waldersee* Bty, 1/1716 Arty Regt.
43. Staffs Yeo War Diary dated 6 Jun 44.
44. Richter, MS # B 621.
45. Feuchtinger, MS # B-441.
46. Stacey, *Official History of the Canadian Army in the Second World War, Vol. III, The Victory Campaign*, p. 109.
47. According to Feuchtinger (MS # B-441), one bty of the 1/155 Arty Regt managed to withdraw before being overrun on 6 Jun but the third was also lost.
48. Appx B to 1 Suffolks War Diary dated 6 Jun 44.
49. One cupola is still clearly visible today. Its armour is 40cm thick.
50. Scarfe, op. cit. p. 81.
51. 5th Bn, The King's Regt.
52. 2 KSLI War Diary dated 6 Jun 44 claimed two. These guns had the new armour piercing discarding sabot (APDS) rounds which were much more effective than standard 6-pdr ammunition.
53. Lébisey wood was in fact half orchard and half wood.
54. 2 Warwicks War Diary for Jun 44.
55. Ibid.
56. Canada made over 600 officers available to the British Army, mainly to make good infantry shortages. More than fifty served in 3 Inf Div. McGregor was the first to be killed.
57. Miller, *History of the 13th/18th Royal Hussars 1922–1947*, p. 103.
58. Ibid.
59. I Suffolks War Diary dated 6 Jun 44 (Appx B).
60. Shulman, *Defeat in the West*, p. 119. If Feuchtinger is correct this would mean he lost a maximum of 36 tks through air attack, naval gunfire & in the fighting against 3 Inf Div on D-Day. Carlo D'Este, *Decision in Normandy*, p. 140, puts the losses at 'over fifty'.
61. Feuchtinger, MS # B-441.
62. According to Ellis, op. cit., p. 204, 'eight Typhoons . . . dive-bombed tanks moving up to join the fight . . . [they] left two in flames and four others smoking'.
63. 22 Pz Regt less No. 4 Coy, 1/125 (SPW) Pz-Gren Regt, 220 Pz Pnr Bn (less one coy) & 3/155 Pz Arty Regt; named after its commander Col Hermann Oppeln-Bronikowski.
64. Two Bns of 192 Pz-Gren Regt, 2/220 Pz Pnr Bn & 2/155 Pz Arty Regt; named after its commander Col Rauch.
65. Capt Hoffmann's 4th Coy.
66. Carrell in his *Invasion – They're Coming!*, p. 101, says ninety-eight tks.
67. 1/192 Pz-Gren Bn.
68. Shulman, op. cit., p. 121.
69. Ellis, op.cit., p. 223.
70. The Americans landed approximately 34,250 men on OMAHA but it must be remembered that their beach was more than twice the width of SWORD and they were landing two Divs rather than one.
71. Whilst commanding an inf Bn in Syria in 1941, Orr had been captured by Vichy French; when that campaign ended he was released and quickly given command of a Bde of the Sudan Defence Force in the Western Desert. His Bde was overrun by Rommel's troops during their advance into Egypt and Orr returned to the UK
72. Report No. 261.

73. This figure includes all attachments less Commandos.
74. An area of ground lying 1km south-east of Plumetot that cannot be seen from strongpoint HILLMAN.
75. Air 37/563.
76. Municipal Information Bulletin, *Caen Normandie 44*, p. 2.

CHAPTER X
The Big Picture at the End of D-Day

(Maps 1 & 3)

Having dealt with the actions of the Blue and Gray and Iron Divisions on D-Day in some detail, it is time now to look at the overall situation in Normandy as darkness fell on 6 June.

The first action in the Allied invasion of Normandy had been the seizure, shortly after midnight on 5/6 June, of the bridges over the Caen canal and Orne river at Ranville by a small glider-borne force of some 200 men from the British 6th Airlanding Brigade. This was followed by the delivery of nearly 24,000 American and British paratroopers to the flanks of the planned 80km beachhead. Sadly, low cloud, poor navigation and enemy anti-aircraft fire led to dispersed drops and landings and to many men being drowned in the sea or, in the case of the Americans, in the flooded areas north-west of Carentan. Nevertheless, by first light on D-Day the American 82nd and 101st Airborne Divisions had secured much of the hinterland behind UTAH beach while the British 6th Airborne Division had established a bridgehead roughly 8km by 8km east of the Orne. The flanks of the planned Allied bridgehead were therefore reasonably secure.

Taking the other invasion beaches from west to east, UTAH has to be considered a major success. By the end of the day the Americans had put ashore 23,000 men and 1,700 vehicles of VII Corps for a loss of only 197 men and, although they had not reached their D-Day objectives, they were in control of a substantial area and were within a few kilometres of linking up with their airborne comrades.

GOLD beach also has to be considered a considerable success. The 50th Infantry Division, part of XXX British Corps, reinforced with an Armoured Brigade, an extra Infantry Brigade and a Commando[1], had established a bridgehead some 10km wide and 10km deep by last light. It had not achieved all its D-Day objectives but it had captured Arromanches and stood on the outskirts of the city of Bayeux.

JUNO beach, like SWORD, was the responsibility of I British Corps and it proved to be the toughest of the three eastern beaches. Ninety of the 306 landing craft were lost on mines or to German gunfire; but despite this and congested landings due to bad weather, the 3rd Canadian Infantry Division, reinforced with a Canadian Armoured Brigade and a British Commando[2], managed to secure a bridgehead 10km wide and to link up with the British on GOLD. By dusk the Canadians, despite more than 1,000 casualties including 335 killed[3], were only 5 or 6km from the northern suburbs of Caen. As far as Tom Rennie and the Iron Division were concerned it was comforting to know that the Canadian 8 Infantry Brigade with an Armoured Regiment in support was firm in Colomby-sur-Thaon and Anguerny, and that a Battalion from the reserve 9 Infantry Brigade with another Armoured Regiment had reached Villons-les-Buissons.

The most disappointing aspect of I Corps' operations on D-Day was the failure of the Canadian and British 3rd Infantry Divisions to link up. As we have heard, it was the corridor between them that the 21st Panzer Division had managed to exploit in the late afternoon and evening of D-Day.

In summary, one can do no better than quote Chester Wilmot:

Between the Vire and the Orne the Allies by dark on June 6th had broken into Hitler's fortress on a front of 30 miles. The enemy had been taken completely by surprise, his coastal defences had been over-whelmed, his air force and navy had been rendered powerless and his armoured reserves had been unable to intervene effectively. But the battle was by no means over. The UTAH beachhead was isolated and no junction between the two American Corps was likely for several days; the penetration at OMAHA was slight and insecure; there was still a gap seven miles wide between the two allied Armies and another three miles between the Canadians and 3rd British; none of the final D-Day objectives had been reached. . . [But] the Allies had gained a striking victory at a cost of fewer than 2,500 lives, and had accomplished the first phase of what Churchill rightly called 'the most difficult and com-plicated operation that has ever taken place'.[4]

Now let us turn to the situation on the German side. To understand this fully we must go back to 0445 hours on D-Day. It was then that Field Marshal von Rundstedt's Chief of Staff had asked General Jodl at OKW to release the Panzer Divisions of the Strategic Reserve to his commander. The request was turned down, for at that time the High Command was still not convinced that the Allied airborne landings were anything more than a feint. Fifteen minutes later, however, the 12th SS Panzer Division Hitlerjugend was attached to Rommel's Army Group 'B', which in turn placed it under General Erich Marcks' LXXXIV Corps at St Lô and at 0545 hours von Rundstedt (CinC West) agreed to an Army Group 'B' request for 12th SS to concentrate around Lisieux.

Throughout the course of D-Day, OKW, von Rundstedt and Rommel remained convinced that the Normandy landings were merely a prelude to a main attack in the Pas de Calais region; as such they were designed to lure major elements of the Fifteenth Army (Map 4) away from the Pas de Calais and thus make landings in that sector much easier. It would therefore be playing into the Allies' hands to move any of the Fifteenth Army's five infantry and two Panzer reserve Divisions from north of the Seine to counter them. Furthermore, as they saw the situation, the American landings in the west were 'a diversion within a diversion'[5] and the only immediate threat was in the Caen sector. They therefore agreed that the Seventh Army would have to use its own resources west of the Orne to contain and then eliminate the American landings in western Normandy but that the threat to Caen would be countered by deploying part of the strategic armoured reserve located west of the Seine – the 12th SS Panzer and Panzer Lehr Divisions. OKW therefore released both these Divisions for use by Seventh Army in the early afternoon. At 1507 hours von Rundstedt took further action; he told Rommel that he was subordinating SS General Sepp Dietrich's I SS Panzer Corps to Seventh Army and placing 12th SS and Panzer Lehr as well as 21st Panzer and what was left of the 716th Infantry[6] under Dietrich's command. Orders were promptly given for 12th SS to change direction and assemble on both sides of Evrecy with the mission of driving 'the enemy who has broken through adjacent to the 21st Panzer Division on the west, back into the sea and destroy him'.[7] Panzer Lehr was to secure the area of Flers–Vire.

It was approximately 1700 hours by the time the 12th SS Panzer Division's Headquarters received the new orders and 1740 hours before Kurt Meyer's 25th SS Panzer-Grenadier Regimental Group was given its new destination. By then it had already arrived in the Lisieux area – in fact it had been there since 1300 hours. Had it been told to go to Evrecy in the first place it could have been there by about 1500 hours and it would have been ready to launch an attack into the Allied bridgehead by not later than 1800 hours. This could have presented a serious threat to the British Second Army. As it was it took until 2100 hours for Meyer's Group to cross the Orne river and until 2300 hours before its first SS Panzer-Grenadier Battalion was able to take up a position near Noyers, to the south-west of Caen. The rest of the Group was to take all night to concentrate in the assembly area. The 26th SS Panzer-Grenadier Group, following up with the Division's Panthers and other units, had an even bigger problem and would not reach its assembly area until the night of 7/8 June – even then some important elements would be missing because of fuel shortages. Allied air power was having a serious effect on German logistics and movement.

Meanwhile, at 1655 hours the senior operations officer at von Rundstedt's Headquarters confirmed to the Chief of Staff Seventh Army that it was 'the wish of the Supreme Command that the enemy bridgehead be destroyed by the evening of 6 June because there was the danger of strong airborne and sea landings [in the Pas de Calais region]'. Not surprisingly he was told this was impossible.[8]

At 2000 hours Sepp Dietrich, commander I SS Panzer Corps, arrived at the Headquarters of the 21st Panzer Division in St Pierre-sur-Dives to assess the situation. To his intense irritation he found no Divisional commander and a Chief of Staff who had himself only just returned from Paris. He was told that in the late morning the 21st had been committed in support of the 716th Infantry Division and that his Divisional commander, Lieutenant General Edgar Feuchtinger, had gone to the 716th's Headquarters at Couvrechef to see his opposite number. Furthermore, the Headquarters of the 21st Division was out of touch with its units, which were operating piecemeal on both sides of the Orne river. And there was worse to come – Feuchtinger had, unbelievably, failed to take a radio with him so there was no way Dietrich could contact him. He was furious. He had been given command of the Division nearly five hours previously but there was still no way in which he could influence or coordinate the use of its eighty-plus Mk IVs and numerous assault guns with the tanks of the 12th SS Panzer Division.

At midnight Headquarters I SS Panzer Corps finally established formal links with the 12th SS and 21st Panzer Divisions and the battered remnants of the 716th Infantry Division. At about this time Dietrich learned that his newly constituted I SS Panzer Corps was to mount a counter-attack into the Allied bridgehead in the sector of the 716th Division using three Panzer Divisions. But there were many problems to be overcome before this could happen. 21st Panzer Division had already been committed to battle by LXXXIV Corps and it would be no easy task to coordinate its use with the 12th SS Panzer Division which had yet to arrive. Dietrich also knew that the Panzer Lehr Division, located over 100km away between Chartres and Le Mans (not shown on Maps), could not possibly arrive before first light on the 7th. Its 196 tanks, including eight Tigers, and forty assault guns, were vital for the success of any counter-attack. It was obvious to Dietrich that it would be impossible to launch a coordinated counter-attack before midday on the 7th at the earliest or even perhaps as late as the morning of the 8th. General Dollmann, the commander of Seventh Army, was so informed by teleprinter message.[9]

Kurt Meyer reported to the tactical Headquarters of General Richter's 716th Infantry Division at midnight. He described it as dug deep into the earth in a sandpit on the north side of Caen, with wounded men from the 716th Infantry and 21st Panzer Divisions lying in the corridors. Feuchtinger of 21st Panzer and a liaison group from the Panzer Lehr Division were also waiting for Meyer and a discussion took place on the possibilities of a coordinated attack by the three Panzer Divisions on 7 June. The officers from Panzer Lehr made it clear that there was no chance of their Division arriving in time and Feuchtinger was pessimistic about the chances of success with anything less than three divisions. The fact that he could not communicate with his own Headquarters at St Pierre-sur-Dives could not have helped matters. Feuchtinger said later:

> About midnight, Kurt Meyer arrived at my Headquarters. He was to take over on my left and we were to carry out a combined operation the next morning. I explained the situation to Meyer and warned him about the strength of the enemy. . . We decided to drive towards Douvres and 12 SS was to take up assembly positions during the night.[10]

Between them Meyer and Feuchtinger had about 160 tanks and five battalions of Panzer-Grenadiers available for the counter-attack and, with a large gap between the British and Canadian 3rd Divisions in the Douvres–Plumetot area, there was every chance of success if only these forces could be refuelled and coordinated in time.

As Meyer was about to leave Richter's Headquarters he received a telephone call from his own Divisional Commander, Fritz Witt, calling from Feuchtinger's Headquarters at St Pierre-sur-Dives. Witt asked for a situation report and then, having already discussed matters with Dietrich, said:

> The situation necessitates speedy action. First of all, the enemy has to be denied Caen and the Carpiquet airfield. It can be assumed that the enemy has already brought his units to order and that they have been readied for defence in so far as they have not deployed for further attacks. Therefore it would be wrong to throw our Divisional units into battle as soon as they arrive. We can only consider a coordinated attack with the 21st Panzer Division. So the Division is to attack the enemy along with the 21st Panzer Division and throw them into the sea. H-Hour for the attack is 7 June at midday.[11]

NOTES

1. 8 Armd & 56 Inf Bdes & 47 Cdo.
2. 2 Armd Bde & 48 RM Cdo.
3. Stacey, *Official History of the Canadian Army in the Second World War, The Victory Campaign*, Vol. III, p. 650.

4. Wilmot, *The Struggle for Europe*, pp. 292–3.
5. Ibid, p. 294.
6. The other Div in I SS Pz Corps, the 1st SS Pz Div Leibstandarte (LAH), located in Belgium, had been ordered by OKW to remain where it was in strategic reserve.
7. Meyer, Hubert, *The History of the 12th SS Panzer Division Hitlerjugend*, p. 33.
8. Seventh Army War Diary for 6 Jun 44.
9. Kraemer, *I SS Panzer Corps in the West*, MS # C-024.
10. Shulman, *Defeat in the West*, p. 121.
11. Meyer, Kurt, *Grenadiers*, p.120.

CHAPTER XI

The Iron Division – 7 and 8 June

7 June

(Map 3)

Since the main German actions against the Allied bridgehead in the first few days of the invasion were to take place in the British Second Army's sector, we will stay with the Iron Division for a few more days and then return to the Blue and Gray.

Before describing the Iron Division's actions on 7 June, and to some extent those of the 3rd Canadian Infantry Division, it is important to look at the German defences south of SWORD beach on D+1. In the case of the 21st Panzer Division it is unfortunate that most commentators have accepted without question the statement made in February 1947 by Edgar Feuchtinger that his defensive posture west of the Orne:

> was particularly difficult for the armoured group [which] had to defend a sector of over 5km in width for which it had only two Panzer-Grenadier Companies, one heavy Panzer-Grenadier Company and one engineer Company. As the whole anti-tank Battalion, with the exception of three guns, had been lost through its subordination to the static Division [716] on 6 June 44 . . . the two Battalions of the 22nd Panzer Regiment had to be fitted into the defence somehow.[1]

This is totally misleading. As we know from the details already provided of the counter-attack by 21st Panzer on the evening of D-Day, Feuchtinger had the whole of his Division west of the Orne on 7 June, less one tank Company, a Panzer-Grenadier Battalion, a Panzer Reconnaissance

101

Battalion, an Assault-Gun Battalion and a company of 88mm anti-tank guns.[2] This latter group formed KG von Luck which was on the east side of the river fighting the British 6th Airborne Division. The bulk of Feuchtinger's Division, which therefore comprised two Panzer Battalions less one Company, the two Battalions of Rauch's 192nd Panzer-Grenadier Regiment, the SPW Battalion of von Luck's 125th Panzer-Grenadier Regiment, the whole of the 220th Panzer Pioneer Battalion and the 2nd and 3rd Battalions of the 155th Panzer Artillery Regiment, was located between Hérouville on the Caen canal and the railway line running from Caen through Epron and Cambes to Luc-sur-Mer.

Turning now to the 12th SS Panzer Division Hitlerjugend, it will be remembered that its formal operation order issued early on the 7th stated that the Division would 'attack the disembarked enemy together with 21st Panzer Division and throw him back into the sea'. The objective was the Channel coast and the boundary between the two Divisions was to be the same railway line from Caen to Luc-sur-Mer mentioned above. H-Hour for the two Divisions, originally planned for midday, had to be delayed until 1600 hours since many of the Hitlerjugend's tanks had failed to arrive in the combat zone. About fifty Mk IV tanks of the 2nd SS Panzer Battalion reached their designated area at about 1000 hours, but the other forty or so were not expected until much later in the day or even after dark and the forty-eight combat-ready Panthers of the 1st SS Panzer Battalion were stranded east of the Orne without fuel. Furthermore, Wilhelm Mohnke's 26th SS Panzer-Grenadier Regiment, the SS Pioneers and some of the artillery Battalions had still to cross the Odon. Until these additional forces could take up their positions on Kurt Meyer's 25th SS Panzer-Grenadier Regiment's left flank there could be no full-scale attack by the Hitlerjugend. It was necessary therefore for the 25th Regiment to adopt temporary defensive positions. Meyer had already ordered a reconnaissance to the north-west of Caen late on 6 June and at 0100 hours on the 7th it reported Carpiquet and Buron clear of enemy, the latter being held by minor units of Richter's 716th Infantry Division, but that Villons-les-Buissons was occupied by enemy forces.[3] Meyer therefore based his Regiment on St Contest and Epron, due north of Caen and next to the 21st Panzer Division in its positions between Lébisey and Blainville. There was, however, a 2km gap between the two German Divisions – a gap that should have been occupied by the British 9th Infantry Brigade on D-Day!

British Actions

As already mentioned, Major General Tom Rennie was expecting a German armoured counter-attack against his Division at about first light on D+1. The ground dictated that any such attack was likely to come in on the same axis as that launched the previous evening, i.e., on his right flank through the gap between his men and the Canadians. It is perhaps unsurprising therefore that 9 Brigade on that flank was ordered to wait until well after first light before advancing on the axis Périers-sur-le-Dan–Mathieu–Cambes. We will come back to its actions shortly. Meanwhile Brigadier K P Smith's 185 Brigade was told to press forward on the left flank with Lébisey as its initial objective, while Cass's 8 Brigade was to clear Lion-sur-Mer, capture Plumetot and Cresserons and close the rear area gap with the Canadians. The Lincolns, who were dug in between Lion-sur-Mer and Hermanville-sur-Mer, were transferred to 8 Brigade for this task and the Suffolks, who were still in the HILLMAN area, took their place in 9 Brigade. Such was the overall plan; unfortunately in the event the urgency that might have been expected in its implementation was sadly lacking.

(Map 13)

Brigadier Kipper Smith decided that the operation to secure Lébisey would be carried out by a single Battalion – the Warwicks, less its D Company which was still guarding the Caen canal bridge at Bénouville. The Battalion was required to clear Blainville by first light, after which A and B Companies were to advance over 3km to secure the eastern half of Lébisey wood. C Company was then to pass through and capture the western half of the wood and the village of Lébisey. The Norfolks and KSLI were not involved and, since the ground was considered too difficult for tanks, no armoured support was to be provided. Three artillery Regiments (battalions) firing on the Lébisey wood east of the Caen–Biéville road, a naval cruiser firing on the wood and village west of the road and more concentrations of naval gunfire south of the wood were considered sufficient support to ensure a successful operation.

The Warwicks secured Blainville without difficulty by first light and at 0730 hours Brigadier Smith met his artillery advisor, Lieutenant Colonel Nigel Tapp, and Lieutenant Colonel 'Jumbo' Herdon, the commanding officer of the Warwicks, in the village to confirm his orders and go over the final details of the fire plan. H-Hour was set for 0845 hours.

The Warwicks' attack has been described by a number of writers including the Regimental historian, Marcus Cunliffe, and the commander of A Company, Captain (later Brigadier) Harry Illing. The latter wrote later that the orders for the attack were given in the dark off a map and that there was no opportunity for a visual reconnaissance of either the objective or the approaches to it. He went on to point out that the Start Line for the attack, on which the artillery fire plan was based, was unsecured and lay nearly half way to the first objective. Be that as it may, a good description of what happened in the initial stages of the attack is recorded in the 185 Brigade War Diary:

A Company came under heavy fire from houses on the canal road towards Beauregard . . . this caused considerable delay and CO [commanding officer] 2 Warwicks requested a postponement of H-Hour. The Brigade commander referred the matter to the Divisional commander who, in view of the importance of capturing Lébisey as quickly as possible, ordered that the delay should not be more than half an hour. The Brigade commander passed this information to CO 2 Warwicks and the supporting arms. Meanwhile B and C Companies had proceeded to the assembly area and owing to a breakdown in communications did not receive orders for the postponement. They then proceeded to attack at the original hour, unsupported.[4]

Not mentioned in the Brigade War Diary is the fact that the Battalion's armoured carriers and 6-pdr anti-tank guns were unable to follow the infantry Companies across the swampy ground between Blainville and the objective and were thus ordered to divert via the road through Biéville.

Meanwhile Lieutenant Colonel Jumbo Herdon, seeing two of his Companies advancing as originally planned, had little choice other than to order A Company, which had by now arrived on the Start Line[5], and his own Tactical Headquarters, to follow B and C Companies – again without artillery support. Matters now went from bad to worse, for waiting in Lébisey wood on the other side of a concave slope were well-prepared and dug-in Panzer-Grenadiers.[6] When the Warwicks were within 200m of the wood they opened fire. One Platoon of B Company on the right flank managed to get into the wood but its commander, Lieutenant Docherty, was killed and most of his men were wounded or taken prisoner. The rest of the Battalion found itself pinned down and it was not long before the commanding officer, Jumbo Herdon, was caught by machine-gun fire and killed. Major Robin Kreyer, the second-in-command, took over but there was little he could do. The Companies held on making use of such cover as was available but any movement brought down merciless fire. At 1150 hours Brigadier Smith asked the Divisional commander to release the Warwicks' D Company from its task of guarding the Caen canal bridge and at about the same time he ordered the Norfolks, who were 4km to the rear at Bellevue, to be prepared to move through the Warwicks to the high ground south of Lébisey.[7] In the meantime the Warwicks 'held on to the edge of the wood from 1200 hours until 1500 hours'.[8]

What of 9 Brigade on the right flank? The overall plan saw an attack in three Phases: Phase I was an advance to le Mesnil by the KOSB; in Phase II the Ulster Rifles, with A Squadron of the East Riding Yeomanry, a machine-gun Company and two medium mortar Platoons of the Middlesex under command, would take Cambes, while the Suffolks with another tank Squadron secured Galmanche; and finally in Phase III the

KOSB would exploit to St Contest. But before anything could happen Lieutenant Colonel Renny's KOSB had to be brought across to rejoin the Brigade from St Aubin-d'Arquenay (Map 3) where they had ended D-Day. The initial advance went well. By 1000 hours the Ulster Rifles group reached Périers which, not surprisingly, they found clear of enemy, and by 1215 hours the KOSB were on the Caen–Douvres road at Mathieu[9]. The latter then moved on down the Caen road to the le Mesnil wood where, at 1400 hours, they were ordered to dig in. The other Battalion in the Brigade, the Suffolks, and the other two tank Squadrons of the East Riding Yeomanry took no part in this advance other than to watch the flanks. Although there had been no direct opposition it had taken the Brigade over five hours to cover less than 5km.

(Map 3)

Meanwhile back in the 8 Brigade sector the Lincolns had been ordered to clear Lion-sur-Mer and capture TROUT. Lieutenant Colonel Welby-Everard decided to use his A and B Companies to clear the Château area on the southern outskirts of Lion-sur-Mer after which C and D would take on the strongpoint. The Battalion moved at 1520 hours and Phase I was completed for a loss of only nine wounded; despite this success, the second phase of the operation had to be cancelled when an order was received for the Battalion to move to the left flank of the Divisional area and take up a defensive position at St Aubin-d'Arquenay. It will be remembered that KOSB had only just been moved out of the village in order to take part in the 9 Brigade advance. Such was the haste of the Lincolns' move that the vehicles used to lift the Battalion were still half full of petrol cans for the re-supply of 27 Armoured Brigade! Fortunately the convoy was not attacked from the air or shelled and on arrival in St Aubin-d'Arquenay the Lincolns were told to send one Company to the Orne bridges. One Company of the Suffolks was already there, having relieved D Company of the Warwicks, but in view of the perceived threat to 6 Airborne Division's bridgehead from KG von Luck[10], this was considered insufficient.

Meanwhile at 1130 hours, single Platoons of B and C Companies of the South Lancs had occupied Plumetot and Cresserons against very light and scattered opposition, following which at 1300 hours the balance of the Companies mounted on the M-10s of 67 Anti-Tank Battery joined them. B Company then went on to take la-Délivrande where it captured an officer and thirty men. It did not, however, attack the fortified radar station south-west of Douvres – this task had been given to a Canadian Battalion.[11] At 1700 hours the Battalion received a warning order for a move to Biéville but twenty minutes later Brigadier Cass countermanded this order and said one company was to complete the Lincolns' mission in

Lion-sur-Mer in cooperation with No. 41 Commando. B Company was chosen for the task and at 1720 hours Lion-sur-Mer was reported clear of enemy. The Company then moved to a position where it could 'contain' strongpoint TROUT. C Company was withdrawn from the Plumetot area to join A Company in Hermanville-sur-Mer at 2330 hours. The third Battalion in 8 Brigade, the East Yorks, relieved the Ulster Rifles on the Périers ridge for their Cambes operation and then spent the day out of action, being reinforced and re-equipped.[12] It will be recalled that they had suffered heavily on D-Day.

(Map 13)

Let us return now to the Warwicks pinned down in front of the Lébisey wood. At about 1500 hours Brigadier Smith held a conference at the Headquarters of the KSLI during which it was decided to bring the Norfolks forward as a matter of urgency. At about the same time the situation in the Warwicks' sector eased slightly. Major Bundock's D Company, having been relieved on the Orne bridges, arrived and mounted an attack on the left flank. This enabled A Company to move forward and secure the north-east corner of the wood; but, 'the Battalion was [then] counter-attacked by tanks and forced to withdraw into a tank-proof locality in a thick part of the wood'.[13] Meanwhile the Mortar, Anti-Tank and Carrier Platoons, plus the only officer able to call for naval gunfire, had been waiting in Biéville for the order to move forward. This came from Brigadier Smith himself who drove up in a jeep and told the group that the Lébisey wood had been captured and their support was needed as a matter of urgency. The Platoons, with the Battalion Adjutant, Captain Pike, set off at once only to run straight into the Germans still in the wood and covering the road. All the vehicles were lost and the commanders of the Mortar, Anti-Tank and Carrier Platoons, Lieutenant Healey and Captains Bannerman and Waterworth respectively, were all captured. A number of the men managed to filter back to British lines during the night.

At 1605 hours Brigadier Smith was informed that the Warwicks were surrounded in Lébisey wood. With the Divisional commander's approval he therefore directed the Norfolks to cover the Warwicks' withdrawal and then to consolidate in as much of the wood as possible with a view to subsequent exploitation by the Brigade. A Squadron of the Staffordshire Yeomanry was to support the Norfolks.[14]

According to the 185 Brigade War Diary the advance by the Norfolks towards the east end of the Lébisey wood began at 1830 hours. The Royal Norfolk Regimental History says the Battalion:

advanced through the village of Hérouville under fire from snipers, crossed the anti-tank ditch in front of the wood and continued through cornfields to the edge of Lébisey wood, all without artillery support. The anti-tank guns and mortars were brought up to a position where they were able to give some support, though the leading companies were under heavy fire from fixed machine-guns and mortars, suffering a number of casualties.

The link up with the Warwicks was achieved but rather than being able to consolidate as ordered, the Norfolks now found themselves similarly pinned down.

Meanwhile, on the right flank of the Iron Division the Ulster Rifles, after a delay of another three hours, joined the KOSB in the le Mesnil wood at about 1700 hours and soon afterwards their D Company under Major John Aldworth and the Squadron of Shermans of the East Riding Yeomanry advanced towards Cambes. Nothing was known of the enemy's dispositions in and around the village, for its wood and park were surrounded by stone walls some 3m high. Aldworth led two of his Platoons into the east side of the Cambes wood and Captain Montgomery took the other two Platoons to the west. Unfortunately for the Ulstermen they ran straight into the 1st Battalion of Kurt Meyer's 25th SS Panzer-Grenadier Regiment, together with an SS Pioneer Company and five Mk IVs. This force had begun its advance towards Anguerny (Map 3) as part of a major counter-attack against the Canadians started two hours earlier by Meyer when he found their 9th Infantry Brigade overextended and highly vulnerable in the Authie area. This counter-attack need not concern us but for those interested full details can be found in the author's book *Steel Inferno*. Suffice to record here that the Shermans of the East Riding Yeomanry and German Mk IVs engaged each other on the completely flat ground to the west of Cambes and all five German tanks were either knocked out or immobilised. SS Panzer-Grenadiers claimed to have knocked out three of the Shermans using Panzerfausts. Despite their tank losses the Germans soon proved too strong for the Ulster Rifles who, after receiving thirty-one casualties[15] including Major John Aldworth killed, retreated back to the le Mesnil position. By now, however, the British artillery coupled with heavy and highly accurate naval gunfire began to take its toll of the Germans and at about this time Meyer became aware of worrying Allied movements on his western flank; as he put it in his book, *Grenadiers*:

Filled with tension, I observe the dust clouds west of the Muc [a stream usually spelt Mue]. Tank after tank is rolling over the high ground towards Bretteville [7km west of Buron]. There are no German troops in that sector that can stop the enemy's advance. Enemy tank forces are thus rolling right into the 26th SS Panzer-Grenadier Regiment's area of deployment. . . The way is open deep into our flank. . . . the 25th Regiment's attack has to be stopped immediately.[16]

Meyer called off his attack and both sides adopted defensive positions. The Ulster Rifles, KOSB and one Squadron of the East Riding Yeomanry were in the area of le Mesnil and its wood, and the Suffolks, 9 Brigade Headquarters and the rest of the Yeomanry tanks around Mathieu.

But what of the joint counter-attack by Feuchtinger's 21st Panzer Division and Kurt Meyer's heavily reinforced 25th SS Panzer-Grenadier Regiment ordered for 1600 hours? As we have just heard, Meyer decided to launch his attack two hours early and this ended any hope of a coordinated attack. In his book, *Grenadiers*, Meyer wrote:

> Whilst with the 1st Battalion, I notice, with some trepidation, that the 21st Panzer Division is not supporting the attack and that its tanks are stationary near Couvrechef. The Regiment's right flank is thus exposed and the enemy tanks are probing the 1st Battalion's flank.

Criticism that 21st Panzer Division failed to support Meyer's counter-attack continued even after the war. In an interview with Milton Shulman in August 1945, Feuchtinger said:

> Artillery fire was so great that a proper coordination of this attack was impossible. Meyer did make a short spurt with some fifty tanks, but was driven back. He never reached the start-line from which our combined attack was to begin. Allied anti-tank guns prevented him from getting into proper position.[17]

Not unreasonably Meyer strongly refuted this statement, but it is perhaps understandable that Feuchtinger was reluctant to attack earlier than the designated H-Hour of 1600 hours. Meyer was undoubtedly a dynamic commander, but his habit of riding around the battlefield on a motor-cycle often resulted in him being out of touch with his Divisional commander. Moreover, sending a despatch rider to tell the commander of the 22nd Panzer Regiment that he was attacking two hours early would, to say the very least, have caused some concern in that officer's mind. In any case there was no intention of 21st Panzer beginning its attack until Meyer's men had come into line and that did not happen until 1615 hours.

On the left flank of Rennie's front it was clear that as darkness approached the Warwicks and Norfolks were in a highly vulnerable state in the Lébisey wood sector and at 2230 hours Brigadier Smith gave orders for the Warwicks to withdraw under the protective fire of two field artillery Regiments (battalions), one medium artillery Regiment (battalion) and a naval cruiser. Captain Illing later described the withdrawal as 'neither coherent nor highly organised', but at least it was successful. The 185

Brigade War Diary records that after the Warwicks started their withdrawal, 'the Norfolks decided to do the same'. Overall the former lost ten officers and 144 other ranks on D+1 and the latter twenty killed, including three officers, and some thirty wounded. According to Kipper Smith's own account of events on this day he personally went off during this time, 'to get an inkling of the situation but got lost and, finding a barn, rested on a bed of straw until dawn'.[18]

So ended D+1. It was clearly a day of missed opportunities and extreme muddle. In the case of 9 Brigade an advance by a single Battalion supported by a Squadron (company) of tanks in the middle of the day while the rest of the Brigade remained idle was hardly likely to lead to the capture of Caen. And on the left flank a similar attack by a single Battalion of Smith's 185 Brigade without tanks was courting disaster and the muddled way in which it was executed guaranteed failure. As the commander of A Company of the Warwicks, wrote later:

> It was galling that the great prize of Caen had not fallen into our hands. Lébisey could in all probability have been captured if a properly coordinated *brigade* [author's emphasis] attack had been put in instead of battalions being committed piecemeal: first a battalion on the evening of D-Day, secondly our own on the morning of D+1, and thirdly by another battalion on the evening of D+1.[19]

(Map 3)

And where was the armoured thrust that Monty had demanded? Where indeed were the tanks of 27 Armoured Brigade? The answer is simple – apart from one squadron of the East Riding Yeomanry, they were doing virtually nothing. The six remaining tanks of A Squadron of the 13/18 H remained near Hermanville-sur-Mer all day, but at 1600 hours B and C Squadrons, accompanied by the M-10 Troop of 67 Anti-tank Battery from the Cresserons area, were sent to cover the Caen canal and Orne river bridges. Reports had been received of a German counter-attack in this area involving Tiger tanks and a battalion of Panzer-Grenadiers.[20] In the event no such attack developed and as darkness fell the Hussar tanks withdrew to a harbour area between Bénouville and St Aubin-d'Arquenay. They were to remain there out of action for the next three days: 'learning how to cook on petrol stoves . . . discovering how to sleep in comparative comfort and safety in shallow pits dug beneath the tanks and how to take a bath in a canvas bucket full of cold water'.[21] As we have heard A Squadron of the Staffordshire Yeomanry was placed in support of the Norfolks in the late afternoon of D+1, whilst the rest of the Regiment remained in a counter-penetration role on the Périers ridge facing south and south-west.

By the end of D+1 only thirty-one tanks had been lost to enemy action. Fifty-eight replacement Shermans were immediately available with another twenty-eight standing ready to be delivered during D+3 and D+4.[22] The fact that eighty-six replacement tanks were in the immediate pipeline gives some indication of the tank casualties expected by the planners in the SWORD beach sector alone.

The performance of Rennie and the commanders of 185 and 9 Brigades on 7 June can only be described as seriously wanting. All three were, of course, infantrymen without previous experience in handling armour. Whilst no one would dispute their proven personal bravery in earlier campaigns, it is clear that they were unprepared, and indeed untrained, for their mission of thrusting inland quickly and in strength. The classic example is Kipper Smith. He had served in WWI and in Africa and India and with the RAF between the wars, but his only previous senior command experience was as the commander of the 1st Infantry Brigade on the island of Malta – hardly the ideal pedigree for the officer destined to lead the main attack on Caen! Smith's pre-D-Day experience with armour was typical of the day:

> We went down to the Tank Corps Depot at Bovington [Headquarters of the Royal Armoured Corps in Dorset] where each of us [senior commanders] was put in the driver's seat of a Churchill tank for a day. It was great fun and I challenged Jim Cunningham to a race which he won when I stalled my engine going up a dune.[23]

Readers will recall that the Staffordshire Yeomanry were equipped with Shermans anyway.

The failure of the British Army to train its senior officers in handling mixed battlegroups of armour, infantry and engineers with supporting artillery was to dog its performance throughout the Normandy campaign and, unbelievably, it was to be another nineteen years before infantry officers were given practical training and experience in this modern form of warfare.[24]

Furthermore, it will not have escaped the reader's notice that the Suffolks, East Yorks, KOSB, KSLI, 13/18H, Staffordshire Yeomanry and the bulk of the East Riding Yeomanry were not engaged on D+1. The only thing that can be said in defence of Tom Rennie is that the nervous reaction of Crocker at I Corps and Dempsey at Second Army to events east of the Orne led to moves to reinforce the Orne bridges at the expense of moves towards the main objective of Caen. Defensive tactics and reaction to events, rather than a seizure of the initiative at a time when the enemy was relatively weak and unbalanced, seem to have been the order of the day. As Feuchtinger put it later:

34. An exhausted GI – 11 June.

35. Generals George Marshall (Chairman US Joint Chiefs of Staff) and Dwight Eisenhower (Supreme Commander Allied Expeditionary Force) and Admiral Ernest King (CinC US Fleet) aboard a DUKW near Vierville – 12 June.

36. Hedgerow fighting.

37. Germans dug in with MG-42.

38. Hedgerow fighting.

39. Dead GIs.

40. 'Hedgebuster' fitted to Sherman.

41. Hedgebusting Sherman.

42. Bulldozer blade fitted to Sherman and used for hedgebusting.

43. Sherman fitted with 'rhino'.

44. Sergeant Curtis Culin of the 2nd Armored Division – inventor of the 'rhino'.

45. Colonel von Oppeln-Bronikowski, commander KG Oppeln on D-Day.

46. Mk IV tank dug in near Lébisey.

47. Major General 'Bolo' Whistler, commander 3rd Infantry Division from 23 June, with Lieutenant General Crocker, commander I British Corps.

48. Officers of 9 Infantry Brigade meet Resistance leaders in Caen – 9 July.

49. Brigadier 'Dutch' Cota being decorated by Monty on 9 July.

50. Ernest Hemingway (on right) with Robert Capa of *Life* magazine and Pfc Olin Tomkins, their driver, in centre.

51. Members of the Blue and Gray pass a dead German and knocked out anti-aircraft vehicle near St Lô.

52. GIs accompany a Sherman into St Lô.

53. US troops pass knocked out Mk IV tank – St Lô.

54. Two members of the Blue and Gray check a dead German's equipment while another keeps watch.

55. Greyhound armoured cars of the Blue and Gray's Reconnaissance Troop in St Lô – 20 July.

56. US vehicles enter St Lô.

57. German armoured car in St Lô – 29 July.

58. The Blanchet mausoleum in St Lô – Tactical Headquarters of the 1st Battalion of the 115th Regiment on 18 July 1944.

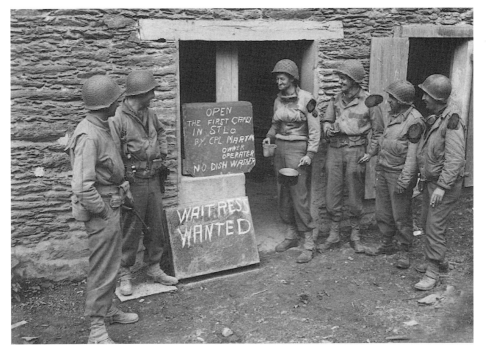

59. Cpl E L Martin opens the first US café in St Lô – 19 July. Blue and Gray shoulder insignia has been eradicated by the censor.

60. Two members of the Blue and Gray mourn their dead. La Cambe cemetery, 11 July.

THIS CEMETERY

was established on 11 June 1944 by the **29ᵗʰ INFANTRY DIVISION. UNITED STATES ARMY.** *as a final resting place for officers and men of that* **DIVISION** *who made the supreme sacrifice on the battlefields of* **NORMANDY.** *We who carry on the fight salute these comrades, and other honored dead of the* **DIVISION** *who could not be buried here. In command of this valiant legion of the* **BLUE and GRAY** *is* **LIEUTENANT COLONEL WILLIAM T. TERRY** (0-185851) **INFANTRY.** *who was killed in action on 17 July 1944.*

20 July 1944

61. La Cambe cemetery in July 1944 – now an official *German* cemetery.

THOMAS D. HOWIE

LE MAJOR DE SAINT-LO

12 AVRIL 1908/17 JUILLET 1944

COMMANDANT LE 3 BATAILLON

116ᵉ RÉGIMENT D'INFANTERIE

29ᵉ DIVISION U.S.A.

62. Memorial to Major Howie in St Lô.

63. Major General Charles Canham – 27 January 1953.

64. Brigadiers 'Copper' Cass, Jim Cunningham and 'Kipper' Smith revisit SWORD beach in 1964.

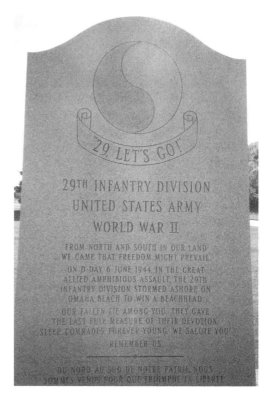

65. Memorial to the 29th Infantry Division, Vierville.

On 7 June 44 it was possible to shape the main line of resistance . . . into one line, to consolidate it, make adjustments and to put it in a state in which it would be able to repel large scale enemy attacks.[25]

One has to wonder what would have happened if George Patton had been in Dempsey's or Crocker's positions on D+1 and Uncle Charlie Gerhardt in Tom Rennie's?

By last light on 7 June the Iron Division had lost 996 men.[26]

Caen on 7 June

At 0230 on 7 June 120 Lancasters of RAF Bomber Command dropped another 440 tons of bombs on Caen.[27] The St Jean district was hit again, as was that of St Louis. The destruction caused proved too much for the Caen fire fighters, many of whom were injured; sixteen were buried under the rubble of the fire station and the resulting fires were to burn for eleven days. Many people fled to the racecourse outside Caen and by 0700 hours some 1,500 people had taken shelter in St Etienne, the church of the Abbaye-aux-Hommes. An estimated 4,000 more[28], including mental patients, some deaf-mute children and many ordinary schoolchildren, had crowded into the huge Convent of le Bon Sauveur, so big that it was known as 'the town within a town'. Hundreds more moved to the quarries at Fleury, 2km south of Caen whilst others fled towards Evercy, 10km to the south-west (Map 1).

Kurt Meyer described the scene as he moved past the city on his way to counter the British and Canadians:

Caen is a sea of flames. Harassed people are wandering through the rubble, streets are blocked, burning smoke is rolling though the town. Venerable churches are converted into heaps of rubble, the work of generations is now a sea of ashes and rubble. Seen from a military point of view, the destruction of Caen is a major mistake.[29]

In improved weather conditions, RAF photographic reconnaissance on 7 June confirmed that the city was on fire, the four main bridges over the Orne impassable and the railway station devastated. It probably did not show that three of the city's hospitals had been hit or, according to one of the nuns at le Bon Sauveur, the many convents and schools that had suffered a similar fate. Detailed assessments by the air staffs, however, deduced that the damage would cause only temporary delays to German military movement. The Orne bridges were therefore targeted again that same afternoon and sixty-three B-26 Marauders dropped 100 tons of bombs. This raid was followed by yet another at 1800 hours when seventy-three Marauders attacked unspecified 'town defences'.

No one is sure how many people died in the air raids on 6 and 7 June but most estimates put the figure well in excess of 600.

8 June

(Map 1)

Montgomery landed on French soil early on D+2 and spent most of the day touring the British sector. During a meeting with Miles Dempsey in the early afternoon he was told that the Canadian and British 3rd Infantry Divisions north of Caen were 'a bit messy' and needed to get their armour and artillery under better control. Once this was done Dempsey wanted I Corps 'to be prepared to operate offensively with a view to capturing Caen from the east [i.e., from the 6 Airborne Division bridgehead] in two or three days time.' [30] Monty disagreed. He was already aware that the situation in front of Caen was unsatisfactory and that evening he wrote to the Director of Operations in the War Office in London:

> The Germans are doing everything they can to hold on to Caen. I have decided not to have a lot of casualties by butting up against the place; so I have ordered Second Army to keep up good pressure at Caen and to make its main effort towards Villers-Bocage and Evrecy and thence south-east towards Falaise.[31]

He also signalled Eisenhower, the Supreme Commander, at 2000 hours:

> Today has been spent in repelling attacks in the Caen sector and in cleaning up centres of resistance existing inside our lodgement area . . . Am organising strong thrust south towards Villers-Bocage and Evrecy. Am very satisfied with the situation.[32]

Monty's statement that the day had been spent repelling attacks in the Caen sector applied only to the Canadian part of the I Corps area. In the case of the 3rd British Infantry Division it was a day of consolidation.

(Map 3)

In 9 Brigade the Suffolks marched from their positions in the HILLMAN area and dug in around Mathieu. They had not been engaged since D-Day. The KOSB and Ulster Rifles maintained their current positions with the only offensive action being a patrol by the Ulster Rifles towards the SS Panzer-Grenadiers near Cambes. The Germans did the same and the two patrols clashed. Five SS men were killed and six SS taken prisoner. The Ulster Rifles lost two killed and three wounded. The tanks of the East

Riding Yeomanry remained in reserve between le Mesnil and Villons-les-Buissons.

In the 185 Brigade sector Brigadier Smith reappeared at his Head-quarters in the Château in Biéville and was revived with a bottle of champagne:

> My HQ was in the ruins of a large chateau which the RAF had destroyed. . . There were enormous cellars with hundreds of empty champagne bottles. Pat Dayley, my BM [Chief of Staff] was naturally wondering what had happened to me but during my absence he had found a full bottle and, returning extremely weary and depressed, the champagne cheered us up considerably.[33]

The Warwicks, after their withdrawal from Lébisey, dug in at Beuville, a little to the north of the KSLI in Biéville, and reorganised. 150 replacements were received and distributed throughout the Companies and a new commanding officer, Lieutenant Colonel Gibbs, took over. The second-in command, Major Kreyer, received a DSO for his leadership during the Lébisey wood battle.

The Norfolks in the woods north-east of Biéville were ordered to send a detachment to the left flank between Blainville and Beauregard where they were to hold a new line some 2km in front of the rest of the Brigade. It consisted of Major Eric Cooper-Key's B Company, three sections of carriers and two SP anti-tank guns, all under the command of the Battalion second-in-command, Major Humphrey Wilson. In the coming days this position, nicknamed 'Duffer's Drift', became a major patrol base. The KSLI spent the day reorganising and integrating 100 reinforcements.

Back in the 8 Brigade area a midday attack by B Company of the South Lancs and four flail tanks of A Squadron of the 22nd Dragoons was launched against strongpoint TROUT. The latter cleared a lane through mines and wire and engaged the enemy at point blank range.[34] Not surprisingly the eighty Germans who had held out in the strongpoint for a day and a half surrendered. Whilst this was happening the rest of the South Lancs moved to Bénouville and at 1330 hours its Companies were in position on each side of the Caen canal and Orne river bridges. The East Yorks, like the Lincolns, spent the day of the 8th resting.

The three Regiments of Brigadier Erroll Prior-Palmer's 27th Armoured Brigade remained in a counter-penetration role and carried out maintenance. The Brigade War Diary records the 8th as 'a quiet day on the whole'.

NOTES

1. Feuchtinger, MS # B-441.
2. 4 Pz Coy, 2/125 Pz-Gren Bn, 21 Pz Recce Bn, 200 StuG Bn & one coy of 88mm guns from 200 JgPz Bn: von Luck, *Panzer Commander*, p. 142 & personally to the author 17 Nov 1981.
3. The tanks of the Canadian Sherbrooke Fusiliers & the North Nova Scotia Highlanders.
4. 185 Inf Bde War Diary dated 7 Jun 44, Appx 1.
5. According to Illing, *No Better Soldier*, pp. 21–2: 'My own company had run into trouble and had a bit of a battle. They had had to divert from their prearranged route and work their way forward and so were late.'
6. 1/125 Pz-Gren Regt.
7. 185 Inf Bde War Diary dated 7 Jun 44.
8. 2 Warwicks War Diary dated 7 Jun 44.
9. Shown incorrectly on the 1944 British maps as Cazelle.
10. See Note 2.
11. At the end of D+1 this task was handed over to 51 (Highland) Inf Div.
12. Nightingale, *The East Yorkshire Regiment in the War 1939/45*, p.188.
13. 2 Warwicks War Diary dated 7 Jun 44.
14. 185 Inf Bde War Diary dated 7 Jun 44.
15. 2 RUR War Diary dated 7 Jun 44.
16. Meyer, *Grenadiers*, pp. 123–4.
17. Shulman, *Defeat in the West*, p. 121.
18. Smith, *Adventures of an Ancient Warrior*, p, 108.
19. Illing, *No Better Soldier*, p. 24.
20. 13/18 H War Diary dated 7 Jun 44.
21. Miller, *History of the 13th/18th Royal Hussars 1922–1947*, p.106.
22. 3 Inf Div Administrative Plan, 2nd Edition, dated 11 May 44.
23. Smith, op. cit., p, 97.
24. The author attended the second of such courses in November 1963.
25. Feuchtinger, MS # B-441.
26. Dupuy Institute (collated from 'A' Branch Situation Reports in 21 Army Group files): 124 killed, 635 wounded and 237 missing. If confirmed D+1 casualties are subtracted from this total of 996, one is left with a D-Day casualty figure of 752.
27. Air 41/24: ABH Narrative, Vol. III, p. 72.
28. These figures are merely estimates made in retrospect by various French writers.
29. Meyer, op. cit., p. 118.
30. Diary of M C Dempsey, PRO London.
31. Hamilton, *Monty Master of the Battlefield 1942–1944*, p. 631.
32. Ibid., p. 633.
33. Smith, op. cit., p, 108
34. *The Story of the 79th Armoured Division*, p. 65.

CHAPTER XII

The Iron Division – 9 to 11 June

(Map 13)

Despite Montgomery's statement that he had 'decided not to have a lot of casualties by butting up against the place [Caen]', 9 Brigade was ordered to launch a major attack on 9 June. Brigadier Dennis Orr's plan, a repeat of that attempted on 7 June, required the Ulster Rifles to capture Cambes in Phase One and the Suffolks to take the hamlet of Galmanche, a kilometre to the south-west, in Phase Two. On the successful completion of these Phases, the Brigade was to go on to capture Mâlon and St Contest. Despite the fact that Lieutenant Colonel Harris's Ulster Rifles would have to advance across a one and a half kilometre stretch of completely open country, the tanks of the East Riding Yeomanry were not to lead the way – C Squadron was to protect the right flank, A Squadron was to 'shoot the Ulster Rifles into Cambes' and then take up a position facing south-west, whilst B Squadron was to be kept in reserve just forward of Ainsy.[1] In fact the whole operation had all the hallmarks of a WWI attack. Massive fire support was to be provided by the whole of the Iron Division's artillery, a naval cruiser, one Company of heavy mortars and another of medium machine-guns from the Middlesex, two troops of M-10s and five AVREs.[2] What the commander of 9 Brigade did not know, however, was that the Ulster Rifles were being pitched against a well-prepared Panzer-Grenadier Battalion in Cambes, supported by tanks of the 21st Panzer Division in la Bijude, and that his Brigade was being 'butted up' against the whole of Kurt Meyer's 25th SS Panzer-Grenadier Regiment. The latter had other Battalions deployed in the northern edge of Galmanche and at Buron; furthermore, two more Panzer-Grenadier Companies of Feuchtinger's Division were defending la Londe and its Château.[3] Put in simple military terms the Germans were holding all the 'vital ground'.

The Chief of Staff of the 12th SS Panzer Division Hitlerjugend, Hubert Meyer, had this to say about the 9 Brigade attack:

> The Royal Ulsters started an attack . . . at 1515 hours in order to capture Cambes. They were supported by preparatory fire from the artillery of the 3rd Division and from a cruiser. That fire landed in no-man's land. When the Battalion had approached to within 1km of its objective, it received concentrated fire from artillery, mortars and machine-guns . . . The enemy suffered significant losses. . . With the arrival of darkness, the King's Own Scottish Borderers moved forward to reinforce the Ulsters. The enemy apparently expected a counter-attack. . . Two

attacks on the neighbour to the right, Panzer Regiment 22 [21st Panzer Division] were reported. The first attack started at 1600 hours resulting in two enemy tanks lost. The second attack began at 2030 hours. The neighbour on the right knocked out fifteen tanks during the attack. The Platoon of the 16th Pioneer Company, in action on the right flank of the 1st Battalion, destroyed a tank in close combat using a Teller mine. . . During the fighting on 8 and 9 June the 1st Battalion lost one NCO and four men killed. Four NCOs and sixteen men were wounded. Of them, four NCOs and five men remained with the unit.[4]

A British version of this attack differs in the number of tanks lost and in pointing out, correctly, that Cambes was in fact captured:

The objective of the two [Ulster Rifles] Companies was to seize the northern half of Cambes through which the follow-up Companies would pass to take the rest of the village. . . A Company on the left under Major 'Digger' Tighe-Wood was especially hard hit; the Company lost all three platoon commanders. . . B Company under Major Hyde also reached their final objective which included the once fine Norman church. D Company under Captain Montgomery went through on the right and secured its objective despite him being wounded twice and with only one officer left. C Company under Major Stewart de Longueuil came through on the left and fought through the wood to their objective. Under command of this Company were five AVREs which engaged the enemy beyond the village until all were knocked out by enemy guns [tanks] firing from la Bijude but not before knocking out one German tank.[5] There then followed five hours of vicious shelling and mortaring as the Battalion consolidated. The War Diary of 9 Brigade reported that the success signal went up at 1610 hours but there was some uncertainty as to the exact state of affairs owing to a breakdown in communications. Plans had been made for the Scottish Borderers to advance into Cambes and stabilise the situation . . . They advanced [from le Mesnil] at 2015 . . . and reached the Ulsters in the grounds of the Château.[6] They helped to clear up the remainder of the village and consolidated. . . The East Riding Yeomanry who had helped the Ulsters into Cambes were shot up from west of the village and had two tanks destroyed; another Squadron protecting the other flank came under fire from la Londe and had a tank knocked out.[7]

During this very valiant attack against Cambes by the Ulster Rifles, for which members of the Battalion received three MCs, one Distinguished Conduct Medal and two MMs, the Suffolks moved forward to their designated assembly area in le Mesnil in preparation for Phase Two – the capture of Galmanche. Unfortunately, however, when the commanding officer, Lieutenant Colonel Dick Goodwin, reconnoitred his Battalion's part in the operation, his armoured carrier was hit by anti-tank fire and he was badly wounded. Soon after this Tom Rennie came forward to assess the overall situation and gave orders for the Suffolks to: 'Firm base where you are.' Caution once more ruled the day and the Battalion went into defence round the le Mesnil farm.

The limited British success on 9 June, an advance of just 2km, was very costly. The Ulster Rifles lost ten officers and 172 men, the KOSB three killed and thirteen wounded and the Middlesex, providing machine-gun support, two officers and a sergeant-major killed. The commanding officer of 33 Field Regiment, Lieutenant Colonel Tom Hussey, was also killed, as were the Battery commander in direct support, Major Brooks, and one of his forward observers, Captain Roose. In the other forward observer party all the personnel were wounded.

As for the rest of Rennie's Division on D+3, Brigadier Kipper Smith's 185 Brigade spent the day patrolling, improving its defensive positions and starting work on an extensive minefield on its western flank designed to protect it from any possible attack directed between Biéville and Beuville. Brigadier Copper Cass's 8 Brigade in the area of St Aubin-d'Arquenay (Map 3) and the Orne bridges was relieved by a recently landed Brigade of the 51st Highland Division, and its Battalions then moved into le Mesnil wood on the eastern flank of the Suffolks and about a kilometre north of le Londel.

There was one further movement by the British before the front immediately north of Caen solidified. During the afternoon of 10 June a patrol of the South Lancs discovered that a group of buildings at le Londel was undefended and at 2100 hours that evening D Company of the Battalion occupied them. By 0300 hours on 11 June the South Lancs were firm in the le Londel position and at 0900 hours elements of the Battalion began to infiltrate south-west towards the farm and out-buildings at la Londe and the Château de la Londe which, as just mentioned, were held by two Panzer-Grenadier Companies of Feuchtinger's 21st Panzer Division. Unfortunately when reports came in of German self-propelled guns and three tanks in the area of la Bijude, the ever-cautious Brigadier Cass called a halt to the operation.[8]

It is time now to return to the actions of the American 29th Division, the Blue and Gray, south of OMAHA beach.

NOTES

1. East Riding Yeo War Diary for Jun 44.
2. 2 Ulster Rifles War Diary for Jun 44.
3. 5 & 7 Companies, 192 Gren Regt (21 Pz Div).

4. Hubert Meyer, *The History of the 12th SS Panzer Division Hitlerjugend*, pp. 62–3.
5. 5 ARRE War Diary for Jun 44 says that three AVREs of 77 Sqn operated with C Coy & two with D Coy. One broke a track, three were disabled by enemy action & one was shot up by the East Riding Yeo. The Sqn suffered five wounded and fourteen missing.
6. The Château no longer exists but the dovecote remains and indicates the approximate location.
7. Lummis, *From Sword to the Seine*.
8. 1 South Lancs War Diary for Jun 44.

CHAPTER XIII

The Blue and Gray – 7 and 8 June

The OMAHA Sector

(Maps 5 & 12)

7 June

When dawn broke on 7 June the situation on and to the south of OMAHA beach was, from the American point of view, far from satisfactory. Despite appalling casualties, the bridgehead was only some 3,000m wide and 1,500m deep at best – about 10% of that planned. In addition, the beach itself was still under enemy artillery fire, only about a third of the obstacles had been cleared and a mere 100 tons of essential supplies, including ammunition, out of a planned total of 2,400 tons had been landed. The commander of the 29th Division, Major General Charles Gerhardt, although ashore in his CP in the Vierville draw, had still not been given command of the 115th and 116th Regiments; however, the overall commander ashore, Major General Huebner of the 1st Infantry Division, did allow him and his Deputy, Dutch Cota, to plan and direct the actions of those two Regiments on the 7th. They were to operate to the west of a line drawn from St Laurent to Formigny, whilst the 1st Division would stay to the east. Cota established a separate Headquarters in St Laurent where he could maintain close contact with the 1st Division. He had had a busy time during the night of D-Day and the early morning of D+1, visiting Huebner and V Corps Headquarters several times and his own commander twice to keep him informed of plans and events. This untidy but essentially practical command arrangement persisted until 1700 hours when Gerhardt officially re-assumed command of his

Division. By then his third Regiment, the 175th, which had started landing at 1230 hours, was more or less complete in the area of the beach north of St Laurent.[1] Its landing had not been easy. Each of its Companies was carried in a different landing craft and the situation off OMAHA, with its jumble of warships and transports, was almost as chaotic as that on the beach itself. One officer of the Regiment described the scene as looking 'like something out of Dante's Inferno'. Nevertheless, during the afternoon the 'Dandy Fifth' was ordered to march, in column of Battalions, via the Vierville draw and village towards the hamlet of Gruchy. This was a complete change of plan and caused some confusion. The Regiment had been expecting to move south after landing and indeed C Company never received the new orders and ended up with the 115th Regiment for three days.

Gerhardt's Division, which still lacked supplies, transport and its normal artillery and armoured support, spent most of the day of the 7th clearing up 'the fragments of enemy units that were shattered but not destroyed by the initial shock of the landings. In some areas small arms fire from groups of enemy riflemen or isolated strongpoints was almost continuous'.[2]

Some idea of the tenacity of the enemy remaining near the US bridgehead can be gauged from the fact that at 0520 hours on the 7th, B Company of the 121st Engineers was forced out of the Château Vaumicel and back into Vierville by a German counter-attack.

The same situation pertained in St Laurent and the surrounding area where the 3rd Battalion of Colonel Eugene Slappey's 115th Regiment had been ordered to mop up. This was achieved by 0900 hours and the Regiment then moved first towards Vierville and then south-west towards Longueville on the Isigny road. Its progress was desperately slow, due in some respects to the fact that it had to carry all its heavy weapons and ammunition but also because communications were very poor and the Battalions were out of contact with each other for most of the day. By last light its 1st and 3rd Battalions had been halted in front of Louvières and its 2nd was in a stream valley a kilometre north-west of Montigny.[3]

Meanwhile, Colonel Charles Canham of the 116th had arrived in St Laurent from Vierville at 0930 hours in order to see Dutch Cota and to try to regain control of his disorganised 2nd and 3rd Battalions. Both units were in poor shape; Major Bingham's 2nd Battalion numbered less than 500 men, Lieutenant Colonel Meeks' 3rd was little better off and both Battalions lacked their proper complement of heavy weapons. Even so Canham ordered the 2nd Battalion to clear the few remaining Germans from the les Moulins draw and the 3rd to sweep the ridgeline between there and Vierville where 'small parties of riflemen, with occasional support from machine-guns and mortars, were reappearing at points

119

along the bluffs to harass the beaches'.[4] No sooner had these operations been completed in the late afternoon, however, than General Gerhardt gave orders that both Battalions, rather than continuing to move westwards, were to 'form a tight defense perimeter around the town [Vierville] and protect the beach and CP [Command Post] installations of 29th Infantry Division'.[5]

At around 2000 hours Vierville was subjected to a 'prolonged concentration by German artillery, judged to be 150mm, which demolished buildings . . . blew up ammunition trucks and destroyed a number of vehicles and at least three AA guns'.[6] Traffic moving up the Vierville draw was also hit, with Lieutenant Colonel John Cooper's 110th FA Battalion losing two howitzers and seventeen men. Immediately following the shelling another German counter-attack in company strength 'carried past the Château [Vaumicel] before being stopped by mortar and rifle fire'.[7]

Before leaving Vierville for St Laurent, Canham had ordered Lieutenant Colonel John Metcalfe, the commander of the 1st Battalion of the 116th, to advance along the coast road to relieve the Ranger force at the Pointe du Hoc. He was to move out at 0800 hours with his own depleted Battalion of some 250 men, and the 5th Ranger Battalion, three Companies of the 2nd Ranger Battalion and ten tanks of B Company of the 743rd Tank Battalion under command. In the event, enemy activity in the Vierville sector necessitated leaving four companies of the 5th Rangers behind. Even so, advancing with the 2nd Rangers in the lead and with tanks on the road between two columns of infantrymen and Rangers, the combined force reached the hamlet of St Pierre du Mont, about a kilometre from the Pointe du Hoc, by 1100 hours. German counter-attacks[8] had pushed the ninety or so survivors there into a strip of headland about 200m deep and 500m wide. Supporting fire from naval destroyers had helped them to hold off the Germans but their situation was now said to be desperate. The 116th Group mounted two attacks during the afternoon of the 7th but accurate German artillery fire damaged two of the Shermans[9] and the rest withdrew leaving the infantry unsupported. After losing thirty to forty men, Metcalfe decided to wait for further reinforcements and attack again the following day. As the US Official History puts it, 'a series of attacks by the relieving force . . . although frustrated by well-placed enemy artillery fire, at least eased the pressure'.[10]

Colonel Paul Goode's 175th Regiment reached the Gruchy area by 2000 hours. The sight of so many bodies still lying exposed on OMAHA beach had done little for his men's morale but the knowledge that additional armour and artillery had been landed gave them some confidence. Twenty-nine guns of the 58th, 111th, 224th and 227th FA Battalions had been brought ashore, as had the tanks of Lieutenant Colonel Stuart Fries' 747th Tank Battalion.

During the night of 7 June Gerhardt told Canham that his 2nd and 3rd

Battalions were to move west soon after first light to catch up with the 1st Battalion and that the whole Regimental Group was then to attack and relieve the Ranger force at the Pointe du Hoc. Gerhardt had already received orders from General Gerow at V Corps at 2100 hours to take Isigny as a matter of urgency and he chose the 175th, formerly in Corps reserve, reinforced by the newly arrived 747th Tank Battalion, less B Company with the 1st Division, for this mission. The 115th Regiment was tasked with protecting the flank of this advance by moving one Battalion to the Formigny area and using the other two to secure the high ground north of the Aure river from Normanville to Longueville. The 116th Group, after it had relieved the Rangers at the Pointe du Hoc, was to continue advancing on the coastal road, clearing any enemy between Grandcamp and Isigny as it did so.

The 175th Regimental Group's advance jumped off at 2130 hours along the minor road leading through Englesqueville to la Cambe. Although the light was beginning to fade, tanks led the way.

The Enemy

The enemy confronting the 29th Division on 7 June still comprised units of Kraiss' 352nd Infantry Division with the remnants of the 726th Grenadier Regiment under command. The following description of the fighting on that day is taken from the Divisional Chief of Staff's account[11] and can be compared with the US version.

Sometime before 1000 hours, Colonel Goth's 916th Regiment reported that its counter-attack towards Vierville was making progress and that the Americans had been pushed back into the northern part of the village. Losses were described as 'considerable on both sides'. This was presumably the attack carried out much earlier that morning against the 121st Engineers in the Château Vaumicel. It was also reported at this time that the 352nd Pioneer Battalion had attacked from Vierville towards St Laurent.

More worrying for Kraiss was the news from the commander of the strongpoint at the Pointe et Raz de la Percée that the Americans had been unloading tanks and artillery on OMAHA during the night 'almost undisturbed'.

By 1300 hours Goth was reporting the enemy advancing with artillery support from St Laurent to the south. Although this move, by part of the 115th Regiment, was of much less concern to Kraiss than the advance in the Bayeux sector (Map 1) by the British, he nevertheless detached the 517th Battalion of the so-called 'Mobile' 30th Brigade to Goth's command. Mounted on bicycles, it arrived in the late evening and was deployed in the Formigny sector. The other two Battalions of the Brigade, also on bicycles, were used against the British.

At about 1700 hours Goth reported that the Americans (1st Infantry Division) had penetrated into the gun positions of the artillery Battalion north-east of Formigny and news also came in that the enemy had 'broken through the ring of obstacles at the Pointe du Hoc and had slightly pushed back . . . the reinforced company of the 914th Regiment'.

In his 2200 hours summary of the day's fighting, the Chief of Staff stated:

> In the 916th Regiment [sector] hard fighting continued until late in the evening. The 517th Battalion is to relieve the completely exhausted 1st Battalion of the 916th Regiment during the night. . . Though it was not possible to fling the enemy into the sea, at least we managed to thwart his probable attack intentions on 7 June. We must expect however, a further reinforcing of the . . . St Laurent bridgehead and a continuation of the attack on 8 June. . . The reinforced 916th Regiment has suffered considerable losses and is severely weakened physically and morally.[12]

St Lô

Dawn on 7 June saw the people of St Lô emerging from the rubble of their houses and shelters. Some headed for 'The Tunnel', a large underground cavity beneath the city ramparts that acted as a communal shelter and First Aid Post, but most of those who could headed for the countryside. But still the destruction was not at an end. At 0830 hours more aircraft appeared overhead; the Police Headquarters and prison were hit again and although some prisoners managed to escape from their cells and release others, many perished.

By now most of St Lô had been destroyed. The Bon Sauveur hospital had also been damaged, but it was still treating patients and since there were no anaesthetics available in the Tunnel and no major operations could take place there, many people sought treatment at the hospital.

8 June and Night 8/9 June

The OMAHA Sector

Recall that the 175th Regimental Group had begun its advance towards Isigny from Gruchy at 2130 hours on 7 June. Soon afterwards it was: 'hit in the flank by enemy machine-gun and artillery fire. Supporting tanks . . . moved up, supported the action to clean up the opposition and the advance continued.'[13] Englesqueville was reached at 0200 hours and a two-hour halt was made for reorganisation. An attempt to enter la Cambe at 0500 hours resulted in one Sherman being knocked out by anti-tank fire.[14] The tanks eventually succeeded in destroying five anti-tank guns and 'during the morning the infantry-tank team [1st Battalion and 747th tanks] succeeded in capturing la Cambe'.[15] Colonel 'Pop' Goode established his Headquarters in the village at 0915 hours but as the 2nd and 3rd Battalions approached la Cambe 'the column was attacked and strafed by aircraft bearing Allied insignia at 0930. Six men were killed, eighteen wounded'.[16] One GI who witnessed the strike wrote later:

> Over our heads zoomed a flight or two of 'Limey' planes, Spitfires, I believe, and suddenly they assumed the nearly vertical and tore down toward the earth to our front, smoke trailing from their wing guns, while the faint, peculiar multiple rat-tat-tat of the aerial MGs drifted down to us after they had already pulled out of their dives. Time after time they dove while we cheered them on. It wasn't until later we found they were hitting our own.[17]

According to the US War Department Publication, *Omaha Beachhead*:

> Enemy resistance stiffened west of la Cambe and artillery fire from 88mm guns[18] disabled six tanks of C Company of the 747th Tank Battalion. A small enemy force supported by a few mobile 88s held the St Germain-du-Pert area. On the other flank an enemy strongpoint protected the radar station at Cardonville. At Osmanville enemy estimated at a company and disposing of anti-tank guns blocked the main highway.[19]

In fact these defences failed to impose any significant delay. By 1600 hours the enemy in St Germain-du-Pert had been pushed back across the Aure by Lieutenant Colonel Edward Gill's 3rd Battalion and, aided by fire from the British cruiser *Glasgow*, Lieutenant Colonel Millard Bowen's 2nd Battalion captured Cardonville in the late evening. Osmanville was quickly cleared and by 0200 hours on the 9th Lieutenant Colonel Roger Whiteford's 1st Battalion was within 500m of Isigny. It is said that Uncle Charlie Gerhardt, the Divisional commander, and his Deputy Dutch Cota played a major part in spurring on this advance.[20]

At 0430 hours the leading Shermans and men of the 1st Battalion[21] entered the partially gutted and burning town – the result of heavy naval bombardments. Cota was amongst the first of the infantrymen to cross the Aure bridge which the 439th Ost Battalion had failed to demolish. There was no organised resistance; the 1st Battalion of the 1352nd Artillery Regiment had been forced to abandon its guns north of the town[22] and some 200 prisoners were taken without a fight. By 0730 hours Isigny was firmly in American hands.

General Omar Bradley visited the town on the afternoon of 10 June:

Isigny lay charred from its shelling. . . A few villagers searched sorrowfully through the ruins of their homes. . . For more than four years the people of Isigny had awaited this moment of liberation. Now they stared accusingly on us from the ruins that covered their dead.[23]

Thirty-four of the townspeople died in the period 6 to 9 June 1944.[24] The capture of the town was a remarkable achievement. In less than thirty-six hours after coming ashore on OMAHA beach, Colonel Paul Goode's Regiment had advanced 20km and eliminated the German corridor between the OMAHA and UTAH bridgeheads. In the face of this rapid advance, the entire enemy defensive system north of the Aure valley, from Isigny to Trévières (Map 5), collapsed. And the whole operation had been achieved on foot – and with little or no sleep and food. The Guardsmen of the Dandy Fifth had certainly won their spurs.

What of its companion Regiments? Early on 8 June, the 2nd and 3rd Battalions of Colonel Charles Canham's 116th Stonewallers, the rest of the Ranger Companies and A and C Companies of the 743rd Tank Battalion joined John Metcalfe's 1st Battalion Group in the area immediately south of the Pointe du Hoc and at 1015 hours a coordinated attack was launched to relieve Rudder's besieged Rangers. The 1st Battalion and Rangers moved cross-country from St Pierre-du-Mont while Meeks' 3rd Battalion and five tanks attacked from due south and south-west with fire support from a destroyer. The right wing of the assault was successful in reaching the Rangers but on the left wing three Shermans of C Company were disabled on mines and two broke down[25], and some elements of the 3rd Battalion ended up engaging friendly troops on the Pointe. Bad radio communications and limited visibility due to the numerous hedgerows added to the attackers' problems and several casualties were incurred before the situation was sorted out. In fact there was little German resistance and by midday the area was clear of enemy.

Soon after noon the 116th Regimental Group continued its advance towards Grandcamp and Maisy. The 1st Battalion, with A Company of the 743rd Tank Battalion, outflanked Grandcamp by swinging south through Jucoville towards Maisy which had been virtually razed to the ground by naval gunfire. The group encountered no resistance until it ran into two pillboxes forming a strongpoint blocking the Isigny road just to the south-west of Maisy.

Meanwhile, the main part of Canham's Regimental Group had moved west along the coast road. A small flooded valley about 100m wide blocked the route to Grandcamp, but although the Germans had failed to destroy the bridge across it, the Rangers leading the column found themselves halted by machine-gun and mortar fire from a defensive position specifically sited to cover this approach at the east end of the small town. Assistance was requested from the navy and artillery, and the

British cruiser *Glasgow* fired 113 rounds between 1455 and 1600 hours and the 58th Armored FA Battalion 123 rounds from positions north of Longueville. Tanks of C Company of the 743rd then led the way across the bridge followed by the 3rd Battalion of the 116th. One Sherman was disabled on a mine and a considerable firefight ensued, but by last light Grandcamp was in American hands. Sergeant Frank Peregory[26] of K Company was awarded a Congressional Medal of Honor for his actions in this fighting.

Colonel Eugene Slappey's 115th Regiment had a rather easier time of it. Recall that its task was to secure the southern flank of the 29th Division's advance to the west. At about 1100 hours the 2nd Battalion found Longueville abandoned by the Germans, and whilst it took up defensive positions just to the west of the village, Slappey established his Regimental Headquarters there. He knew that the flooded Aure valley would present a major obstacle to any further advance and during the afternoon he sent out a reconnaissance patrol of platoon strength. This was led by Lieutenant Miller of E Company. The patrol lasted some eighteen hours but it established that men could indeed cross the valley on their feet and that there were few if any Germans left in Colombières (Map 5) to prevent a general advance in that area. Miller received a Distinguished Service Cross for this action. Meanwhile, the 1st Battalion had reached Ecrammeville without difficulty and Gillespie's 3rd Battalion, after securing Montigny at midday, went on first to Deux-Jumeaux and then to Canchy, which it reached at midnight. The 110th FA Battalion fired 178 rounds in support of the 115th Regiment during the 8th.

The Enemy

It is hardly surprising that the German account[27] of events south and west of OMAHA on 8 June is lacking in detail. It concentrates mainly on the sector to the east where the threat from 1st Infantry Division and the British was seen as much more dangerous.

At 0900 hours the 916th Regiment was reporting simultaneous attacks to the east, south and west, and by midday it said that enemy tanks had broken through its main line of resistance and were advancing down the Vierville to Grandcamp road. It also reported that the enemy had reached the northern outskirts of Formigny. At the same time the 914th Regiment said the enemy had 'attacked the positions just east of Grandcamp but had been repelled'.

At 1500 hours the Americans were reported advancing from Formigny towards Longueville and as a result the 914th Regiment was ordered to use mobile elements to hold the latter and send the bulk of its 1st Battalion, reinforced by parts of the 726th Regiment's 439th Ost Battalion, to hold the la Cambe sector and prevent a breakthrough there. It was later claimed, correctly, that the enemy had been successfully halted, although only temporarily, just east of both la Cambe and Grandcamp. All units were ordered to hold their positions, particularly on the eastern flank where an armoured counter-attack was planned for 9 June. This operation will be discussed in a later chapter.

The final 352nd Divisional synopsis for 8 June says it had:

> been possible to prevent a breakthrough, especially to the south, despite the manifold superiority of the enemy in every respect. However, it is doubtful whether this same infantry soldier will hold up the more powerful enemy attack on 9 June. As far as numbers are concerned, on 9 June there would be . . . in the 916th Regiment's sector about 800 men and six light artillery pieces and in the 914th Regiment's sector about 1,000 men . . . and twelve artillery pieces.[28]

St Lô

By the morning of 8 June there were some 700 casualties within the walls of the damaged Bon Sauveur hospital in St Lô, including a number from Carentan.[29] Then, at 0830 hours, the kitchens of the hospital were hit in yet another air raid and three nuns and two patients killed. Despite the fact that 200 of the patients were unable to walk, orders were given for the hospital to be evacuated yet again. Most were taken to a rescue centre at le Hutrel, 2km south of St Lô in the parish of St Thomas.

Nor surprisingly, it is impossible to be certain about the total number of civilian casualties suffered during the first three days of the invasion. To the 132 names on the city memorial, one must certainly add most of the 700 or so patients being cared for in the Bon Sauveur hospital on the 8th. One thing is certain, by the evening of that day St Lô was a chaotic wasteland. The few remaining citizens who had not fled were either sheltering in the Tunnel or their own cellars, or were wandering helplessly through the rubble looking for relatives or friends. Apart from its importance as a military objective St Lô had ceased to exist.

NOTES

1. According to the 29 Div's AAR, several of F Coy's and one of L Coy's boats were lost to underwater mines and MG fire during the landing.
2. Harrison, *Cross Channel Attack*, p. 340.
3. The area was defended by the 352 Pnr Bn which had been brought up from the south.
4. CMH Pub 100-11, *Omaha Beachhead*, p. 122.
5. 116 Inf Regt AAR dated 23 Jul 44.

6. Ibid.
7. CMH 100–11, op. cit., p. 123.
8. Initially by part of 3/726 Inf Bn & later by 1/914 Gren Bn.
9. 743 Tk Bn AAR dated 20 Jul 44.
10. Harrison, op. cit., p. 341.
11. Ziegelmann, MS # B-433.
12. Ibid, pp. 5 & 7.
13. 175 Inf Regt AAR dated 21 Jul 44.
14. Harrison, op.cit., p 353.
15. CMH Pub 100-11, p.127.
16. 175 Inf Regt AAR dated 21 Jul 44.
17. Gordon, *One Man's War*, p. 12.
18. There were no 88mm guns in this area; they would have been 75mm.
19. CMH Pub 100-11, *Omaha Beachhead*, p.127.
20. Balkoski, *Beyond the Beachhead*, pp. 170–2.
21. Balkoski, op. cit., p. 172–3 says LTC Gill's 3rd Bn was the first to enter the town; the 175 Regt AAR dated 21 Jul 44 says it was LTC Whiteford's 1st Bn.
22. Ziegelmann, MS # B-145.
23. Bradley, *A Soldier's Story*, pp. 284–5.
24. Town authorities 1 Mar 2002.
25. 743 Tk Bn AAR dated 20 Jul 44.
26. He never knew of this award as he was killed six days later.
27. Ziegelmann, MS # B-434.
28. Ibid.
29. 312 civilians were killed and 65% of the buildings were destroyed in Carentan by the RAF raid during the night 5/6 Jun 44.

CHAPTER XIV

The Blue and Gray – 9 and 10 June

From Aure to Elle

(Map 14)

Major General Leonard Gerow had issued his V Corps Field Order No. 2 at 2115 hours on 8 June. It directed that a Corps attack with three Divisions, the 1st, 2nd and 29th, was to begin at noon on the 9th. The 2nd Infantry Division had begun landing on 7 June and had two Regiments operational by the evening of the 8th. Its mission was to seize the Cerisy Forest whilst Hueber's 1st Infantry kept pace on its left flank towards Balleroy. The Blue and Gray's part in this Corps attack was to capture Isigny and make contact with VII Corps in the Carentan area, and at the same time to cross the Aure and close up to the Elle valley between la Communette and the Vire – an advance of some 15km.

As we have heard, Isigny had already been captured by the 175th Regiment and the 747th Tank Battalion before dawn on the 9th. The Regimental Group continued its advance at 1305 hours on the axis: la Hérennerie, la Forêt and Lison, with la Fotelaie as its final objective for the day. The men of the Blue and Gray were now entering the 'bocage' – a soldier's nightmare already described in Chapter IV.

Scattered opposition from men of the 1352nd Artillery Regiment acting in an infantry role was encountered at la Hérennerie and again at la Forêt, where the advance was halted by 'stragglers and men from the supply services' defending a supply dump. This rag-tag group had 'built up a thin front . . . and in spite of their inexperience in combat . . . even managed to hold up tanks'.[1] A delay of several hours was imposed on the US column allowing the dump to be successfully evacuated. An estimated 125 Germans were killed in this fighting.[2] The 747th Shermans eventually continued the advance but 'although Lison was bombed and strafed by Allied planes, an enemy force of about a company delayed the advance for a [further] few hours'.[3] Nevertheless, the 3rd Battalion of the 175th, less K Company, was able to occupy the final objective of la Fotelaie by last light. This was hardly surprising since at 2000 hours the 914th Regiment, with strength of only some 700 men and no artillery, had been ordered to withdraw to a new defensive line south of the Elle. The Germans occupied this line by 0600 hours the following day. 'Since explosives were not available . . . troops were ordered to do what damage they could to all the bridges crossing the Elle and Vire rivers or else to block them by laying mines'.[4]

In the meantime K Company of the 175th had been tasked with seizing the bridge over the 20m-wide Vire near Auville-sur-le-Vey, 3km west of Isigny, and making contact with units of VII Corps; however, the bridge was found to have been burned and the Company took up defensive positions on the east bank. The following morning, 10 June, Captain John King's Company was ordered to wade the 12m-wide, but shallow, Vire river and secure Auville; but when it attempted to do so it was held up by mortar and machine-gun fire from elements of the 2nd Battalion of the 914th Regiment[5] on the high ground immediately to the west of the river. Some hours later General Gerhardt appeared on the scene and ordered King to attempt another crossing that evening and capture Auville. He provided reinforcements in the form of a tank platoon and the 29th Reconnaissance Troop (company) and beginning at 1800 hours, with covering fire provided by the Reconnaissance Troop, King's Company and the tanks waded the Vire and entered Auville. A large number of prisoners were taken[6] – most of them non-Germans from the 439th Ost Battalion. Although King was wounded in both legs and K Company suffered about a dozen casualties, this success enabled engineers to start bridging the river and a patrol of the Reconnaissance Troop, after moving west through Catz, to make contact with elements of the 101st Airborne Division, part of VII Corps. The Dandy Fifth had thus completed all its missions.

Colonel Eugene Slappey's 115th Regiment, supported by A and C Companies of the 743rd Tank Battalion, also achieved its missions by first occupying Bricqueville, Colombières and the Calette wood and then going on to secure la Folie and le Carrefour, 7km and 5km respectively from the Elle – but not without having to deal with some serious problems. The 3rd Battalion under Major Victor Gillespie, supported by the Regimental Cannon Company, started out across the flooded Aure valley from Canchy at first light but made little headway until A Company of the 121st Engineers was brought up to provide improvised footbridges. Even so it took several hours for the Battalion to cross. Only spasmodic rifle fire was encountered during and after the crossing and so by 1020 hours the Battalion was in Colombières, one of the largest and most prosperous villages in the area. It remained there, inactive, for the next seven hours. At 1830 hours the commanding officer was sacked and under its new commander, Captain Grat Hankins, it finally reached la Folie at 2300 hours. It is interesting that the Chief of Staff of the 352nd Division, Lieutenant Colonel Fritz Ziegelmann, later offered the following criticism of the 29th Division: 'An exaggerated feeling of superiority was . . . apparent . . . the careless way the enemy troops rested as soon as an objective was reached instead of making full use of the success'.[7]

The 2nd Battalion of the 115th, in the wake of the 3rd, completed its crossing of the Aure by 1100 hours and then turned west, running into scattered opposition at Vouilly and subsequently spending some three hours clearing the Calette wood. The Battalion still had 7km to go to reach la Carrefour but it got lost on the way and ended up covering 10km before it arrived there exhausted at 0230 hours on the 10th. Then disaster struck. The After Action Report of the Regiment provides the following account of what happened:

At approximately 0245 hours, 10 June 1944, a closing force of German armor and infantry which had been by-passed and cut off to our rear and was attempting to retreat to its own lines, stumbled on the rear of the 2nd Battalion to the surprise of both units. Opening fire with their MGs, mortars and 88s, a heavy and confused action occurred in the dark with severe losses on both sides. Two enemy tanks were knocked out, plus a 150mm field piece. The 2nd Battalion was left in a dispersed and disorganised state and control was not regained until daylight. Battalion CO, Lt Col William E Warfield, was found dead, believed to have been killed at approximately 0300 hours.

129

The 2nd Battalion had temporarily ceased to exist – overall losses were eleven officers and 139 men.[8] The statement that the German column contained tanks and 88mm guns cannot be correct. There were no tanks or 88mm guns with the 352nd Division or the 726th Regiment of the 716th Division under its command. The so-called 'tanks' could only have been StuG IIIs – 75mm assault guns.

Whilst all this was going on, the Divisional commander had turned up at Slappey's Headquarters in Colombières at about 0200 hours, only to find Slappey missing and his staff unaware of his whereabouts or those of his three Battalions and the 743rd tanks. He resolved to replace Slappey at the first suitable opportunity.[9]

In what can only be described as a remarkable achievement, the 2nd Battalion was reformed soon after daylight under the command of Lieutenant Colonel Arthur Sheppe and, after receiving 110 replacements, it moved to a reserve position at l'Epinay-Tesson during the afternoon. By then the other two Battalions were on the Elle – the 1st Battalion having moved forward from Bricqueville to St Marguerite while the 3rd covered the road junction a kilometre to the east of that village. The two Sherman Companies of the 743rd Tank Battalion appear to have played little or no part in the previous day's activities. They had bivouacked for the night 2km north of the Elle after apparently encountering 'little opposition' but 'terrain rather difficult due to numerous hedgerows'.[10]

(Map 12)

Colonel Canham's battered 116th Regiment spent the morning of the 9th clearing the Maisy area[11] and another German defensive position at Géfosse-Fontenay. At 1500 hours the Regiment was placed in Divisional reserve. In the period 7/9 June it had suffered a further 203 casualties, including twenty-six killed.[12] The eighty hours since it had begun landing on OMAHA had been a costly and harrowing experience for everyone involved but without doubt, the Stonewallers had earned their place in history.

By midnight on 10 June the Blue and Gray and its attached units had lost a total of 2,189 men. 280 had been killed or died of their wounds and 889 were reported missing.[13] Of the latter, some were later found to be prisoners of war, some turned up again in American lines but others were never found. 86% of these casualties occurred in the three infantry Regiments.

NOTES

1. Ziegelmann, MS # B-435.
2. 175 Inf Regt AAR dated 21 Jul 44.
3. CMH Pub 100-11, *Omaha Beachhead*, p. 145.
4. Ziegelmann, MS # B-435.
5. Ibid. This Bn was completely separated from, and out of contact with, its parent 352 Inf Div.
6. Balkoski, *Beyond the Beachhead*, p. 182.
7. Ziegelmann, MS # B-435.
8. CMH Pub 100-11, p. 145.
9. Balkoski, op. cit., p. 187.
10. 743 Tk Bn AAR dated 20 Jul 44.
11. 743 Tk Bn AAR dated 20 Jul 44 says its B Coy had to deal with pill-boxes south of the village and that 125 PWs were taken without loss.
12. 29 Inf Div AAR dated 23 Jul 44.
13. 29 Inf Div G-1 Periodic Reports dated 11 Jun 44 and figures provided by the Dupuy Institute. *The D-Day Encyclopedia* on the other hand gives a total of 2,210 including 280 killed or died of wounds, 1,027 wounded, 896 missing and seven POW.

CHAPTER XV

The Blue and Gray – 11 June to 6 July

Crossing the Elle

(Map 1)

By 11 June Major General Gerow's V Corps had won enough ground to ensure the security of the OMAHA beachhead. In the western half of the Corps sector, the 29th Division was on the line of the Vire and Elle rivers; the 2nd Infantry Division had come into line in the centre and had secured the Ceresty forest (Map 14), and on the eastern flank the 1st Infantry Division was well positioned to seize the vital Caumont ridge. The 2nd Armored Division was in Corps reserve in a counter-attack role. There remained, however, the need to effect a strong junction with VII Corps in the area of Carentan which since 10 June had been under attack by the 101st Airborne Division.

It will be remembered that the primary aim of Omar Bradley's First Army in this phase of the invasion was the capture of Cherbourg. It was therefore important to divert German attention and reinforcements away from the VII Corps' operations in the Cotentin peninsula by continuing the V Corps advance towards St Lô and Caumont. This would also assist the British Second Army in an attempt to outflank the German defence in the Caen sector – an operation that will be described in the next Chapter.

At 1700 hours on 11 June, General Gerow issued Field Order No. 3. It directed that on 12 June a strongly reinforced 1st Infantry Division was to seize the high ground astride Caumont, the 2nd was to advance south towards the strategically vital Hill 192[1] (Map 16), whilst the Blue and Gray was to take the villages immediately south of the Elle (Map 16) as a preliminary to advancing on St Lô, just 11km away to the south-west. At the same time the Division was to secure two bridges over the 10m wide Vire–Taute canal (Map 14), a task designated rather strangely as 'a reconnaissance in force'. It was designed to protect the slender link between the V and VII Corps from a possible counter-attack from the south.

The 8km advance by the reinforced 1st Infantry Division met almost no opposition and before last light on the 12th the strategic ridgeline astride Caumont was firmly in American hands. This, as we shall see in the next Chapter, was to have a dramatic effect on British operations farther to the east. The right-hand Regiment of the 2nd Division on the western flank of Hueber's Division had a similarly easy time in reaching its objectives.

(Map 16)

The picture farther to the west, however, where the 23rd Regiment of the 2nd Division and the 115th Regiment of the Blue and Gray were operating, was very different and the opposition encountered was a portent of things to come. It soon became clear that the Germans were going to defend Hill 192 and the approaches to St Lô with the utmost tenacity. The 23rd Regiment suffered 211 casualties and was still more than 3km north of Hill 192 by the end of the 13th.

What of the Blue and Gray? Gerhardt's task was to attack across the Elle in conjunction with the 2nd Division and seize the villages of St Clair-sur-Elle and Couvains.[2] In doing so he would provide vital protection for the right flank of the 23rd Regiment in its advance on Hill 192. With the 175th defending the west flank of the Corps and Canham's 116th Stonewallers in Corps reserve, he had no choice other than to order Slappey and the unfortunate 115th to carry out this task. The 747th Tank Battalion, which had now replaced the 743rd as the dedicated tank unit[3] of the Division, was kept in reserve in a counter-attack role. H-Hour for the attack was set for 0500 hours on the 12th and four artillery Battalions[4] were available to provide close support. The Elle was only 3m wide but its banks were steep and the area to its south was bocage at its worst.

American artillery pounded the 115th's objectives during the early hours of the 12th and then, following a twenty-minute barrage on suspected enemy positions on the south side of the river, Slappey attacked with his 1st and 3rd Battalions abreast. German tactics dictated that forward lines of defence were to be only lightly held, with main defensive positions being sited in depth behind which reserves could be positioned in a counter-attack role. This tactic largely negated the effect of the opening barrage. To add to this problem K Company, leading the 3rd Battalion, believed that the thirty-two casualties suffered during the early stages of the advance, including the Company commander, Captain Louis Hille, killed, were caused by friendly artillery rounds falling short. This proved incorrect but the Company's morale was badly affected and the advance stalled. Eventually one platoon of K Company and the other two rifle Companies got across the Elle near St Jean-de-Savigny and by 0830 hours the Battalion had advanced about a kilometre. The 1st Battalion, however, had failed to cross in the face of small arms and mortar fire which inflicted nearly 100 casualties including twenty-one killed. This left the 3rd Battalion advancing out on a limb with open flanks. Somewhere south of St Jean-de-Savigny, in the vicinity of les Fresnes, it too was halted by enemy fire. At around midday Germans with some armoured vehicles approached from Couvains and in the early afternoon Captain Hankins ordered the Battalion to pull back north of the Elle. Some elements of the unit apparently failed to receive the order and it was another two hours before the remnants recrossed the stream 'in some disorder'. The line of retreat was littered with discarded equipment and many of the badly wounded had to be left behind. The 3rd Battalion lost 130 men on this day.

Gerhardt was dismayed at the failure of the 115th to take its objectives and soon after 1200 hours he ordered the 1st Battalion to attack again, but this time with two Platoons of Shermans spearheading the assault. It made no difference. The Germans were not to be moved and three tanks were lost in the process. Gerhardt was furious; he removed Slappey from command and replaced him with his own Chief of Staff, Colonel Godwin Ordway. At the same time he sacked the commanding officer of the 1st Battalion, Major James Morris, and replaced him with Major Glover Johns.

At 1700 hours Gerhardt ordered Colonel Charles Canham's 116th Regiment, which had been released to him from Corps reserve, to take over the attack. The Stonewallers went in at about 1930 hours and by 2200 hours the 1st and 2nd Battalions, together with the depleted 3rd Battalion of the 115th which had been placed under Canham's command for the operation, had achieved a 2km-deep bridgehead over the Elle. The defenders in this sector were part of the 916th Regiment and according to the Chief of Staff of the 352nd Division, Lieutenant Colonel Ziegelmann, 'the enemy succeeded in taking possession of St Jean, despite the fact that . . . all available reserves had been committed in counter measures'.[5]

The American advance was renewed at first light on the 13th and later that morning Major Sidney Bingham's 2nd Battalion captured St Clair-sur-l'Elle and Lieutenant Colonel John Metcalfe's 1st Battalion took Couvains. The Divisional artillery fired over 3,000 rounds in support of this advance. It is interesting to note Ziegelmann's comment on the tactics employed by the Americans at this time:

> It became noticeable that the enthusiasm which previously had prevailed during attacks was lessening, a fact that could be attributed to the lack of open view in this territory – the greatest visibility was 100 metres. It became a practice with the enemy to spray each hedge with his machine-guns for longer and longer periods of time, wasting great amounts of ammunition.[6]

(Map 14)

Let us look now at the 29th's secondary task of securing the two road bridges over the Vire–Taute canal. In order to achieve his mission Colonel Paul Goode, the commander of the 175th Infantry Regiment, decided with good reason that he could not do this without first clearing the village of Montmartin-en-Graignes. He placed his Executive Officer, Major Anthony Miller, in charge of the operation and gave him a Task Force (TF) consisting of C and E Companies, each with a section of heavy machine-guns and 81mm mortars, all of which, together with ammunition, had to be manhandled. The Deputy Divisional commander, Dutch Cota, accompanied E Company – no doubt to the embarrassment of Major Miller.

The crossing of the Vire was meant to take place before first light on the 12th, but the trucks of C Company of the 121st Engineers carrying the assault boats were late reaching the crossing sites. Not that this mattered – neither infantry Company had arrived anyway. This was unsurprising since in the case of C Company at least the Company commander, Captain Alex Pouska, had not been warned for his mission until after midnight and he then had to get his men up, brief them on what little he knew about the situation and then march them 9km to the Vire crossing site! It then transpired that there were only four boats for each Company instead of the expected eight[7] and the crossings over the tidal river had to be made in a series of waves.

The operation eventually began at 0645 hours. E Company and Brigadier General Cota crossed near the railway bridge over the Vire and C Company about a kilometre to its south. Fewer than a dozen casualties were incurred from spasmodic and long-range rifle and machine-gun fire, mostly as the men climbed over the 3m-high dyke on the west side of the river, but communications within the TF failed and the Companies ended up operating as independent sub-units with E Company going for the western bridge and C the eastern.

E Company of the Dandy Fifth approached Montmartin-en-Graignes at

0800 hours but, without waiting for C Company to catch up, Cota decided to bypass the village to the north-west and go straight for the western bridge.

> In approach-march formation, Company E started south down a road banked with deep hedgerows. . . before they had gone a hundred yards, heavy enemy fire from machine-pistols and rifles came out of the hedges on both sides of the sunken road. Caught in an ambush of the type easily set in hedgerow country, Company E was cut up and badly scattered. . . . Some of the Company went all the way back to the river and recrossed.[8]

The remnants of E Company joined C Company which had also been ambushed when trying to advance on the Vire side of the village. Cota was determined to try again but at about 1100 hours the joint force ran into more opposition some 300m south-east of Montmartin and was halted. Supporting fire from Lieutenant Colonel Clinton Thurston's 224th FA Battalion failed to dislodge the Germans, estimated at no more than a company in strength, and despite a further attempt to go round the village to the north and reach the bridges that way, the operation was called off just before darkness fell. Cota ordered the TF, by then reduced to some 150 men, to take up positions firstly in the village but later in an orchard on a small hill to its south-west. There are conflicting reports about a Battalion of the 327th Glider Infantry[9] that may or may not have joined the Cota TF during the afternoon. The *Omaha Beachhead* account claims that no contact was made between the two groups 'other than by patrols'[10]; on the other hand, the Official History says that after interviewing Cota the *Omaha Beachhead* account had to be 'slightly modified' and that the Glider Battalion was indeed part of the force located on the high ground south of Montmartin.[11] Yet another version claims that about sixty members of the 101st Airborne Division joined the TF at about 1800 hours.[12]

At 2200 hours Colonel Goode decided to personally accompany Captain John Slingluff's G Company of the 2nd Battalion, reinforced with heavy machine-guns and mortars, to reinforce Cota and the original TF on the other side of the Vire. Unfortunately the group, moving south in very close country near the river and in darkness, missed Cota's position. It is not entirely clear what happened next. One version says:

> south of Montmartin they ran into a German bivouac and inflicted many casualties in a surprise encounter. Rallying, the Germans came back and surrounded Company G, which fought until its ammunition ran low.[13]

The Regimental After Action Report merely says, 'Company G recrossed the river Vire, having run into stiff opposition', but a third account based apparently on a later interview with Captain Slingluff would have us believe that the Company ended up at first light some 2km south-east of Montmartin at a hamlet on the Vire called la Raye. From there his Company moved to a position overlooking the eastern bridge where it was counter-attacked and virtually overrun. Only about thirty men found their way back across the Vire, rejoining their parent Battalion shortly after midday. The survivors west of the river, including Slingluff who was wounded and Colonel Paul Goode, became prisoners.

During the morning of the 13th ammunition and rations were dropped by air to the Cota TF, but according to the 175th's After Action Report when:

> an enemy Panzer Division was reported to be approaching Montmartin, it was consequently felt that in spite of the fact that the task force was on high ground south of Montmartin, the village must be shelled. The battleship *Texas* shelled the town with its 16-inch batteries, without hitting the task force.'[14]

This was an extraordinary thing to do – there were no Germans in the village and it placed the nearby Americans in great danger. The so-called 'Panzer Division' was in fact the 17th SS Panzer-Grenadier Division which had begun to arrive south-west of Carentan on the 11th with the mission of securing, or if necessary counter-attacking, the town. Not surprisingly the Cota TF was ordered back across the Vire and at midnight 110 men rejoined the Regiment. It had not been a good episode for the Dandy Fifth – the Germans had taught it a painful lesson. As Dutch Cota said later, the whole operation had been 'ill-conceived [by V Corps], ill-planned [by the 29th Division] and ill-executed [by the 175th]'.

Gerhardt's battered Division was now less than 9km from the city of St Lô but it had received another 547 casualties in the two days fighting on the Elle and west of the Vire, bringing its total to some 2,700[15] – over 16% of its authorised strength. As previously mentioned, nearly all these casualties had occurred in the cutting edge of the Blue and Gray – the Infantry Regiments. They were hardly in a condition to continue the advance, particularly with Hill 192 (Map 16) on their left flank still in German hands.

It was perhaps as well therefore that at the end of 13 June General Omar Bradley ordered the attack by V Corps towards St Lô to be halted. As the US Army Official History puts it:

> In calling off the southward push, General Bradley was influenced by the desire to avoid a general engagement of V Corps which might

absorb resources needed for First Army's main effort – the VII Corps attack to cut the [Contentin] peninsula and take Cherbourg. . . Furthermore XIX corps was just becoming operational . . . and it was necessary to adjust troop alignments between the corps.[16]

When told by his Chief of Operations that Gerhardt wanted to push on to St Lô, Bradley replied bluntly:

If Gerhardt could take St Lô without breaking the back of his 29th I wouldn't object. But I doubt very much that he could. . . We're not going to spend a division just to take a place name. We can get along very nicely without St Lô at this time. . . Nobody's going anywhere until Joe [Collins, VII Corps commander] gets Cherbourg.[17]

The following day at noon the Blue and Gray was transferred from Gerow's V Corps to Major General Charles Corlett's XIX Corps. Its partner in this new Corps would be another National Guard Division, the 30th Infantry. 'Old Hickory', as it was nicknamed, had started disembarking during the night of 13/14 June and was to be committed to the west side of the Vire to reinforce the tenuous link between V and VII Corps. This news delighted Uncle Charlie Gerhardt who realised that with his right flank secured he would be able to concentrate the 29th against St Lô. During the several days it would take for the 30th to come into line, however, there was no option for the Blue and Gray other than to go firm in its current positions and maintain whatever pressure it could by aggressive patrolling. Needless to say Gerhardt took this tactic to the extreme and decreed that every forward Company was to send out at least one patrol each day and every forward Battalion was to capture at least one prisoner each day. It was not a popular decision.

And the Germans? The 352nd Division had suffered about 200 casualties in the recent fighting[18], bringing its total losses to somewhere in the region of 3,000.[19] By coincidence, on the same day that the US 29th Division changed Corps, Kraiss's Division left LXXXIV Corps and joined the 3rd Parachute Division in General Eugen Meindl's II Parachute Corps. It was shortly to be reinforced by KGs from the 275th, 266th and 353rd Infantry Divisions. Meindl's task was to defend St Lô and its approaches.

Toujours l'Attaque

(Map 17)

Author's Note

In this and subsequent Chapters mention is made of various 'Hills', e.g., 'Hill 90'. This indicates that the highest point in that particular area is 90m above sea level; however, except in the case of Hill 192 already mentioned, anyone visiting one of these 'Hills' should not expect to find a prominent feature but rather an area of ground slightly higher than the surrounding countryside.

Despite Bradley's order that Corlett's XIX Corps and Gerhardt's 29th Division were to 'hold their ground'[20], and the fact that their ammunition was deliberately rationed by First Army[21] to give priority to the Cherbourg campaign, both commanders were determined to press ahead towards St Lô. Similarly, Gerow of V Corps still had his eyes set firmly on Hill 192. On 14 June both Corps commanders issued warning orders for attacks that were aimed at securing 'better defensive positions, although commanders hoped that larger rewards might be reaped'.[22] Specifically, the 2nd Division of V Corps was to secure St Georges-d'Elle, Hill 192 and the high ground 2km to its east, whilst the 29th was to take St André-de-l'Epine and Hill 150, 6km to the east of St Lô and Hills 90 and 97, 3km to the north-west of the city. All three commanders recognised that if this 10km thrust to the south succeeded, the 29th Division would be vulnerable to a counter-attack from the west across the Vire. It was hoped, however, that an advance by Corlett's other Division, the 30th Infantry, on the west side of the Vire just before the planned attack would draw any German reserves in that direction.

(Map 14)

Major General Leland Hobbs' 30th Division was far from complete in Normandy when his attack, designed to reach the line of the Vire–Taute canal, jumped off on 15 June. Only one Regimental Combat Team[23] was available and, despite support from five artillery battalions, naval gunfire and ground attack aircraft, progress was very slow. At the end of the day the designated objectives of Montmartin-en-Graignes and the high ground north of the Vire–Taute canal had been reached but it would take until the following day for the line of the canal to be finally cleared. Hobbs was then ordered to go firm and build up his Division for a forthcoming offensive.

(Map 17)

The attack by Gerow's 2nd Infantry Division on 16 June also had very limited success. One Battalion got to within 600m of the crest of Hill 192 where it was able to hold on, but at the end of the day the vital hill, St Georges-d'Elle and the high ground to its south were still in German hands and the Division had lost more than 300 men.

The main effort by the Blue and Gray[24] was to be made by Charles Canham's 116th Regiment, still with the 3rd Battalion of the 115th Regiment under command, and sixteen Shermans of the 747th Tank Battalion. Its mission was to support the 2nd Division's attack on Hill 192 by advancing with its 1st Battalion and eight tanks from the area of Couvains on the eastern flank to take the plateau to the east of the Bois de Bretel. After this it was to reorganise and be prepared on order to seize St André-de-l'Epine and Hills 147 and 150. On the western flank the 3rd Battalion of the 115th, with the other eight Shermans, was to cut the main St Lô–Isigny road at la Fossardière and prepare the high ground in that area for defence. The 2nd Battalion of the 116th, after breaking contact at St Clair-sur-l'Elle, was also to advance from the Couvains area, pass through the other two Battalions and, after securing Hill 115, go on to take the stretch of the main St Lô–Isigny road near la Luzerne.

Concurrent with Canham's attack, the 175th Regiment, now under the command of Lieutenant Colonel Alexander George, was to secure the right flank of the Division on the Vire and advance to take Hills 90 and 97 to the north-west of St Lô. The 115th Regiment, less its 3rd Battalion with Canham, was to be held in XIX Corps reserve in the St Marguerite-d'Elle sector on the first day of the attack but was expected to join in sometime on the 17th.

The advance by Canham's 116th Regimental Group was led by the 3rd Battalion of the 115th at 0800 hours. It made some progress, but after four hours and some 2km it had been halted by an estimated two companies of enemy east of les Foulons. During the afternoon the Battalion reported the loss of two Shermans and shortly afterwards it pulled back about a kilometre. The 1st Battalion of the 116th, with the advantage of starting farther south near Couvains, did much better. By midday it was only 1,000m short of St André-de-l'Epine.[25] At this point, however, it was stopped by accurate artillery fire and then counter-attacked. The 2nd Battalion was then committed towards la Fossardière but could get no farther forward than a point just to the east of Villiers-Fossard. Shortly after 1800 hours the Corps commander decided to call off the advance and orders were given for all three Battalions to dig in where they were and renew the attack the following day. Both Gerhardt and Canham were far from satisfied with their performance. At his own request, the commanding officer of the 3rd Battalion of the 115th Regiment, Grat Hankins, was relieved of command and Major Charles Custer took over.[26] That night Canham admonished his subordinates. He told them that in future their units should advance on a much broader front and:

> get around the sniper and machine-gunner and wipe him out. . . If you allow your unit to bunch up behind a hedgerow and wait for hours you are only playing into Jerry's hand. He will move around where he can enfilade you or drop artillery or mortar fire on you. . . It is time to get over the jitters and fight like hell.[27]

After relief by units of the 30th Infantry Division during the early hours of 16 June, the 1st and 3rd Battalions of Lieutenant Colonel Alexander George's 175th Regiment began their advance from a start line on the ridge south of Moon-sur-Elle at 0800 hours. Despite small arms, mortar and artillery fire from elements of the 914th Regiment, good progress was made and just after 1100 hours Lieutenant Colonel Edward Gill's 3rd Battalion captured its first objective in the vicinity of Amy. Two hours later Major Shorey's 1st Battalion cut the road from la Mauffe to St Clair-sur-l'Elle. Both Battalions then halted and dug in, confirming Ziegelmann's criticism that the men of the 29th Division often 'rested as soon as an objective was reached instead of making full use of the success'.[28]

The following morning at 0730 hours, George's Regiment continued the attack with the 1st Battalion targeted on Hill 108. It was held up at 1045 by a German counter-attack against its right flank, but this was beaten off by Lieutenant Colonel Millard Bowen's 2nd Battalion and by last light it had advanced more than 2km and was just short of Hill 108 and les Buteaux. During this advance the Regimental commander was seriously wounded by an enemy hand grenade whilst leading an assault against an enemy machine-gun position.[29] Lieutenant Colonel William Purnell took over.

> By 2210 hours on the night of 17 June, the 1st Battalion [of the 175th Regiment] was only 600 yards from its objective [Hill 108] but encountered determined resistance. Patrols located the German position about this time and after artillery and mortar preparations, an attack was made. [The enemy position] was occupied just as it became dark. An 88mm, a 150mm mortar, a 20mm gun and much miscellaneous equipment was captured and fifteen prisoners taken. Under continued enemy fire a temporary defensive position was assumed for the night. At 0820 the following morning, while preparation of a defensive position as ordered by the Division was under way, the Germans delivered a strong counter-attack. Although many casualties were suffered, including the Battalion commander [Lieutenant Colonel Whiteford] and Executive Officer [Major Miles Shorey took over

command] the ground was held with the exception of 200 yards. . . . During the entire remainder of the day until after dark that night the Battalion was completely isolated by enemy mortar and artillery fire from the balance of the Regiment. . . During the night [18/19 June] . . . the 3rd Battalion [which after advancing from Amy had entered la Meauffe at 1100 hours on the 17th, was brought forward and] relieved the 1st, and the latter was withdrawn to a less exposed position immediately to the rear of the defended area.[30]

The 1st Battalion, after losing 250 men on Hill 108, including sixty killed, was awarded a Presidential Distinguished Unit Citation. Not altogether surprisingly, the men christened it 'Purple Heart Hill'.

The enemy in the sector from Hill 108 through Villiers-Fossard to la Luzerne was a new formation – KG Böhm of the 353rd Infantry Division. It had just arrived from the Brest area of Brittany to reinforce Major General Dietrich Kraiss's very depleted 352nd Division. It comprised Colonel Böhm's own 943rd Grenadier Regiment, less a Grenadier Battalion, but included Anti-Tank and Infantry Gun Companies and the 353rd Division's Fusilier Battalion. The infantry were mounted on bicycles and the KG fielded ninety machine-guns, eighteen mortars, three 75mm anti-tank guns, two 150mm and five 75mm infantry guns.[31] The men were mostly from Pomerania and with many veterans of the Eastern Front the KG was to prove a formidable adversary.

There is a German report that towards midday on the 17th a light American Task Force:

made a thrust west of les Buteaux toward the south and had reached the first farmhouses of le Mesnil-Rouxelin. The buildings of the Divisional [Kraiss's 352nd] CP, located under cover, were under machine-gun and mortar fire.'[32]

The report goes on to say that a small KG of thirty men, 'staff guard, reinforced by messengers and office personnel . . . succeeded in pushing back the light enemy forces' to les Buteaux, but that Kraiss's CP moved back into the northern outskirts of St Lô. There is, however, no mention of this incident in any US report that the author could find. Similarly, a German claim that KG Böhm was 'able to take back the village of Villiers-Fossard'[33] would seem to be an exaggeration. There is no report on the American side that they had ever captured it!

Meanwhile, the Stonewallers' attack on the 17th, re-launched at 0400 hours, was soon halted by heavy machine-gun and mortar fire. 'The worst spot was in the gap of about 1,000 yards developed in the previous day's attack between the 116th and 175th. There in the vicinity of Villiers-Fossard, the enemy [KG Böhm] was strongly entrenched'.[34]

At 1840 hours Gerhardt committed the 115th Regiment, less the 3rd Battalion with Canham, to fill the gap between his leading Regiments in the area between Villiers-Fossard and la Fossardière. The attempt failed – one Battalion lost direction and the other never left its assembly area.

Still determined to prevail, the following day Gerhardt massed eight Battalions of artillery to support his attack on the Germans holding the 4km line in front of the 115th and 116th Regiments. Even so the seven-minute artillery concentration by nearly 100 guns:

> had little effect in softening the enemy defenses. At noon the 115th reported that the general advance had been stopped. The troops were getting mortar, 88mm, 105mm and 20mm explosive fire and found it impossible to determine the exact location of the enemy.[35]

As for the 116th, it was exhausted by the attacks of the first two days. The 1st Battalion commander reported that he could not attack as he had 'hardly anyone left'. His Executive Officer added that: 'Everyone is done out physically, no leaders left. No reorganisation possible'.[36]

During the desperate fighting on the 18th, Gerhardt received a telephone call from Headquarters XIX Corps. He was told to hold the line achieved and prepare it for defence. His Corps commander had come to the conclusion that the 29th Division was exhausted. This was true. It had reached the limit of its endurance and it needed rest and time to assimilate new blood. The Germans, using all the advantages of the 'hedgerow country', had exacted a dreadful toll. It is impossible to be precise about the total number of casualties suffered by the Blue and Gray in the twelve days since 6 June, but a figure in the region of 4,000 men killed, wounded, evacuated sick or missing would not be unreasonable.[37]

Between 11 and 30 June Gerhardt's Division received over 3,000 replacements.[38] These men were received by Replacement Battalions initially attached to each Corps, but from 16 June controlled by First Army, and then despatched in 250-man packages to the Regiments on an as-required basis decided by the Division. The system worked well but the operations officer of the 116th Regiment noted that:

> The new men are green. They need time to get to know the old men and officers and learn to work with them. This can't be accomplished simply by putting the Regiment in a defensive position. They must be pulled out of the line and given a chance to effect a real organisation.[39]

Unfortunately there was no chance of the Blue and Gray coming out of the line; any reorganisation and integration had to be carried out within range of German guns.

There were also problems of combat exhaustion and inadequate training. Not surprisingly after their experiences on OMAHA and then spending nearly two weeks fighting their way through the bocage, many of the riflemen in the 29th were at the very least jumpy or in some cases clearly victims of battle fatigue. Battalion administrative areas, several kilometres behind the front line, began to see men who had left their foxholes without orders. One officer in the 116th described these areas as 'the skid row of the battle zone'. The First US Army Medical Report put the increasing numbers of combat exhaustion cases down to the difficult terrain, mud, hedgerows, etc., the stiff resistance offered by the enemy and troops remaining in combat for excessive periods. The situation for the replacements was not helped by the fact that they often witnessed the dead and wounded of the Division as they moved inland from OMAHA to the forward areas; and when they arrived there they inevitably found themselves with total strangers and without knowledge of their leaders. Many of these reinforcements joined the Division during actual combat. An artillery lieutenant colonel recalled:

> I saw replacements headed for an infantry Regiment brought in under cover of darkness. By midnight they were in a foxhole, at 0500 hours they had to attack. By 0530 hours some of them were coming back on stretchers – dead.[40]

Another sap on morale was the obvious skill of the enemy. All credible studies of WWII combat effectiveness[41] have shown that the German soldier in Normandy consistently inflicted casualties at a considerably higher rate than his enemies. One even goes so far as to suggest, without contradiction as far as this author is aware, that:

> On a man for man basis, the German ground soldier consistently inflicted casualties at about a 50% higher rate than they incurred from opposing British and American troops in all circumstances. This was true when they were attacking and when they were defending, when they had numerical superiority and when, as was usually the case, they were outnumbered.[42]

It often seemed to the GI in the hedgerow country that no matter how much firepower was expended, he would still be facing bullets, mortar and artillery rounds as he got out of his foxhole to engage his enemy.

And then there was the question of training. No one had foreseen or could possibly have envisaged the conditions that prevailed on OMAHA on 6/7 June; and indeed no one had anticipated the difficulties of fighting in the bocage. As a result, the officers and the men of the Blue and Gray were unprepared mentally and physically for those conditions and difficulties. The tactics they had been taught and practised had come to naught in the hedgerow country, and although they had managed to advance some 30km, it had been at a terrible cost. But why were they so unprepared for the bocage? Basically because its closeness did not show on military or civilian maps and because those studying the wealth of excellent air photographs were not looking for orchards, sunken lanes and small fields with high banks – they were concentrating on the coastal defence belt and looking for signs of German units farther inland capable of counter-attacking the planned beachhead. In addition, the majority of the aerial photographs had been taken in the winter and early spring before the thick foliage was visible.

As soon as Gerhardt was ordered to adopt a defensive posture he decided to set up a Divisional re-training centre under the direction of Brigadier General Dutch Cota near Couvains – one of the few places in that part of Normandy with flat and relatively open ground. It was clearly time to employ different tactics and the Division quickly adopted the slogan 'One squad, one tank, one field'. The aim was to teach the men to overcome their fear of the bocage and to work closely with tanks. Many must have wondered why they had seen so few tanks operating with them in the various advances from OMAHA and they were not alone in this thought. The Germans too were astounded that American infantry successes were not exploited by armour. As Fritz Ziegelmann put it:

> It was also noticed with surprise that the advance of the American infantry was well supported by Jabos [fighter-bombers] and artillery spotter planes but was not followed up by tanks. If on 16 June the roads, which had been opened up, had been used for that purpose, St Lô would no longer have been in German hands at the end of that day.[43]

The reason for this, as already mentioned in Chapter VI, was quite simply that in June 1944 infantry/tank cooperation in American infantry divisions was still in its infancy and the men of the Blue and Gray, like their British counterparts, had not been trained to operate closely with armour. They often had no way of communicating with the tanks they could see only a stone's throw away. The installation of a field telephone in a simple metal box on the back of a tank so that someone outside could talk to those inside did not begin until very late in June and even then it took a brave infantryman to stand close to the back of a tank, knowing that the crew were probably unaware of his presence – especially when under fire. The problem of communications was further aggravated by the fact that there was simply not enough room in a Sherman for an extra radio set through which to talk to men on the ground. Relationships were not helped either when tanks withdrew at last light for maintenance and refuelling, leaving the infantryman in his foxhole with nothing between him and the enemy. But whereas the tank crews could see the miseries being suffered by the infantry, the latter had little comprehension of the stench, heat and claustrophobic atmosphere overwhelming those confined for hours on end in their steel mastodons. The two combat arms were operating together but in very different worlds.

This then was the problem that Cota was told to solve. But there was another technical problem. The tanks were restricted to roads because there was simply no way they could break through the wide hedgerows of the bocage. As already described, the irregular small fields, usually little more than 100 square metres in size, were separated by high earth banks, on top of which grew dense bushes and trees. Running along these banks were sunken tracks, often overgrown and some so narrow that once in them tanks could not turn or even traverse their guns. Unless a way could be found to overcome this problem, there was no way tanks could operate closely with infantry and rout out the German defences that were inevitably based on these hedgerows.

One solution, devised sometime in late June by Lieutenant Charles Green, a tank officer in the 29th Division, consisted of a bumper for the Sherman made from salvaged railroad tracks that the Germans had used for beach obstacles. Ziegelmann described the Shermans as having 'a new kind of shovelling apparatus attached to their fronts which dug breaks in the hedgerows'.[44] Whilst a considerable help in breaking through small embankments, this device was insufficient to break through the majority of the hedgerows and certainly not the double hedgerows flanking nearly all the narrow tracks. Sergeant Curtis Culin of the 2nd Armored Division invented a more effective and better-known device, called the 'rhino'. It comprised two iron prongs welded to the final drive housing of a Sherman. The tank would charge the hedgerow and either get through or at least make two deep holes into which engineers could place explosives.[45] In the After Action Report of the 116th Regiment, chosen by Gerhardt to lead the next major advance on St Lô, there is a description of the combined arms training undertaken in the Couvains camp:

> Coordination exercises were staged in the rear. This series of exercises, formulated to season the men for the operation to come, found a platoon of infantrymen, a platoon of tanks and a demolition team [engineers] working as one unit and advancing on a limited objective. . . The infantrymen, in a line of skirmishers, push ahead to a hedgerow to provide a base of fire to enable the tanks to advance. The demolition team then blow gaps in the hedgerow to permit the tanks to storm through the openings and knock out emplacements which . . . might otherwise slow up the attack. The coordination exercises proved invaluable when our troops took up the main attack in July.

Although the second half of June and first week of July saw the Blue and

Gray basically holding the line reached on 18 June, it was not entirely devoid of offensive action. Both Gerhardt and his Corps commander considered the KG Böhm[46] salient north of Villiers-Fossard a dangerous finger pointing into the heart of the Divisional area. The KG had been reinforced during the night of 19 June by the 513th Battalion of the 30th Mobile Brigade, about 200 men, and three StuGs of the 352nd Panzerjäger Battalion. Accordingly the 115th Regiment, supported by Shermans of the 747th Tank Battalion, was ordered to eliminate it. Colonel Godwin Ordway tasked his 1st and 3rd Battalions, but the ill fortune that seemed to dog this Regiment struck again and the attack, carried out on the 20th and 21st, failed at a cost of some forty casualties. The Regimental After Action Report does not even mention the attack, although the Germans say that on 19 June the Americans 'achieved penetrations so that the main line of resistance was changed once more'.[47] The Report of the 747th Tank Battalion has this to say:

At 0600 Company B moved forward, with the engineers blowing gaps in the hedgerows and the infantry following. The infantry was pinned down and tanks could not move further forward. But they were on part of their objective. Tanks were forced to withdraw due to heavy anti-tank fire and bazooka fire. One tank was knocked out and the crew of five were wounded. The tanks kept trying to move forward but got stuck. And the infantry stayed pinned down. Another tank was hit. On order of the Regimental commander four tanks forced their way through fire to the objective. No infantry followed. Two tanks returned; anti-tank guns knocked one out. The other was stuck so that the crew had to abandon the tank as no help could reach them. The infantry withdrew 900 yards and took up defensive positions. The tanks covered the withdrawal.

The lack of trust between the tank crews and infantry so evident in this report is a good example of the lack of training and experience already mentioned above. Nevertheless, it is perhaps worth noting that the 747th lost nineteen tanks on 19 June.[48]

On 23 June Gerhardt made some changes amongst his commanders – particularly in the 115th Regiment. Lieutenant Colonel Sheppe, having handed over the 2nd Battalion to Major Maurice Clift, took over the 3rd Battalion from Major Custer. The latter was the third commanding officer of that Battalion to be sacked in as many weeks. At the same time, Colonel Ollie Reed assumed command of the Dandy Fifth and Lieutenant Colonel Purnell resumed his duties as Regimental Executive Officer. Reed was the fourth commander of the 175th in less than three weeks – one of his predecessors (Goode) having been captured on 13 June and another (George) wounded on the 17th.

On 26 June Major General Corlett decided to use part of the recently arrived 3rd Armored Division in yet another attempt to eliminate the KG Böhm[49] salient at Villiers-Fossard and during the night of the 28th Combat Command A (CCA) of the Division passed through the 115th Regiment's lines. CCA comprised an armored Regiment and an armored infantry Regiment, neither of which had been in action before; however, they had trained together, were well practised in infantry/tank cooperation and were supported by an armored artillery Battalion, a TD Battalion and an armored engineer Company.[50] 'The 23rd Armored Engineer Battalion was to make all tank dozers available to CCA and prepare necessary demolitions for blowing hedges to let the tanks pass through.'[51]

... following bombardment and supporting fire, [the attack] jumped off at 0900 [hours] 29 June. By 1130, TF 'X' [a Task Force of CCA] had reached a line la Forge–Bois de Bretel [to the east of the St Lô–Isigny road] where they were ordered to remain. By 1300 part of TF 'Y' [another Task Force of CCA attacking to the west of the St Lô–Isigny road] had reached the stream north of Villiers-Fossard [the only stream in the area is some 2km north of the village], the right flank of the force being held up by difficult terrain and stubborn enemy resistance. By 1600 the entire Task Force had reached the stream and assaulted enemy strongpoints south of the stream. . . The attack resumed at 0800, 30 June. By 1200 TF 'Y' was moving forward slowly. TF 'X' continued its advance against stubborn enemy resistance from small arms and AT guns. At 1245 enemy armor was observed in front of TF 'X', either tanks or SP 88mm guns (estimated at 5 to 10) and the line stabilized along the road leading from la Forge to Bois de Bretel. . . At 1500 the . . . line had been stabilized and no further advances were made.[52]

The Chief of Staff of the 352nd Division, Lieutenant Colonel Ziegelmann, had this to say about the action:

The enemy started his attack at about 0900 hours, supported by groups of tanks. . . At first the attacks were repelled; the enemy withdrew again under the cover of fog. At 1100 hours the enemy renewed his attack and reached the area just east of Villiers-Fossard. The village of la Forge changed hands frequently. At about 1530 hours the enemy attacked for the third time, supported by numerous Jabos [fighter-bombers], artillery [spotter] planes, strong artillery and mortar fire and numerous tanks and gained possession of Villiers-Fossard and la Forge. The fighting south of Villiers-Fossard continued until dark. . . . Losses on the German side were heavy. . . On 30 June . . . at about 0900, 1100 and 1400 hours the enemy made attacks in approximately battalion strength,

147

supported by tanks, from the area Villiers-Fossard on the German hastily constructed positions to the south and south-west.[53]

Readers will have noticed that whereas Ziegelmann's account says Villiers-Fossard fell to the Americans on the 29th, the US After Action Report indicates that, if this happened at all in this period, it was more likely on the 30th. The author has been unable to resolve this mystery.

By midnight on 30 June CCA of the 3rd Armored Division had been pulled back to its original assembly area and the Blue and Gray had assumed responsibility for the ground gained – less than six square kilometres. The cost to the 3rd Armored had been heavy – 329 men and twenty-eight Shermans.[54] The German salient had been dented but not eliminated and Corlett and Gerhardt had to be content.

Gerhardt's orders for the relief of CCA of the 3rd Armored Division were as follows:

29 Inf Div [with] attached: 747th Tank, 803rd TD, 821st TD, 823rd TD, 459th AAA Battalions [and] Company B, 81st Chemical Battalion, [will] advance . . . with Regiments abreast from right to left: 175th, 115th, 116th. Strong deliberate defenses will be prepared, based upon the occupation of the position for the next four days, against enemy counterattack involving the use of armor in mass.[55]

'Strong deliberate defenses' meant erecting protective barbed wire fences and laying numerous anti-personnel minefields.

During the last few days of June and, despite Gerhardt's concern about a possible enemy armoured counter-attack, in the first week of July, reserve Companies replaced those in the forward positions and every infantry soldier in the Blue and Gray spent some time in a so-called 'rest area'. 'During this period, each Battalion was successively placed in Regimental reserve for 48 hours, about three miles behind the front lines for a much needed rest'.[56] But in Charlie Gerhardt's Division real 'rest' was out of the question and he gave orders that uniforms and equipment were to be smartened up and: 'snappy drill, callisthenics [physical exercises], mass commands etc, were [to be] conducted to maintain the esprit de corps and splendid status of . . . units'.[57] One has to wonder whether this and the statement that: 'All in all, the men were in a happy frame of mind during their short stay in the rear' was entirely true, particularly when the men saw their Divisional commander watching them as they paraded at the crack of dawn in a Normandy pasture. But there was method in Uncle Charlie's apparent madness. An infantryman's horizon is inevitably very limited and he is usually unaware of anything going on outside the immediate vicinity of his own Company. At least the parades disproved rumours of severely depleted Companies and

Battalions – the men could actually see that their units were more or less up to strength – even if many of the faces were new.

On 2 July Generals Eisenhower and Bradley visited the 29th's Divisional Headquarters near St Clair-sur-l'Elle. Gerhardt, in his usual flamboyant way, lined up most of his Regimental and Battalion commanding officers in clean uniforms and even had a band to welcome his distinguished visitors. Bradley's ADC noted that the 29th was the only Division in Normandy to greet the Supreme commander with a formal ceremony. One officer missing from the line up was Lieutenant Colonel John Metcalfe, the commanding officer of the 116th Regiment's 1st Battalion. He had been seriously wounded and replaced by Major Thomas Dallas on 30 June.

During the first week of July preparations began in earnest for the long planned American offensive on the western flank of the Allied beachhead – Operation COBRA. The first requirement was to create the space needed for Lieutenant General George Patton's Third Army and to this end Bradley ordered an attack to secure the line Coutances–St Lô (Map 1). XIX Corps' part in the operation was to take St Lô. To this end the 30th Infantry Division, supported by the 113th Cavalry Group, was to make an initial advance on the west side of the Vire and threaten the city from the west, whilst a newly arrived National Guard Division, the 35th, together with Gerhardt's 29th, would advance two days later from the north-east. The prize of St Lô itself was to be awarded to the Blue and Gray.

The Enemy

By 27 June the strength of the 352nd Division, the main adversary of the Blue and Gray for the past three weeks, was only 3,480 men.[58] These were formed into three KGs and two reserves. Three days later the Division's Artillery Regiment, after losing four 105mm and three 150mm howitzers to direct hits, was down to just fifteen guns.[59] Manpower losses between 6 and 24 June amounted to 5,407 officers and men and by 11 July this figure had increased by another 2,479[60], leaving it, despite reinforcements, with only 3,360 men.[61] The only significant increase in strength in this period was four companies of Mk IV tanks from the 2nd SS Panzer Division Das Reich. These joined the 352nd on 1 and 2 July.

The reinforcement and reorganisation of Corlett's XIX Corps in the first days of July was to bring the Blue and Gray into direct contact with a new enemy – Lieutenant General Richard Schimpf's 3rd Parachute Division. It had a strength of 17,420[62] and its organisation is shown at Appendix L. Suggestions that it was much better equipped than normal Army infantry divisions are incorrect. One writer has even gone so far as to say it had over 1,000 machine-guns as against the US 29th Division's 157. In reality it had 382, admittedly 40% more than the Blue and Gray but nearly 100 less than Kraiss's 352nd Infantry Division. It was, however, strong in medium mortars, fielding 124, but this was to make up for its weakness in artillery. It had only one Battalion with twelve 105mm howitzers. Another major weakness was its lack of mobility. Nominally motorised, it had only 45% of its authorised vehicle holdings. This meant that when it was ordered from Brittany to the St Lô area on 7 June, only one reinforced Regiment could be lifted. The bulk of the Division had to begin marching some 300km to the battle area.

It was 10 June before the first KG of the 3rd Parachute Division arrived in St Lô and midday on the 11th before it took up a position between Berigny and St Germain-d'Elle on the right flank of the 352nd Division. Two days later the main part of the Division reached the St Lô area and by 22 June the Division was complete in Normandy. Unlike most German units moved to the front in June, it arrived almost intact. 'By marching only at night, avoiding the main roads and maintaining strict march and camouflage discipline, they [the Regiments] almost wholly escaped air attack.'[63]

Schimpf's Division was an elite formation. General Eugen Meindl, the commander of II Parachute Corps, to which the Division was attached, had this to say about it:

At the time of the Normandy fighting, there is little doubt that 3 FS [Fallschirmjäger] [Parachute] Division was the best of the German FS divisions. The Division consisted entirely of volunteers whose average age was 22. . . From 15 Jan 44 until 8 Jun 44, the Division trained extensively in thinly populated areas of Brittany, paying particular attention to hedgerow combat, close-in fighting, defence and attack by small groups on a self-sufficient basis, and firing all weapons – particularly Panzerfausts. The Regimental and Battalion commanders were hand picked and were of top-notch quality. Almost all of them had been in the fighting at Crete, Cassino, and the drops of 10 May 40, and were young, vigorous and infused a spirit of leadership in the troops.[64]

St Lô

In late June a number of the citizens of St Lô returned to see what, if anything, remained of their properties and to try to salvage some of their belongings. Many feared they would be mistaken for looters and possibly shot by either the French or German authorities. Inevitably some looting had already taken place – the French claiming that the Germans were much more thorough in that they set fire to the already ruined houses afterwards.

A few officials of the city Administration also returned in a vain attempt to salvage office records and supplies and to establish some sort of local government – but it was too late; St Lô was about to be engulfed in the fighting. According to one French historian[65], at 2145 hours on 8 July the Germans gave orders that any civilians remaining in the city were to leave at once and that anyone found there after 1100 hours the following day would be summarily executed. Ziegelmann, however, claimed later that the evacuation was carried out much earlier – on 27 June. 'The civilian population [was moved] to a line running approximately 7km south of St Lô . . . without particular incidents.'[66]

Let us now catch up with events in the British and Canadian sectors.

NOTES

1. In answer to the question, 'Of what tactical significance did you regard Hill 192', Gen Meindl, commander II Parachute Corps, replied as follows: 'Not very much. It lacked importance to us because there were other hills south of the St Lô road which were better points of observation.' – ETHINT 78, dated 12 Jan 46. Be that as it may, Hill 192 has commanding views to its north and north-east.
2. Couvains had been bombed during the night of 7 Jun; seventeen civilians were killed.
3. 743 Tk Bn was transferred to 1 Inf Div between 10 & 12 Jun & then to 30 Inf Div on 14 Jun 44.
4. One of these was the 230 FA Bn of 30 Inf Div which had come ashore on 10 Jun. It replaced the 111 FA Bn of 29 Div which had lost all its guns on D-Day.
5. Ziegelmann, MS # B-437.
6. Ibid.
7. This was possibly because HQ 29 Div was unaware that Goode had decided to send two Coys on this mission rather than the single coy ordered by V Corps.
8. CMH Pub 100-11, *Omaha Beachhead*, p. 158.
9. 1st Bn.
10. CMH Pub 100-11, op. cit., p. 158.
11. Harrison, *Cross Channel Attack*, p. 364.
12. Balkoski, *Beyond the Beachhead*, p. 200.
13. CMH Pub 100-11, p. 159.
14. 175 Inf Regt AAR dated 21 Jul 44.
15. CMH Pub 100-11, p. 163, gives a figure of 2,440.
16. Harrison, op. cit., p. 376.
17. Bradley, *A Soldier's Story*, p. 295.
18. Ziegelmann, MS # B-437.
19. Zetterling, *Normandy 1944*, p. 278.
20. Bradley, op.cit., p. 295.
21. 'When Pete Corlett came into line with his XIX Corps, he objected to the skinflint ration that had been allotted to his guns. "Pete," I remonstrated, "I hate this rationing as much as you do. But remember, we've got no choice. Either we ration it now or we shoot what we've got, packup, and go home." ' – Bradley, op.cit., p. 306.

22. Harrison, op. cit., p. 377.
23. 120 Inf Regt with tks of 743 Tk Bn.
24. By 16 Jun the 803 TD and 459 AAA Bns had joined the Div.
25. In MS # B-438 Lt Col Ziegelmann, Chief of Staff of 352 Div, claims that the Americans actually entered St André but this is not confirmed in any US report that the author could find.
26. 115 Inf Regt AAR dated 23 Jul 44.
27. 116 Inf S-3 Journal.
28. Ziegelmann, MS # B-435.
29. 175 Inf Regt AAR dated 21 Jul 44.
30. Ibid.
31. Zetterling, op. cit., p.281.
32. Ziegelmann, MS # B-438.
33. Ibid.
34. Harrison, op. cit., p. 382.
35. Ibid, p. 383. The difficulty in locating the enemy is not surprising; the ground in this area is a maze of small, twisting valleys, streams and hedgerows.
36. 116 Inf Regt S-3 Journal dated 18 Jun 44.
37. The June casualty figures given in the AARs of the three Inf Regts total 3,155, including 899 dead but excluding 'lightly wounded'. Using data from SHAEF, 12th Army Gp & First Army Casualty Reports, the Dupuy Institute provides a figure of 3,790 for the whole Div.
38. 29 Div G-1 Periodic Reports dated 18 & 25 Jun & 2 Jul 44.
39. 116 Inf Regt Unit History, June–Dec 44.
40. Balkoski, op. cit., p. 224.
41. Dupuy, Numbers, Predictions and War & Zetterling, Normandy 1944.
42. Dupuy, A Genius for War, pp. 253–4.
43. Ziegelmann, MS # B-438.
44. Ziegelmann, MS # B-439.
45. A 'rhino' was demonstrated to Bradley on 14 July and he immediately gave orders that several hundred were to be made available for Operation COBRA, the American breakout, scheduled for 20 Jul.
46. Ziegelmann, MS # B-241
47. Ibid.
48. Dupuy Institute.
49. By this time the KG was down to 980 men – Ziegelmann, MS # B-439.
50. 32 Armd & 36 Armd Inf Regts and 803 TD & 54 Armd FA Bns.
51. 3 Armd Div AAR dated 23 Jul 44.
52. Ibid.
53. Ziegelmann, MS # B-439.
54. Dupuy Institute.
55. HQ 29 Inf Div, FO#17 dated 301500B June 44.
56. 115 Inf Regt AAR dated 31 Jul 44.
57. 116 Inf Regt AAR dated 23 Jul 44.
58. Ziegelmann, MS # B-439.
59. Ibid.
60. Zetterling, op. cit., p. 278.
61. Ziegelmann, MS # B-439.
62. Zetterling, op. cit., p. 216.
63. MS # B-541.
64. ETHINT 78 dated 12 Jan 46.
65. Lantier, Saint-Lô au bûcher.
66. Ziegelmann, MS # B-241.

CHAPTER XVI

The British and Canadian Sector – 10 June to 6 July

(Map 15)

Readers will remember that the Operation Instruction issued by Lieutenant General John Crocker's I British Corps before D-Day stated that:

> Should the enemy forestall us at Caen and the defences prove to be strongly organised thus causing us to fail to capture it on D Day, further direct frontal assaults which may prove costly, will not be undertaken without reference to I Corps. In such an event 3 Brit Inf Div will contain the enemy in Caen.

They may also recall that by the evening of 8 June Montgomery had decided to encircle the city by making a major thrust to the west of Tilly-sur-Seulles, leading to the high ground north-east of Villers-Bocage and thence east to Evrecy on the far side of the Odon. It is time therefore to look, if only in outline, at the actions designed to achieve that encirclement.

The initial move towards Villers-Bocage failed when forces[1] under the command of the 7th Armoured Division were halted on the line Verrières–Tilly-sur-Seulles. This happened on 10 June and the following day another Infantry Brigade supported by tanks[2] was ordered to attack on the east side of the Seulles river with the aim of bringing the 50th Infantry Division into line with the 7th Armoured and supporting its further advance.

On this same day, 11 June, General Dempsey was warned by Allied intelligence sources that the Germans were concentrating for a counter-attack out of the Caen area. He was unaware that Rommel had already decided to delay this attack because of insufficient forces, but in view of this information and in order to help the British push towards Villers-Bocage, Dempsey ordered Lieutenant General John Crocker, commanding I Corps, not only to concentrate his armour on the high ground south of Douvres where it could counter the expected German attack, but at the same time to launch an attack with his Canadian troops. This concentration of armour soon became known to the Germans because their radar station at Douvres, which was still holding out against all attempts to capture it, reported during the morning of the 11th:

'Continuous movement, heavy and medium tanks, towards south-west. More than eighty tanks counted in one hour.' And at 2045 hours it reported: 'Urgent. In Anguerny area assembly of up to now 200 medium enemy tanks with transport echelon facing south.'[3] These reports were not exaggerated. Montgomery had written to his Chief of Staff:

> We are VERY strong now astride the road Caen – Bayeux about the junction of 3 Div and 3 Canadian Div, and if the enemy attacks he should be seen off: I have 400 tanks there.[4]

Both sides were therefore expecting major attacks in this sector on 11 June.

For reasons that need not concern us the British and Canadian attacks failed.[5] Nevertheless, they caused serious anxiety in the German command because the troops earmarked to fill the widening gap between Waffen-SS General Sepp Dietrich's I SS Panzer Corps east of Tilly-sur-Seulles and General Marcks's LXXXIV Corps west of Balleroy had yet to arrive. Marcks reported to Seventh Army on the 11th that his 352nd Division: 'Now has small combat value and the gap between it and its right flank neighbour [the Panzer Lehr Division] is constantly increasing'.[6] It was planned to fill the gap with the 3rd Parachute and 2nd Panzer Divisions, though the tanks and wheeled vehicles of 2nd Panzer were not expected to arrive before 14 June or to be ready for action until the 15th at the earliest. In the meantime the gap would have to be filled by light reconnaissance forces.

When Dietrich briefed his commanders on the situation he told them that he no longer believed a concentrated counter-attack against the British was possible and that he had no reserves left. In fact Dietrich did have one reserve that was about to arrive in the sector and play a dramatic part in forthcoming events – the 101st SS (Tiger) Heavy Panzer Battalion.

Operation PERCH

The crisis for the Germans came on 12 June when the American 1st Infantry Division advanced and captured Caumont on the US left flank. This small town stands on a prominent ridge between Villers-Bocage and St Lô and dominates the surrounding area. General Marcks himself was killed on this day in a fighter-bomber attack when leading a group of hastily assembled minor units in a last attempt to defend this vital ground. But it was too late and by nightfall, after an advance of 8km, the Americans entered Caumont.

The news that the Americans had found a gap to the west of Tilly-sur-Seulles electrified the British command. General Dempsey, the Second Army commander, learned about the American advance on Caumont at 1145 hours on 12 June when he met the commander of XXX Corps,

Lieutenant General Bucknall. He wrote in his personal diary: 'I told him to switch 7 Armd Div from their front immediately, to push them thro' . . . and endeavour to get to Villers-Bocage that way.'[7] And Montgomery sent a message to his Chief of Staff that night: 'Thrust line was switched quickly further to the west and Div. . . will move on Villers-Bocage and Noyers tomorrow. All this very good and Pz Lehr may be in grave danger tomorrow.' As Monty saw it PERCH, as the operation was code-named, could be a 'turning point in the battle'.

Major General Bobby Erskine, commander 7 Armoured Division, knew that this deep probe around the back of the Panzer Lehr Division would mean advancing on a very narrow front with an exposed left flank, but he also knew that Dietrich's Panzer Divisions were fully committed and that there were no immediate German reserves. An ULTRA decrypt on the 12th indicated that 2nd Panzer was on its way to support Panzer Lehr in the neighbourhood of Villers-Bocage but it still had some way to go to reach the battle area. The British generals had every reason to expect success on 13 June – but then none of them knew about the fourteen newly arrived Tigers of the 101st SS Heavy Panzer Battalion!

The battle of Villers-Bocage has been described in virtually every book written about the battle of Normandy – with varying degrees of accuracy. It will not be repeated here but this author's version of events can be found in his book *Steel Inferno*. Put in very simple terms, Waffen-SS Panzer ace, Michael Wittmann, and other members of the 101st SS Heavy Panzer Battalion routed the leading combat group of the 7th Armoured Division and this led to Villers-Bocage remaining in German hands for a further two months and caused Montgomery to revise his plans yet again. The day following the disaster Monty wrote to the British Chief of Staff: 'I am going to put all my offensive power, ammunition and so on, into an offensive . . . on the right of Second Army.'

Operation EPSOM

Montgomery's new offensive, known as operation EPSOM, was originally scheduled for 23 June but, quite unexpectedly, in the early hours of 19 June a violent summer storm developed in the Channel and lasted three days. The interruption to the landing of men and supplies meant that EPSOM had to be postponed. The scale of the interruption can be judged by the following figures: in the period 15 to 18 June, before the storm, the British landed 15,774 soldiers, 2,965 vehicles and 10,666 tons of stores; in the period of the storm, 19 to 22 June, the figures dropped to 3,982 men, 1,375 vehicles and only 4,286 tons of stores.[8] As well as causing a postponement of the planned offensive, the storm had another positive effect for the Germans – the poor flying weather allowed them to carry out resupply and troop movements without fear of attack by fighter-bombers.

The aim of EPSOM was to cross the Odon and Orne rivers and capture the high ground astride the Caen–Falaise road, north-east of Bretteville-sur-Laize, thus isolating Caen and exposing the German right flank in Normandy. It was to be executed by three Corps, totalling 60,000 men and 600 tanks. Phase I, beginning on 25 June, saw XXX Corps capturing the commanding ground around Rauray and then, after taking Noyers, exploiting south to Aunay-sur-Odon. With its right flank thus protected, the recently landed VIII Corps was then, in Phase II beginning on 26 June, to carry out the main thrust. As the operation progressed I Corps, including the British and Canadian 3rd Infantry Divisions, was to apply pressure north of Caen and capture Carpiquet airfield; and there was to be a concurrent thrust out of the 6 Airborne Division's bridgehead east of the Orne. The main attack by VIII Corps was to be supported by over 900 guns, three naval cruisers and the fighter-bombers of the Second Tactical Air Force.

As readers will appreciate, EPSOM was an extremely complicated operation and we need not go into the details – again they are clearly set out in *Steel Inferno*. The fighting lasted until 1 July and by then VIII Corps, which had borne the brunt of the fighting, had suffered 4,020 casualties. It was clearly a major effort to break through the German defences to the west of Caen and in that it failed. Nevertheless, EPSOM was highly successful in two vital aspects. First, it had destroyed any chance the Germans might have had of launching a major counter-attack towards Bayeux and second, it had forced them to commit their armour 'piecemeal and in haste'.[9] In fact by the end of June seven and a half of the eight Panzer Divisions in Normandy were deployed against the British Second Army. Monty was under strong criticism for failing to capture Caen, but his strategy of keeping the German reserves, particularly armoured reserves, away from the planned American breakout in the west was clearly working.

Operation WINDSOR

One of the aims of EPSOM had been the capture of Carpiquet village and its airfield by the Canadians; however, the failure to expand the British bridgehead across the Odon led, on 30 June, to the postponement of this part of the operation. Nevertheless it was still considered to be an essential prerequisite to the capture of Caen and on 4 July the Canadians were ordered to attack. The operation was code-named WINDSOR and involved supporting fire from twenty-one artillery battalions and the battleship HMS *Rodney*. Two squadrons of 'tank-busting' aircraft were on call if needed. The village of Carpiquet was captured by 1400 hours, although attempts to advance across the airfield and capture the southern hangars and control tower ended in failure. Even so the Canadian advance into the flank of the 12th SS Panzer Division Hitlerjugend was seen by both Sepp Dietrich, commanding I SS Panzer Corps, and Kurt Meyer, now commanding that Division[10], as a threat to Caen itself and a night counter-attack was ordered to regain the village. This was beaten off and both sides went firm on the line of the main Caen–St Lô road.[11]

It was now clear to both Montgomery and Dempsey that Caen would after all have to be taken by frontal assault. German occupation of the city was blocking the way to the Bourguébus Ridge, some 6km to its south-east, and subsequently to the Falaise Plain. This latter feature was desperately needed, not just for airfield construction, but more impor-tantly for the eventual Allied breakout. The closer the hinge for this breakout could be located to the city of Falaise, the greater the threat to the German forces to the west of that hinge. In addition, four German infantry divisions were known to have reached Normandy in early July, and if they were able to release the Panzer divisions for their classic counter-attack role and operations against the Americans, Monty's overall strategy would be in jeopardy.

The most important consequence of the Hitlerjugend's tenacious defence of Carpiquet airfield was that it led Dempsey to believe that it would be impossible to take Caen quickly and without unacceptable casualties unless the attack was assisted by RAF Bomber Command. I British Corps had by this time been reinforced to a strength of 115,000 and, almost exactly a month after Caen should have fallen to the Iron Division, planning began in earnest for an onslaught that would see the total destruction of the once beautiful city.

Having described in outline the events in the British and Canadian sector between 10 June and 7 July, we can now revert to the detailed actions of the Iron Division.

NOTES

1. 22 Armd Bde & 56 Indep Inf Bde.
2. 69 Inf Bde & 8 Armd Bde.
3. Douvres Radar Radio Log for 11 Jun 44.
4. Demi-official Correspondence of CinC 21 Army Gp, PRO London.
5. For those interested full details are given in the author's book *Steel Inferno*.
6. Wilmot, *The Struggle for Europe*, p. 306.
7. Dempsey Diary, PRO WO 285/9.
8. Ellis, *Victory in the West, Vol. I, The Battle of Normandy*, p, 275.
9. Wilmot, op. cit., p, 348.
10. Fritz Witt had been killed on 14 Jun 44.
11. Full details of Operation WINDSOR can be found in *Steel Inferno*.

CHAPTER XVII

The Iron Division – 12 June to 11 July

Stalemate

(Map 13)

We come now to a period of static warfare in the Iron Division's sector, reminiscent of WWI. 185 Brigade was on the eastern flank from Blainville on the Caen canal to Biéville, 8 Brigade was in the centre holding from exclusive Biéville to the le Mesnil wood east of the main Caen to Luc-sur-Mer road, and 9 Brigade was defending the le Mesnil wood to the west of the Caen road and the Cambes-en-Plaine sector. On 12 June the 13/18 H crossed to the east side of the Orne leaving only the Staffordshire Yeomanry and East Riding Yeomanry under Rennie's command.[1] Protruding into the Division's front was the German salient at la Londe. There were no continuous trench lines but both sides were dug in and both sides resorted to a pattern of patrolling and shelling – and in the case of the British to rotating battalions from front to rear and back again. For example, the Warwicks took five-day turns with the KSLI moving from Beuville to Biéville and back again. A good account of what it was like for the infantrymen of the Division during this period, based on individual reminiscences, can be read in Patrick Delaforce's book *Monty's Iron Sides*.

The British were able to produce a much heavier weight of shellfire owing to the presence of the Royal Navy's ships offshore; these included the battleship HMS *Rodney* with her 16-inch guns, and a more than adequate supply of ammunition. The History of the KSLI describes how it was the custom to fire 'one minute's worth of hate' at Lébisey several times a day with at least five battalions of artillery, naval ships and all the machine-guns and mortars within range. An example of the weight of fire produced can be gauged by the fact that in just two days, 21 and 22 June, the 33 Field Regiment alone fired 8,700 rounds. The extent of the casualties caused by this constant harassing fire is unknown but Feuchtinger spoke of 50% losses in his infantry forces 'during these defensive battles' due to shelling and bombing. He went on to say:

The supply problem was particularly difficult for the defence in this sector as British heavy naval artillery kept the supply routes under fire far into the hinterland. . . After 12 June the ammunition dumps within reach of the supply columns no longer had the most important types of ammunition in stock and these now had to be collected in trips of several days' duration. . . The Division received no reinforcements of any kind.[2]

One British officer said later:

> We wondered how it was possible for human nerves to stand such an onslaught. We began to realise the extreme toughness and tenacity of the Germans who lay across the wasted fields, so near to us and apparently resolved never to be dislodged.[3]

But just as the Germans were suffering, so the German shelling and patrol clashes caused numerous casualties to the British – the Lincolns for example reporting 124 casualties and the KOSB 122 in the period 10 to 27 June. The most significant casualty was the Divisional commander himself. On 13 June Tom Rennie was on one of his frequent visits to the forward area and unwisely agreed to take a short cut to get to Cambes-en-Plaine. An officer described how Rennie's jeep appeared in the village 'from the hostile end' and hit a British mine. The General was wounded and had to be evacuated to England. Brigadier Copper Cass took command of the Division and Lieutenant Colonel Foster of 76 Field Artillery Regiment took over 8 Brigade.

The Fighting for la Londe

It will be remembered that during the night of 10 June the South Lancs had been able to move into the group of buildings at le Londel, 2km north of Lébisey and Epron, but that a plan to infiltrate south-west and occupy the Château and farm buildings at la Londe had been vetoed by Brigadier Cass. Subsequent patrols confirmed that la Londe was strongly held and that Mk IV tanks were present. This was hardly surprising since the position held commanding views towards Biéville to the east, Lébisey to the south-east and the high ground overlooking Caen to the south. Any future advance towards the city would necessarily involve the capture of this vital area.

After spending a week in reserve whilst the East Yorks took over the sector, the South Lancs came back into the line on 21 June. By then the area immediately north of Caen was strongly held by the 21st Panzer Division. A Panzer-Grenadier Battalion[4] with Mk IV tanks was in the village of Lébisey and its wood and another[5] with two companies of Mk IVs was in and around la Bijude and Epron. Eight 88mm guns of the Division's Panzerjäger Battalion occupied positions alongside and between the two Battalions. More Panzer-Grenadiers, Pioneers[6] and Mk IV tanks were holding la Londe and its Château.

At 0030 hours on 22 June B and C Companies of the South Lancs launched a silent (no preparatory fire) night attack against la Londe. C Company was soon held up by heavy machine-gun fire but B Company established itself in the south-west corner of the enemy position and A

Company was then ordered to reinforce it. Unfortunately, before this could be completed the Germans launched a counter-attack from the area of the Château supported by artillery and mortars. The Battalion's anti-tank guns had yet to arrive and tanks overran Captain Murison's B Company. The operation cost the South Lancs two killed and thirty-four wounded, plus another seventy-three missing, at least sixty-two of whom were later found to be prisoners of war.

The day after the South Lancs' attack against la Londe, a new General arrived to take command of the Iron Division. He was Major General Lashmer 'Bolo' Whistler. As the commander of 131 (Queen's) Infantry Brigade in the North African and Italian campaigns he had earned Monty's tribute of being 'probably the finest fighting Brigadier in the British Army'. A holder of three DSOs, Whistler had been wounded and captured by the Germans in WWI and was known as 'Bolo' as a result of serving with the Archangel expedition in 1919 against the Bolsheviks, or 'Bolos' as they were called. In January 1944 he had written in his diary: 'Am not fit for an Armoured Division. . . will do whatever providence dictates as well as possible', and then in early June he added: 'Am windy of a Division [infantry] and more so of an armoured Division where I may easily go. I trust my best will be good enough for this next job.'

Readers may recall that as part of operation EPSOM (25 June–1 July), Lieutenant General John Crocker's I Corps had been tasked with applying pressure on the front directly north of Caen. This mission inevitably fell to the Iron Division and Whistler chose Brigadier Cass's 8 Brigade for an initial operation which was code-named MITTEN. It involved the capture of la Londe and its Château, la Bijude and Epron. Following this a second operation code-named ABERLOUR was to be launched by Brigadier Dennis Orr's 9 Brigade with the East Riding Yeomanry under command. It was to be made in conjunction with an attack by the Canadian 9th Infantry Brigade on its right flank. ABERLOUR had the incredibly ambitious aim of reaching the Caen–Bayeux road.

The 8 Brigade attack was to begin at 1530 hours on 27 June. Copper Cass's plan required the South Lancs in Phase I to take la Londe and its Château and then a second Phase in which the East Yorks and Suffolks would pass through and capture la Bijude and Epron. Armoured support was to be provided by the Shermans of the Staffordshire Yeomanry, four flame-throwing Churchill tanks from the 79th Division and sixteen anti-tank guns of 67 Anti-Tank Regiment, and the fire plan was to be executed by the whole of the Iron Division's artillery plus guns of the Canadian 3rd and British 51st (Highland) Divisions, some additional Second Army medium and heavy artillery battalions and the machine-guns of 2nd Middlesex. The attack had all the hallmarks of a WWI operation on the Somme.

The South Lancs came under shell and mortar fire and suffered casualties even as they formed up for their Phase I attack. Nevertheless they crossed the Start Line on time and despite heavy resistance Captain Sussex's D Company managed to reach the wood on the north side of the Château by 1610 hours; however, C Company on the left flank was soon pinned down and both Companies took serious casualties. A Company was moved up from le Londel on the left flank and a platoon under Lieutenant Eddie Jones got as far as a bank leading directly to the Château wall on its north-east side. He was supported by one of the flame-throwing Churchills but a salvo of mortar rounds put most of one of his sections out of action and at about the same time the turret on the tank was blown off and the tank and trailer went up in flames. The Panzer-Grenadiers holding the Château and its surrounding woods were clearly not going to give up easily and at 2200 hours, with casualties still mounting, it was decided to withdraw the forward Companies. By then the new commanding officer, Lieutenant Colonel Stone, and the C Company commander, Major Johnson, had both been wounded. The decision was then taken to try again at dawn, 0415 hours, the following day, with the East Yorks, now under the command of Lieutenant Colonel Dickson, taking the Château and the Suffolks advancing over open cornfields to secure the left part of the Château grounds and the open area to the east. Artillery and machine-gun support was to be the same as on the 27th but despite a request by the attacking Battalions for close armoured support, none was provided.

At 0407 hours on the 28th the supporting artillery opened fire. Private Richard Harris of B Company of the Suffolks writing six years after the event gave this description: 'The very ground shuddered under the impact and the scene resembled a gigantic and terrible firework display with black smoke and fumes being wafted towards us as shell after shell thundered down.'[7]

The Start Line for the East Yorks' attack was a track running parallel to the forward edge of the le Londel wood and it was under heavy fire even before the Companies moved up to cross it. Major Sheath of B Company was wounded but his men and A Company reached their objectives. As they were consolidating the inevitable counter-attack came in led by Mk IV tanks and although A Company was partially over-run the attack was beaten off. By then C and D Companies had come forward and with help from the Suffolks the position was eventually stabilised. Meanwhile the Suffolks had been attacking on the left flank. B and C Companies, under Major McCaffrey and Major Boycott respectively, reached their objectives behind the Château by 0530 hours and started to dig in. They too had suffered serious losses. Boycott had been wounded and of his Platoons, one had only its commander and seven men left, another only eight men and the third Platoon just one section (squad). Major John Waring, commanding a Battery of 76 Field Regiment in support of MITTEN, re-called later:

As the advance reached the area of the Château the ground became rougher, there being ditches, hedgerows and walls. In this area the Suffolks met their stiffest resistance; all gaps in fences, hedgerows etc and every conceivable place was booby-trapped and mined and every yard of ground had to be fought for. Many men lost their lives or limbs pushing their way through hedges or climbing over ditches. I was proud to be an Englishman that day.

Needless to say another counter-attack soon developed. Six German tanks accompanied by about thirty Grenadiers attacked B Company and lacking anti-tank support, two of its Platoons were forced to surrender. McCaffrey and one of his Platoon commanders, 'seeing they had lost control . . . managed to avoid being discovered by the Germans. After several hours they were able to get away back to Battalion Headquarters'.[8] The survivors dug in near the Château wall. C Company, now under the command of a Canadian officer, Captain Brown, was also attacked by two Mk IVs but both were knocked out by PIAT fire.

Concurrent with the fighting around the Château, D Company of the Suffolks moved forward to le Londel, but as it started to dig in south-west of the farm buildings it was subjected to an intense bombardment during which the Company commander, Major Philip Papillon, was fatally wounded. It was now after 0530 hours and Captain Albert Claxton, who had taken over the Company, was ordered to follow the line taken by the East Yorks and attack the Château. The Company advanced across a cornfield, linked up with the B Company survivors under Captain Warwick Archdale and then went on to attack the Château, taking several prisoners and releasing some twenty-five men of the East Yorks who had been taken prisoner earlier. By now it was about 1300 hours and, although Operation MITTEN had achieved its immediate objectives, the positions held were still under heavy shell and mortar fire. Private Harris, one of the B Company survivors, described later how: 'the twenty men in the position had all been killed including Captain Archdale and Company Sergeant-Major Broom. Many still had shovels in their hands.'

The Suffolks suffered 161 casualties including three Company commanders during the la Londe fighting[9] and the East Yorks fourteen killed, eighty-four wounded and thirteen missing – most of whom were later accounted for. This brought the latter's total for June to 372.[10] Was the price paid by these infantry Battalions for a gain of less than a square kilometre of enemy territory worth it? The reader will have to make up his own mind after reading the rest of this story. Needless to say Operation ABERLOUR, which was dependent on 8 Brigade's attack being success-fully concluded, was cancelled.

During June 1944 the Iron Division fought a battle of attrition rather than manoeuvre and even the most conservative estimate would put its casualties at over 3,000 officers and men. This author has calculated a provisional figure of 3,508 – 417 killed, 2,280 wounded and 811 missing.[11] In the same period the 21st Panzer Division is said to have lost 2,854 men – 472 killed, 1,606 wounded and 776 missing[12] and the 12th SS Panzer Division Hitlerjugend a total of 2,662.[13]

Operation CHARNWOOD

By 7 July I Corps had been reinforced to a strength of 115,000 and, as we have heard, Montgomery and Dempsey had decided to use it, in conjunction with Air Marshal Sir Arthur Harris's Bomber Command, to take Caen by frontal assault. The declared mission was to clear Caen as far as the Orne and to establish bridgeheads across that river. The Iron Division was to attack on the eastern flank. Whistler retained the Staffordshire Yeomanry under command but the 13/18 H, having returned from the 6th Airborne Division's sector, and the East Riding Yeomanry were detached to the British 59th (Staffordshire) Infantry Division. It was to attack in the centre with la Bijude, Epron and St Contest as its objectives. On the right flank Major General Keller's 3rd Canadian Infantry Division, with the 2nd Canadian Armoured Brigade under command, was tasked with capturing Buron and Carpiquet airfield and then entering Caen from the west. Specialist tanks from the British 79th Armoured Division supported all three Divisions and additional artillery was to be provided by the guns of two Army Groups Royal Artillery and the Guards Armoured and 51st (Highland) Infantry Divisions, reinforced by naval gunfire from HMS *Rodney*, a monitor and two cruisers.

Sir Arthur Harris agreed with the ground commanders that for safety reasons bombs would be dropped no nearer than 6,000 metres to the attacking troops. This meant that the bombs would fall over 5km behind the German forward defences and virtually guaranteed that the vast majority of the defenders of Caen would survive unscathed. Since the attacking troops would be unable to follow the bombing closely, it was further decided to mount the air attack the evening before the ground attack with the fuses of 20% of the bombs set to detonate six hours later. It was hoped that the destruction thus caused would prevent the Germans from bringing reinforcements through the city. Suggestions that the bombing was carried out the evening before the attack because of a forecast of bad weather for 8 July are incorrect.[14]

As early as 16 June Lieutenant General Karl Sievers' 16th Luftwaffe Field Division had been ordered from Holland to Normandy to relieve Feuchtinger's 21st Panzer and it was this Division that would be standing in the way of Whistler's men in Operation CHARNWOOD. Its strength on arrival in the Caen sector is uncertain. One document states that it had only some sixty to seventy men in each of its infantry companies since it was required to leave soldiers in Holland to man static weapons there. Another document, however, states that the Division left the Netherlands with 9,816 men, twenty-eight artillery pieces and thirty-two anti-tank guns.[15] Whatever the truth its basic organisation was three infantry Regiments, each of two Battalions with fifty-six machine-guns and eight mortars, and an anti-tank company with six anti-tank guns and two 20mm Flak guns. In addition there was an artillery Regiment of three Battalions with a total of twenty-eight guns and howitzers, a Panzerjäger Battalion with twenty-three guns including two StuGs, a Pioneer Battalion and a Fusilier Battalion. Its mobility was limited as it had only 57% of its authorised number of horses and 50% of its vehicles.[16] Nevertheless, the 16th Luftwaffe Field Division reached Normandy with few losses, its trains having escaped air attack on the way. It is not clear exactly how much of the Division was deployed west of the Orne in the 21st Panzer Division's sector but Niklas Zetterling in his meticulously researched book *Normandy 1944*, estimates one Regiment of eight infantry companies and other sources indicate that this Regiment was the 31st.

The bulk of the 21st Panzer Division had been relieved by 1800 hours on 5 July and moved into Fifth Panzer Army reserve on both sides of the Dives river east of Vimont (Map 1). But in order to give the in-coming Luftwaffe formation more 'teeth', its 1st Panzer and 200th Panzerjäger Battalions remained behind in the Lébisey–Epron sector and its Anti-Aircraft Battalion and two Battalions of its Artillery Regiment remained in support on both sides of the Orne.[17] In addition, the heavy mortars of the 12th SS Panzer Division Hitlerjugend and another heavy Mortar Battalion[18] were sited north and west of Caen. The combat-ready tank strength of 21st Panzer on 6 July was sixty-seven Mk IVs but it is unlikely that more than half of these were in support of the 16th Luftwaffe Field Division.

Also on 5 July a Brigade of the British 59th Infantry Division relieved the 9th Infantry Brigade in the Cambes-en-Plaine area and at 2200 hours Brigadier Dennis Orr's Headquarters moved to Bénouville to take over from 185 Brigade. The Ulster Rifles moved across to the eastern flank the following morning and the KOSB followed on the 7th. This realignment of the Division was necessary because Major General Bolo Whistler's plan for CHARNWOOD envisaged 185 Brigade advancing at dawn on the 8th to take Lébisey and Point 64 on the northern edge of Caen; then 9 Brigade, less the Lincolns but with the 101st Anti-Tank Battery under command, was to pass through to enter the city from the north and east. Lieutenant Colonel Welby-Everard's Lincolns had been placed under 185 Brigade's command on 5 July. They were tasked with taking Hérouville down by the Orne canal on the morning of the 8th in order to protect the left flank of 185 Brigade's advance – a difficult task because they would be in full view of the German observation posts in the Colombelles factories on the other side of the Orne. The mauled 8 Brigade in the area of la Londe was not to take part in the Iron Division's final assault on Caen.

By 7 July Brigadier Kipper Smith had been sacked and Brigadier Eric Bols was commanding 185 Brigade. Smith was convinced that Monty had 'had it in for him' even before D-Day:

> On returning to England [from the Middle East] he [Monty] had a long list of senior officers, undoubtedly including myself, he was going to sack and replace by his favourite Eighth Army commanders.[19]

Following the failure to reach Caen during early June Montgomery:

> suggested [to Bolo Whistler] that I was on the old side [he was 46] and not up to the stresses which lay ahead. In his report, Bolo confirmed Monty's doubts but said I . . . should retain my rank as Brigadier. . . Understandably I was broken-hearted at leaving my beloved Brigade.[20]

The aerial onslaught on Caen began at 2150 hours on 7 July and lasted until 2230. It was carried out by 467 Lancaster and Halifax heavy bombers[21], covered by fifteen Spitfire squadrons and followed by ground attack aircraft that attacked specific point targets. Some 6,000 actual bombs (2,276 tons) were dropped, 1,000 of which were fitted with delayed action fuses and they completed the destruction of the St Sauveur, St Julien, St Pierre and le Vaugueux districts, set fire to the University, destroyed the Hôtel de Ville, blocked all routes north of the Orne and killed several hundred French civilians.[22] Fortunately the Cathedral, the Abbaye-aux-Hommes and the Hôpital du Bon Sauveur, where many civilians were still sheltering, survived. German casualties were minimal although a 21st Army Group intelligence summary dated 11 July, based on the interrogation of prisoners and confirmed after the war by French sources[23], states that '31 German Air Force Regiment lost its head-quarters'.[24] One effect of the bombing was to raise an enormous cloud of smoke and dust that was blown by the prevailing wind over the British lines, darkening the sky and causing darkness to fall half an hour early.

At 2300 hours the 656 guns of I Corps began firing on the villages on or just behind the German front line, including Lébisey. Every known German battery of guns and mortars was targeted and this pounding continued throughout the night. Apparently, and incredibly, the morale of many of the German soldiers remained high, particularly those of Kurt Meyer's 12th SS Panzer Division, sustained to some extent by, as they saw it, the rather pathetic results of the bombing. Meyer's own comments on this aspect of the attack are interesting:

The air raid seems to be the prelude to the main assault. Every last Grenadier is at the ready. The gunners standby for orders to lay down a curtain of fire in front of our own lines. We wait. The phones are silent. We stare tensely out into the night awaiting the enemy ground force's attack. Minutes pass without the silence being broken. It is inconceivable but true. The Allies are making no attempt to exploit the tremendous bombing operation.[25]

The Attack

H-Hour for Operation CHARNWOOD was 0420 hours on 8 July. It began with a shattering artillery barrage by 656 guns, behind which the two British Divisions advanced towards their objectives. The battleship HMS *Rodney*, the monitor *Roberts* and the cruisers *Belfast* and *Emerald* were also in support. In the case of the Iron Division, the Warwicks and Norfolks, supported by two Squadrons of the Staffordshire Yeomanry and two Troops of flails of the 22nd Dragoons, advanced on time from a Start Line 400m north of the Lébisey wood secured by the KSLI. The commanding officer of the latter, Lieutenant Colonel Jack Maurice, had been killed by shellfire the day before and the second in command, Major Wilson, had taken over.

The various Regimental Histories and War Diaries provide little detail of the fighting on this very hot and sunny day but it is clear that the artillery barrage had, not surprisingly, pulverised the German defences and the Warwicks and Norfolks were able to make good progress, pushing through Lébisey and its infamous wood by 1100 hours. One German report stated that the infantry element of the 16th Luftwaffe Field Division located west of the Orne suffered 75% casualties on 8 July.[26] Certainly the remaining pockets of resistance were easily mopped up and the Warwicks and Norfolks then started digging in south of Lébisey. The Warwicks were shocked to find the unburied bodies of their comrades who had died in the first attack on the village a month previously – 'the heavy reek of death lingered everywhere'. Meanwhile on the left flank, the Lincolns had suffered heavy casualties clearing Hérouville in the face of stiff opposition.

At 1200 hours the I Corps commander, elated by the success of the 3rd Division's attack, decided to reinforce it with two tank Regiments from his armoured reserve, the 33rd Independent Armoured Brigade, and Whistler in turn moved the KSLI from 185 Brigade to 9 Brigade for the move into Caen itself.[27] It was, however, another three and a half hours before the KSLI could be assembled for a further advance to the high ground around ring contour 60 and Point 64.[28] C Squadron and the Reconnaissance Troop (platoon) of the 1st Northamptonshire Yeomanry (33 Armoured Brigade) were to join them in this task. The unfortunate Germans in this area had already been subjected to the weight of HMS *Rodney*'s 16-inch guns. The battleship fired twenty-nine 930kg shells with great accuracy and not surprisingly the opposition encountered was minimal. By 1600 hours Point 64 had been secured and the soldiers looked down on the effects of the RAF raid:

> large tracts of an area of about two and a half square miles had been devastated by the concentrated bombing. In open ground the craters were practically contiguous. With one exception, all roads through the bombed area were completely blocked.[29]

Nevertheless, the area around Point 64 was exposed and in full view of German observers in the Colombelles factories and on the high ground on the far side of the Orne. It was also well within range of German artillery and heavy mortars and all three Battalions of 185 Brigade, the Ulster Rifles of 9 Brigade and the tanks of the 1st Northamptonshire Yeomanry that were following up and had reached the same area by 1800 hours, came under heavy, accurate and continuous fire. It seems likely that had these four infantry Battalions continued their advance into Caen they would have incurred no more, or possibly even fewer, casualties than they did – over 350. The Warwicks lost 151 men including twenty-six killed, the Norfolks 116 with twenty-five killed, the KSLI fifteen killed and twenty-five wounded and the Ulster Rifles in the region of forty.[30] The Staffordshire Yeomanry lost one Sherman, three men killed and one wounded.

At 1630 hours the commander of the 21st Panzer Division, Edgar Feuchtinger, in reserve to the east of the Orne, received the following orders:

> Following heavy air attacks on the positions north of Caen the enemy has succeeded in breaking through and advancing as far as the northern outskirts. The situation there is not clear. Get a rough overall picture of the situation at the Command Post of the 16th Luftwaffe Field Division, then relieve the Divisional commander who is in Caen and take over command of all parts of that Division that are west of the Orne. . . Whatever the situation you will equalise it by counter-attacking.[31]

At 1900 hours when he took over command in Caen:

> The Battalion from the 16th Division [its only reserve] received orders to occupy the north-east rim of Caen while the 192nd Panzer-Grenadier Regiment was to counter-attack from the region south of Hérouville. These orders were carried out in the late hours of the same evening [but see below]. For this attack the available tanks of the 22nd Panzer

Regiment were put under the command of the 192nd Panzer-Grenadier Regiment, while the remaining tanks [of the 1st Panzer Battalion], still surrounded, were fighting south of Epron. Late the same evening, after connection with the 12th SS Division had been made, it was found that the right wing of this Division was retreating towards the Orne via St Germain [St Germain-la-Blanche-Herbe]. . . This greatly endangered the position of the 21st Panzer Division in Caen. . . At 0200 hours the Corps gave orders to retreat to the eastern bank of the Orne.[32]

The counter-attack by the single Battalion of the Luftwaffe Field Division does not seem to have developed but the Lincolns, on the exposed left flank in Hérouville, were certainly subjected to a counter-attack by elements of the 192nd Panzer-Grenadier Regiment. This will be described in sequence.

It will be remembered that the original British plan had seen only the Ulster Rifles and the KOSB of 9 Brigade moving through 185 Brigade and entering Caen on the first day of CHARNWOOD, but with the additional tanks now available it was decided instead to try to rush the Orne bridges with an armoured column. Accordingly, at 2025 hours, B Company of the Ulster Rifles under Major Hyde and two Troops of Shermans of B Squadron of the Northamptonshire Yeomanry advanced into the outskirts of the city, only to find their way through the narrow streets obstructed by deep craters and mountains of rubble from the bombing. According to the 33 Armoured Brigade War Diary two Northamptonshire tanks were hit by enemy fire and at 2317 hours the Regiment reported 'progress was almost impossible'. At 2350 hours it was decided to withdraw the tanks; by then the Ulster Rifles had lost eight men killed and forty-six wounded, many to sniper fire, and it was deemed too hazardous to continue the advance in the dark. In the meantime, over on the left flank in Hérouville the Lincolns had been counter-attacked twice by two Panzer-Grenadier companies and three tanks. The attacks were beaten off and one of the tanks knocked out, but by the end of the day the number of casualties suffered by the Battalion had risen to twenty-five killed and 119 wounded.[33] The commander of C Company, Major (later Major General) Glyn Gilbert said afterwards:

> . . . my company strength was reduced to 40 [men]. We . . . assumed a defensive position in an orchard on the southern edge of the village, and twice German tanks and infantry counter-attacked us. Fortunately we repelled both attacks and destroyed one tank, but with further losses including a very fine young Canadian officer, Lt John Richardson, who was killed in the afternoon. The remainder of the day was relatively quiet although the ever present mortars at Colombelles harassed us.[34]

In the rest of the I Corps sector the British 59th Division committed seven infantry and two tank battalions and the Canadians nine infantry and two tank battalions during the 8th; but despite further air attacks between 0545 and 0945 hours by 183 medium bombers of the US Ninth Air Force against strongpoints, gun areas and suspected Headquarters, the Panzer-Grenadiers of Kurt Meyer's Hitlerjugend Division men fought on with their usual tenacity and there was no breakthrough. Allied hopes of reaching the Orne bridges in Caen with light reconnaissance elements[35] were dashed when they came under fire and ran into mines in St Germain-la-Blanche-Herbe. Despite this failure to breach the German lines the situation as seen by Kurt Meyer was extremely serious. When he returned to his Headquarters in the early evening he reported to his commander, Sepp Dietrich, by telephone that his men had been forced to give up la Bijude and that the British had reached St Contest, cutting off his SS Panzer-Grenadiers in Galmanche and Buron. A counter-attack at 1730 hours by two Panther platoons had failed to relieve the crisis and seven tanks had been lost in the process. Authie, Franqueville and Carpiquet airfield (Map 3) had all fallen to the Canadians and since the 16th Luftwaffe Field Division (in front of the Iron Division) had collapsed, his right flank was dangerously exposed. Meyer knew that his tired and depleted Division was being overwhelmed and he begged for permission to withdraw what was left of his command. Dietrich refused, saying a Führer Order demanded that Caen be held at all costs. Meyer was furious, but his Chief of Staff pleaded with his opposite number at I SS Panzer Corps and finally Fritz Kraemer said the magic words: 'If you are thrown back to the southern banks of the Orne while fighting a superior enemy, it could never be considered to be a withdrawal contrary to orders.'[36] This was enough for Meyer and he gave the necessary instructions. His Division had suffered 423 killed, wounded and missing.[37] This figure does not include those of one of his battalions or those of an attached SS Panzer-Grenadier Battalion of the 1st SS Panzer Division Leibstandarte at Franqueville. A conservative estimate would add a further 200 to this total. A Hitlerjugend strength return dated 9 July shows only eighteen Panthers and ten Mk IVs operational, indicating a probable loss, for one reason or another, of ten Panthers and twenty-two Mk IVs on 8 July.

At 1915 hours Rommel approved the withdrawal of all heavy weapons from the Caen bridgehead and a regrouping south of the Orne.[38] The operation was carried out with typical German efficiency and a new defence line established along the southern bank of the river. Meyer wrote later that if the Allies had continued their attacks during the night his Division would almost certainly have been destroyed.

And so did the final air attack on Caen achieve anything of military value, other than to lift the morale of the Allied soldiers as they watched wave after wave of aircraft streaming over them the evening before the attack? Professor Solly Zuckerman, scientific adviser to Air Chief Marshal

Sir Arthur Tedder, Eisenhower's Deputy, and a supposed expert on Allied bombing policy, visited the target area immediately afterwards and reported that there were almost no signs of German equipment or dead. Later remarks by Montgomery's chief operations officer, Major General David Belchem[39], that the area was known to contain enemy defensive and headquarters locations and that the bombing caused extensive damage to those headquarters and eliminated many enemy gun emplacements, are quite simply not true. As a 3rd Infantry Division report stated later: 'No enemy dead and no destroyed equipment had been found during the advance into the town and no indication of road blocks being erected or strongpoints being built had been seen'.[40] Tedder refused to give Zuckerman's report a wide circulation on the grounds that, 'He had never read a more demoralising document'.[41]

Mission Accomplished

On 9 July the British 59th Infantry Division was ordered to deal with the numerous pockets of German resistance still holding out north of Caen in places like Galmanche whilst Bolo Whistler's men and the Canadians cleared the city itself. The Ulster Rifles sent platoon-sized patrols into the eastern and north-west outskirts early in the day but both platoon commanders and a total of seven men were wounded by sniper fire. Nevertheless, at 1030 hours, the Ulster Rifles and KOSB moved into the city using as their axes the Avenue Clemenceau and the rue Basse and the leading elements reached the centre of Caen around 1300 hours. Bulldozers followed them in an attempt to clear routes through the rubble for accompanying tanks and anti-tank guns.[42] The War Diaries of both Battalions record how the soldiers were relieved by the great welcome they received from civilians coming out of their cellars:

We received a most moving and touching welcome from the civilians. Unbroken by the terrible sufferings they had endured under our bombing assault, apparently indifferent to the destruction of their homes, they rose to meet us in tumultuous welcome, pressing flowers and wine and fruit upon us as they emerged from the cellars in which they been sheltering. It was a deeply humbling, enlightening and unforgettable experience to meet these people.[43]

While the KOSB consolidated in the centre of Caen, the Ulster Rifles pushed on to reach the Orne river at about 1800 hours. There they made contact with the Canadians who had moved in from the west after clearing St Germain-la-Blanche-Herbe.[44] The troops were surprised to find a railway bridge across the river still intact[45] but with Hitlerjugend troops in position on the south bank there was no possibility of rushing it. The ruins of the St Jean district and the open area known as La Prairie soon became a dangerous no man's land.

Meanwhile the Lincolns, still north of the Orne canal at Hérouville, lost a further thirteen killed and thirteen wounded to shellfire on the 9th, bringing their total casualty figure during Operation CHARNWOOD to 170 – the highest of any Iron Division unit.

Montgomery's men had finally reached their D-Day objective. They were over a month late and, although the main part of Caen was in Allied hands, the Germans were in firm control of the south bank of the Orne. The bridgeheads demanded in the I Corps order had yet to be achieved. And the cost had been appalling – the Official British History says 'about 3,500' casualties.[46] Although this is probably an exaggeration it is a fact that the 3rd Canadian Division, which had been fighting Kurt Meyer's Hitlerjugend, lost 1,194 men (more than it lost on D-Day[47]), and the Iron Division in the region of 580. With regard to the latter, readers are already aware that the bulk of its casualties were suffered by the four Battalions of 185 Brigade and the Ulster Rifles of 9 Brigade as they attempted to advance into Caen late on 8 July, and that most of these casualties were due to shelling and mortaring rather than direct fire. It also has to be pointed out that, other than two Companies of the East Yorks putting in a subsidiary attack on Epron to help the 59th Division capture the village on 8 July, 8 Brigade was not directly involved in CHARNWOOD.

On 11 July the British handed over responsibility for Caen to the Canadians and pulled back to a rest area near Luc-sur-Mer. Only the artillery remained in place to support other units. Lieutenant Colonel George Renny's KOSB left the city with a typical show of defiance by marching out with bagpipes playing. It is this author's estimate that the Iron Division lost nearly 4,000 men in achieving its D-Day mission.[48]

Caen – 12 June to 16 August

By the morning of 12 June only about 20,000 civilians remained in Caen north of the Orne. As described earlier the majority had fled or been evacuated to the outlying parts of the city or to places as far away as Evrecy (Map 1). The following day the Germans ordered a further evacuation and on the 14th another 12,000 people are said to have left the quarries and dock area and the village of Colombelles.

French sources say that various parts of their city were shelled by the Allies, including the furnaces at Mondeville, on 16, 17, 18, 22, 23, 24 and 25 June and that another fourteen air raids took place in the period up to 7 July. On 28 June the Germans forcibly evacuated everyone from the right bank of the Orne and further evacuations from the main part of the city took place on 2 July.

Following the final devastating Allied air attack on 7 July and the liberation of the northern part of the city on the 9th, it was to be another ten days before the Canadians freed the rest of Caen (Operation ATLANTIC). By then the Germans had added to the appalling destruction by bombing the area north of the Orne on the 10th, the night of the 13th/14th, shelling it on the 15th, 16th and 17th, and then bombing it again on the 18th and 19th. But even then Caen was not to be left in peace; another three air attacks took place before the last raid on 16 August, by which time 9,000 dwellings had been totally destroyed, 5,000 seriously damaged and only 1,000 remained intact.[49]

The total number of civilian casualties in Caen during the period 6 June to 16 August was originally estimated at 10,000 but this figure was later reduced to an 'official' total of 6,000. No one knows how many people really died – only some 2,500 have known graves.

Having seen how the Iron Division finally achieved its D-Day mission, it is time now to return to the American sector and follow the Blue and Gray to St Lô.

NOTES

1. According to the 13/18 H War Diary the Regt came under the command of 6 Airborne Div on 13 Jun.
2. Feuchtinger, MS # B-441.
3. Delaforce, *Monty's Iron Sides*, p, 66.
4. 1/192 Pz-Gren Regt.
5. 1/125 Pz-Gren Regt.
6. 5/2/192 Pz-Gren Regt & 1/220 Pz-Pnr Bn.
7. Lummis, *Sword to the Seine*.
8. Ibid.
9. Ibid.
10. Nightingale, *The East Yorkshire Regiment in the War 1939/45*, pp. 188–9.
11. Calculated from Div, Bde & unit Casualty Returns & War Diaries & Regimental Histories. On the other hand the Dupuy Institute, using the A Branch Casualty Reports of 21 Army Gp, has calculated a total of 3,001 – 307 killed, 1,997 wounded & 697 missing. However, all these sources are known to contain errors and often contradict one another. It is most unlikely that precise figures will ever be known.
12. Zetterling, *Normandy 1944*, p. 373.
13. Details are given in *Steel Inferno*.
14. Ellis, *Victory in the West, Vol. I, The Battle of Normandy*, p. 310.
15. Zetterling, op. cit., p, 226.
16. Ibid.
17. Feuchtinger, MS # B-441.
18. 3/83 Werfer Bn.
19. Smith, *Adventures of an Ancient Warrior*, p, 102.
20. Ibid., p, 109.
21. Bomber Command War Diaries, *The Battle of Normandy: June to August 1944*, p. 539.

22. Professor Henry Contamine, *Souvenirs Civils sur la bataille de Caen*, January 1946, estimated between 300 and 400.
23. André Heintz, a citizen of Caen and a noted authority.
24. Stacey, *Official History of the Canadian Army in the Second World War, Vol. III, The Victory Campaign*, p. 158.
25. Meyer, Kurt, *Grenadiers*, p. 145.
26. Zetterling, op. cit., p. 227.
27. 9 Inf Bde War Diary for Jun 44.
28. The whole of this area is now a modern industrial and shopping complex and it is impossible to visualise it as it was in Jul 44.
29. Air Historical Branch Narrative 41/24, Vol. III, p. 23.
30. These figures are taken from the unit War Diaries but may not be 100% accurate.
31. Feuchtinger, MS # B-441.
32. Ibid.
33. 2 Lincolns War Diary for Jun 44.
34. *2nd Battalion of the Lincolnshire Regiment* web site, Sep 02.
35. The British Inns of Court and Royal Canadian Hussar Recce Regts.
36. Meyer, Hubert, *The History of the 12th SS Panzer Division Hitlerjugend*, p. 147.
37. Ibid., p. 150.
38. Panzer Group West War Diary.
39. Belchem, *Victory in Normandy*, p. 150
40. Cabinet Office Historical Section Narrative 44/248: *Liberation Campaign North-West Europe*, Book I, Chapter III, Appx C.
41. D'Este, *Decision in Normandy*, p. 317.
42. The majority of streets in the centre of Caen remained blocked until the autumn.
43. History of the 1st Bn KOSB.
44. 9 Cdn Inf Bde War Diary dated 9 Jul 44.
45. André Heintz, a member of the French Resistance in Caen, told the author in Oct 2002 that he saw German tanks still using this bridge shortly after first light the following morning without interference from the British or Canadians.
46. Ellis, op. cit., p. 316.
47. Stacey, op. cit., p. 163
48. The Dupuy Institute gives an exact figure of 3,919 for the period 6 Jun to 10 Jul 44.
49. Municipal Information Bulletin, *Caen Normandie 44*, p. 6.

CHAPTER XVIII

The Blue and Gray – 7 to 19 July

7 – 10 July

(Map 17)

We will first catch up with Major General Leland Hobbs' reinforced 30th Infantry Division which readers will recall was preparing to advance on the west side of the Vire as part of Bradley's attempt to create enough space for George Patton's Third Army. To this end the Division launched a preliminary attack early on 7 July with one Regiment thrusting south-west across the Vire towards St Fromond and another due south across the Vire–Taute canal (Map 14). The immediate objective was the area of St Jean-de-Daye and by 2330 hours this had been achieved and a bridgehead secured running roughly north-west along the ridge from St Fromand through St Jean-de-Daye. The units involved were then told to reorganise and continue the attack the next morning. The success gained in the first half of the day:

> gave the Army commander [Bradley] reason to believe there was a good chance for local breakthrough by an armored force. . . Accordingly the 3rd Armored Division was ordered to make a 'power drive' through the bridgehead and on to the high ground south-west of St Lô [in the area of St Gilles].[1]

By 2230 hours on the same day forty-five armoured vehicles an hour were rolling across the Vire, but when the attack was renewed the following morning the tanks of Brigadier General John Bohn's CCB advanced south-west across the front of two of the 30th Infantry's Regiments and the result was chaos. Even a cursory terrain analysis should have indicated to the American commanders the unsuitability of the ground in this area for an advance by armoured forces. It is bocage at its worst, broken by narrow valleys and numerous waterways. By last light on 8 July the bridgehead had been expanded less than 4km and the Shermans of the 3rd Armored were still 12km short of their objective.

Over the next two days the 30th Division, with CCB of the 3rd Armored Division under command, continued its slow, chaotic and costly advance in appalling weather. By last light on 10 July Brigadier General Bohn had been sacked and the combined force, after losing 1,093 men[2], was still several hundred metres short of Pont Hérbert and the dominating high ground just to the west at Haut-Vents[3]; it was also well over 8km short of

St Gilles – a point where it could be said to be threatening St Lô. Nevertheless, the drive by the 30th Infantry and CCB had, as we shall see later, caused consternation on the German side and attracted German forces that might otherwise have been used in the direct defence of St Lô.

The slow progress of the 30th Infantry and the time needed to bring the 35th into line on Gerhardt's right flank, caused Corlett to postpone the attack by the rest of his Corps for two days – first from the 9th to the 10th and then again until the 11th. General Charlie Gerhardt of the Blue and Gray was not disappointed. The arrival of Major General Paul Baade's 35th Division shortened his frontage from 8km to 4km, gave him a secure right flank and allowed him the luxury of a complete Regiment, the Dandy Fifth, in reserve.

The Enemy

(Map 1)

The Germans had expected the attack by the 30th Infantry across the Vire–Taute canal (Map 14) on 7 July, but at that time their attention was focused more on the situation farther west where, as they saw it, VII US Corps was posing a much greater threat. They resolved therefore to stand firm with their existing forces in the St Jean-de-Daye sector, move another Parachute Division[4] from Brittany to the west flank at Lessay and assemble the Panzer Lehr Division between Périers and St Lô for an armoured counter-attack.

By 8 July the advance by the 30th Infantry and CCB of the 3rd Armored Division had created a situation which the Germans considered 'unquestionably critical' and it was decided to assign the Panzer Lehr Division to the St Jean-de-Daye sector. The Army Group commander, Field Marshal Rommel, came forward to the German Seventh Army Headquarters to discuss its commitment. However, Allied air activity on 9 July continued to delay the arrival of the Division and the situation became so critical that a hasty counter-attack had to be launched that same afternoon against the 30th Division's right flank by the 2nd SS Pioneer Battalion of 2nd SS Panzer Division Das Reich. It was beaten off.

On 10 July Lieutenant General Fritz Bayerlein, the commander of the Panzer Lehr Division, received orders to annihilate the American bridge-head south of the Vire–Taute canal. His Division was an elite formation with an original strength on 1 June of 14,699 men and 237 tanks and assault guns.[5] However, it had already been in action against the British and by 30 June had suffered 2,972 casualties.[6] The available strength for the counter-attack due to take place on 11 July was a Panzer Battalion of thirty-one tanks, four Panzer-Grenadier Battalions and twenty assault guns, supported by three 105mm artillery Battalions.[7]

The Big Picture in the American Sector – 10 July

By 10 July the plan for the American breakout on the right flank of the Normandy front, Operation COBRA, had been born. Omar Bradley, First Army commander, described it thus:

> From a rubble heap that marked the ancient citadel of St Lô, a road ran straight as an arrow for 20 miles through the Normandy bocage to the small town of Périers and beyond to the west shore of the Cotentin neck. This St Lô–Périers road was . . . the line of departure for our breakout. . . A few miles outside St Lô I marked off a rectangular carpet on the Périers road, three and a half miles wide, one and half deep. Two principal roads ran south through that carpet together with several unimproved ones. . .After saturating the carpet with air . . . a motorized infantry and two armored divisions would lunge through that hole in the line. . . [and then] the armor would dash towards Avranches and turn the corner into Brittany.
>
> Since COBRA could not go until first we closed to the Périers road, I concentrated Collins' Corps in a narrow sector and pointed it toward the St Lô carpet. Corlett was to break into St Lô.[8]

11 July

(Map 18)

The First Army attack plan scheduled for 11 July was designed to bring the Americans to their line of departure for Operation COBRA and it gave the primary role to Major General Corlett's XIX Corps. The main effort was to be made by the Blue and Gray towards the ridges running north of, and parallel to the axis of the St Lô–Bayeux road and then against the ruined city of St Lô itself. On the 29th's right flank the 35th Infantry was to exert pressure between the Isigny–St Lô road and the Vire, with the right bank of the Vire north-west of St Lô as its final objective. This advance was also designed to cover the left flank of the 30th Infantry Division west of the river. The inter-Divisional boundary between the 35th and the Blue and Gray ran along a line drawn from just west of Villiers-Fossard to just west of Hill 122. On the eastern flank, the 2nd Infantry Division of V Corps was to finally secure Hill 192, thus protecting the 29th Division's left flank and denying the Germans this dominating observation point.

How did Uncle Charlie plan to execute his mission? He chose Colonel Charles Canham's 116th Stonewallers to lead the attack which was directed initially south along the Couvains–la Calvaire road, bypassing St André-de-l'Epine, and then west along the Martinville ridge towards St

176

Lô. Colonel Godwin Ordway's 115th Regiment, which was thinly spread on a 4km front north-east of Hill 122, was to make a diversionary attack down the Isigny–St Lô road with la Luzerne as its initial objective. Gerhardt hoped the attack by the Stonewallers from the east would so threaten the Germans on Hill 122[9] that they would withdraw rather than risk being cut off. The third Regiment of the Blue and Gray, Colonel Ollie Reed's Dandy Fifth, was to be held in reserve, ready to exploit success by either the 115th or, more likely as Gerhardt saw it, the 116th.

Canham chose Major Sidney Bingham's 2nd Battalion to lead the Stonewallers' attack and he in turn decided to advance on a two-Company (E and F) front. Each assault Platoon in these Companies was teamed up with a Platoon of Shermans from A Company of Stuart Fries' 747th Tank Battalion and, in accordance with Divisional doctrine, each infantry squad and supporting tank had a squad of engineers from Lieutenant Colonel Robert Ploger's 121st Engineer Battalion operating with it.

In terms of artillery Gerhardt was able to call on the firepower of 120 guns – his own four Battalions plus one extra 155mm Battalion attached, plus one 8-inch and four 155mm Artillery Battalions and a 4.2-inch Mortar Battalion placed in support from XIX Corps artillery.[10] The initial fireplan called for a preparatory barrage on known enemy positions from H–20 to H-Hour (0600 hours).

The 'enemy counter-attack involving the use of armor in mass', mentioned by Gerhardt in his order of 30 June, was launched, not against his Division, but against the 9th and 30th Divisions to the west of the Vire. Recall that the Panzer Lehr Division had received orders to eliminate the American salient south of the Taute–Vire canal (Map 14) and in the early hours of 11 July, the very day chosen for the XIX Corps offensive against St Lô, it launched its counter-attack. It failed. The details are unimportant but:

> Joint effort of air and ground force neutralized the Panzer Lehr breakthrough by 1600 . . . The net effect of the German counter-attack had thus been little more than to cause a day's loss in the 9th Division's schedule of advance. The effects on the 30th Division's front were even less; here, 11 July saw notable gains by the Division in one part of its zone, in addition to complete defensive success against Panzer Lehr's right wing column.[11]

The commander of Panzer Lehr, General Bayerlein, blamed the failure on the exhausted condition of his men even before the attack and the difficulty of operating tanks in the bocage.

In support of the Panzer Lehr counter-attack, the Germans launched two diversionary attacks east of the Vire during the early hours of 11 July. One by the 9th Parachute Regiment of Schimpf's 3rd Parachute Division

177

hit the Blue and Gray's 115th Regiment at 0130 hours and the other, by the 5th Parachute Regiment, was made in the Bérigny sector against part of the 2nd Infantry Division. Fortunately for Gerhardt and the Stonewallers, this latter attack did not disrupt the 2nd Division's assault on Hill 192.

Although the attack on the 115th Regiment was limited in size[12] it badly delayed Colonel Ordway's advance towards Hill 122 and la Luzerne. Major Glover Johns' 1st Battalion of the 115th bore the brunt of it.

> Two platoons were reported cut off and destroyed . . . some Germans penetrated to the mortar positions and drove back their personnel. Col Godwin Ordway . . . organised some of the retreating weapons [4.2-inch mortar crews] men as infantry to protect the rear areas. On his left, the 116th Infantry was alarmed by the possibility of a breakthrough in the gap between its units and the 115th and took steps to fill the hole. . . [Despite being] cut off and apparently surrounded, the remnants of A and B Companies held their positions.[13]

The 1st Battalion lost over 100 men but by 0700 hours the German paratroopers had pulled back. They had failed to break through the American lines; nevertheless they had severely disrupted the 1st Battalion's intended attack – instead of advancing at 0600 hours as ordered it would take another five and a half hours to reorganise Major Johns' Battalion for offensive action.[14]

Following the artillery barrage already mentioned, the attack by Major Sidney Bingham's 2nd Battalion of the Stonewallers and A Company of the 747th Tank Battalion went in right on time – at 0600 hours. The initial objectives were Hill 150, a kilometre south of St André-de-l'Epine, and then Hill 147 a couple of kilometres farther to the west.

> At the outset, progress was slow. This was due to the fact that the enemy was in a position to follow the movement of our troops from Hill 192 [the objective of the 2nd Infantry Division]. . . Our tanks experienced considerable difficulty crossing the high and ever-present hedgerows and the sunken roads.[15]

> The tank, infantry and engineer teams moved from hedgerow to hedgerow under extremely heavy artillery fire [and] . . . stiff enemy infantry rifle and machine-gun fire.[16]

Adding to their problems the Stonewallers ran into minefields and booby traps and flanking fire from St André-de-l'Epine and the Martinville ridge. After five hours and heavy artillery support Bingham's men and the Shermans had penetrated only six hedgerows – less than 500m. But then, suddenly, the resistance weakened and the 2nd Battalion was able to advance without difficulty to the road junction near la Calvaire leading to Martinville and then wheel right towards Hills 150 and 147. This sudden collapse of the German resistance was almost certainly due to the success of the 2nd Infantry Division's attack towards Hill 192.

As soon as Canham learned of Bingham's breakthrough to the south, he ordered Lieutenant Colonel Meeks' 3rd Battalion, with some of A Company's Shermans, to advance towards la Boulaye on the ridge running along the St Lô–Bérigny road about a kilometre south-east of Hill 147. This move, which began at 1300 hours, had two aims: first, it would protect Bingham's left flank and, second, it would result in two infantry Battalions and a tank Company being ideally positioned for an advance westwards towards St Lô along the two parallel ridges. And waiting in reserve was Canham's 1st Battalion, ready to advance between the other two Battalion groups as soon as the opportunity presented itself. There was, however, a major drawback to Gerhardt's plan of attacking along the Martinville and St Lô–Bérigny road ridges and outflanking Hill 122 from the east – his men would be moving through open fields and orchards towards a well entrenched enemy in positions running more or less south-east to north-west across their front, and at the same time they would be under mortar and long-range machine-gun fire from their left flank. Readers will recall that General Schimpf had said that 'there were other hills south of the St Lô road which were better [than Hill 192] points of observation' (Chapter XV, Note 1). These 'other hills' on the south side of the St Lô–Bérigny road became known to the Americans as the '101 Ridge'. And there was yet another drawback to Gerhardt's plan; just to the west of the tiny hamlet of Martinville the narrow road descends into another maze of broken, low ground, with extremely limited visibility.

Although Bingham's Battalion group had broken into and partly through the German main line of resistance, Schimpf's paratroopers were far from beaten. Despite Gerhardt's orders, issued at 1920 hours, for the Stonewallers to 'push on, if possible take St Lô', by last light the 2nd Battalion was facing strong resistance and was still 200m short of Hill 147. Similarly, the 3rd Battalion was still more than 1,500m short of la Boulaye, but it was at least successfully dug in near Hill 150 overlooking the St Lô–Bérigny road. During the evening the 2nd Battalion of the Dandy Fifth, which had been following the Stonewallers' advance, took up a defensive position near St André-de-l'Epine and was temporarily placed under Canham's command. Gerhardt was concerned that a German counter-attack might drive a wedge between his men and those of the 2nd Division who had just won the battle of Hill 192: 'By close of 11 July . . . every enemy position on the hill had been reduced and the St Georges-d'Elle defenses had been smashed.'[17] The cost, however, had been heavy. Major General Walter Roberts' 2nd Infantry Division suffered sixty-nine killed, 328 wounded and eight missing.

The After Action Report of Schimpf's 3rd Parachute Division[18] describes the intensity of the fighting by the 5th Parachute Regiment in defence of Hill 192 and the 9th Parachute Regiment's resistance to Canham's Stonewallers on 11 July:

> Parachute Regiments 5 and 9, and especially the 2nd Battalion of Regiment 9 suffered heavy losses owing to the enemy's enormous superiority of materiel. The Division was compelled to commit, first the 12th Assault Gun Brigade and then the Divisional Reconnaissance Company in order to halt the breakthrough. When these last reserves were found insufficient, the 3rd Battalion of the 8th Parachute Regiment was thrown into battle. However, all these combined forces were only able to stem the advance near the main road [St Lô–Bérigny]. It was impossible to reach the old MLR [Main Line of Resistance]. After enemy penetrations had widened the gap in the old CP area of the 9th Parachute Regiment, the Division was compelled to commit the 3rd Parachute Pioneer Battalion as a last reserve. By dark we had succeeded with all these forces in forming and holding a new MLR.

This new MLR faced east and north-east, running across the Bérigny road near la Boulaye and the Martinville ridge to link up with the defenders of Hill 122.

What of the attack by the 115th Regiment? The orders called for the 1st Battalion to secure the low-lying hamlet of Belle-Fontaine and the very broken ground and close country between there and St André-de-l'Epine. This was considered an essential preliminary to the 3rd Battalion's attack through la Forge towards la Luzerne. Colonel Ordway was under intense pressure from Gerhardt all morning to get his attack going, but following the earlier German counter-attack this could not be done until Major Glover Johns had reorganised his Battalion. The advance finally began at 1130 hours. Major Maurice Clift's 2nd Battalion remained in position holding the right flank between KG Böhm at Villiers-Fossard and the main St Lô–Isigny road.

Unlike Canham's Stonewallers who had the advantage of tank and engineer support and a very narrow attack frontage, Ordway had neither tanks nor engineers and a frontage three times as big. One has to question Gerhardt's judgement in this respect since the St Lô–Isigny road offered the only reasonable axis for armour in his whole Divisional sector.

Needless to say things did not go well for the 115th. The advance was carried out under direct observation from Hill 122 and Johns' already depleted Battalion gained only a few hedgerows at a cost of sixty men. 'By 2200 hours an advance of 500 yards was made.'[19] Although Ordway brought his 3rd Battalion into the attack in the middle of the afternoon and, at Gerhardt's insistence, Clift's 2nd Battalion was also ordered to advance west of the St Lô–Isigny road, neither unit could prevail. The advance ground to a complete halt. In the case of the 1st Battalion, Glover Johns wrote later:

> [I] did not ask for permission to halt the advance. . . [I] had no idea where the other units of the Regiment were. . . [the men] had been fighting alone with no support on the flanks for so long that they felt as if the war was a private affair between only themselves and the paratroopers they faced. . . The Battalion had about had all it could handle, merely looking after itself.[20]

Although Gerhardt had not achieved the breakthrough he had hoped for and his Division had suffered another 455 casualties[21], the day had gone reasonably well for the Americans as a whole, and as it ended Uncle Charlie ordered the Dandy Fifth to be prepared to pass through the Stonewallers the following morning and drive hard for St Lô.

12 July

First light on 12 July found Canham's 2nd and 3rd Battalions ready to advance west along the Martinville and St Lô–Bérigny road ridges respectively and his 1st Battalion, which had moved up during the night, preparing to advance in the valley between them. Once the ridges were secured this covered approach was seen as offering the best chance of success. The orders were for the 1st Battalion to push ahead towards the high ground between la Boulaye and la Madeleine, whilst the 2nd and 3rd Battalions secured Hill 147 and la Boulaye respectively. Meanwhile Colonel Ollie Reed's 175th Regiment was to advance at 1130 hours, pass through the 1st Battalion of the 116th and take the high ground south of the St Lô–Bérigny road on the outskirts of St Lô.

Things did not go well for the Blue and Gray on 12 July. Communications were bad and units became intermingled. The 2nd Battalion of the Stonewallers under Sidney Bingham achieved its mission by 1300 hours but then ran into heavy resistance and ended the day about half a kilometre west of Hill 147. A Company of the 747th Tank Battalion which had been operating with it since the beginning of the attack 'was relieved on the 12th and returned to the Battalion bivouac area [just south of Couvains]'.[22] Major Thomas Dallas's 1st Battalion, moving along the valley between the two ridges, made little progress. It suffered a German counter-attack supported by three tanks and by last light it was still short of a line drawn between Hill 147 and la Boulaye. Similarly Meeks' 3rd Battalion fought hard but unsuccessfully to get to la Boulaye and onto the 101 Ridge just to the south of the St Lô–Bérigny road.

The Dandy Fifth, with B Company of the 747th Tank Battalion attached but less its 1st Battalion in Divisional reserve, had even less success. Both its Battalions got mixed up with those of the 116th and never even reached their jumping off positions. The 3rd Battalion was unable to pass through the Stonewallers' 3rd Battalion and it was late in the day when it finally reached a position to the left rear of the latter's 1st Battalion. The 2nd Battalion managed to reach Hill 147 behind its counterpart in the 116th, but a plan for it then to attack towards la Boulaye never got off the ground. Heavy German artillery and mortar fire only added to the general confusion.

Colonel Ordway's 115th Regiment did slightly better. Major Johns' 1st Battalion finally took Belle-Fontaine at 1600 hours[23], by which time the 3rd had secured la Luzerne. Only Major Maurice Clift's 2nd Battalion on the west side of the St Lô–Isigny road failed to gain ground. It advanced through thick apple orchards, across a stream and through a small hamlet known as Bourg-d'Enfer, but on reaching a point less than a kilometre from the top of Hill 122, it came under intense machine-gun and mortar fire. Shortly afterwards an enemy counter-attack caused one Company to panic and pull back and soon the whole Battalion was in full retreat. The original line of departure was eventually restored but Gerhardt felt Clift had failed as a commanding officer and the following morning he replaced him with Major Asbury Jackson, the S-2 of the 116th. He was the Battalion's third commanding officer since D-Day. Uncle Charlie was also becoming very worried about the Regimental commander, Colonel Godwin Ordway, who he suspected was suffering from battle fatigue.

The 29th Division suffered another 489 casualties on 12 July.[24]

13 – 14 July

Gerhardt's main attack on 13 July was to be carried out by the Dandy Fifth with a Company of Shermans under command and with air support. The St Lô–Bérigny road was to be the main axis and the objectives remained the same as for the previous day. Ordway's luckless 115th was to continue pushing towards Hill 122 whilst the 116th Regiment was to dig in and hold its current positions. During the day the Stonewallers learned that Colonel Charles Canham, who had led them onto and from OMAHA beach, had not surprisingly been promoted to the rank of Brigadier General and was to become the assistant commander of the 8th Division. Colonel Philip Dwyer was to assume command. The 3rd Battalion of the Regiment also found it had a new commanding officer – Major Thomas Howie, the Regimental S-3. He replaced Lieutenant Colonel Lawrence Meeks who was moved back to Divisional Headquarters.

Although the After Action Report of Lieutenant Colonel Fries' 747th Tank Battalion claims that its B Company 'was in contact with the enemy, sustaining slight losses in personnel and vehicles' on 13 July, other accounts say that the 175th Regiment 'started its attack without the expected tank support (the tanks had fueling difficulties)'[25] and 'lack of proper coordination prevented the tanks from refueling and immobilized them for the duration of the attack'.[26] Yet another report says the tanks had not even been resupplied with ammunition.[27] And to compound problems bad weather prevented the planned air strike.

Ollie Reed attacked at 0800 hours with his three Battalions in column but in the knowledge that his 1st Battalion, as Divisional reserve, could only be committed with Gerhardt's permission. Things went wrong right from the start. The Germans had registered their artillery on the main St Lô–Bérigny road over which they had full observation from the 101 Ridge. Any movement off the road found the men facing a series of hedgerows. It took the whole morning for Lieutenant Colonel Edward Gill's 3rd Battalion to cover just half a kilometre and come into line with the 1st Battalion of the 116th on the outskirts of la Boulaye. Lieutenant Colonel Millard Bowen's 2nd Battalion, after also coming under heavy fire, ended the day facing south towards the 101 Ridge behind Gill's Battalion. According to the Deputy Divisional commander, Dutch Cota, coordination between the two Battalions failed because 'All of the 175th's communications just got shot to hell'.[28] Counter-battery fire by American artillery, including the use of white phosphorus smoke rounds, did nothing to lessen the enemy bombardment and a request by Reed to use the Divisional reserve (his own 1st Battalion) against the Germans on the 101 Ridge was refused. Although the 2nd Battalion of the 116th was eventually committed in a diversionary attack along the Martinville ridge, it too failed to gain ground.

On the 115th Regiment's front on the Division's right flank, all that could be achieved was to bring the 1st Battalion forward into line on the northern flank of the 3rd Battalion. The latter spent most of the day fighting for a five-acre apple orchard just to the south of la Luzerne. When darkness fell the 2nd Battalion, under its new commanding officer, was still short of Bourg-d'Enfer. The Regiment suffered another 105 casualties during the day.

The After Action Report of Schimpf's 3rd Parachute Division sums up the fighting on 13 July as follows: 'Notwithstanding their superior materiel and heavy weapons the Americans did not gain any ground. In the evening the 9th Parachute Regiment was relieved by the 8th.'

Perhaps the most surprising aspect of the American actions at this time was their persistence in launching daylight attacks in full view of a dug-in enemy. The Dandy Fifth suffered another 152 casualties on 13 July[29] and not surprisingly Uncle Charlie was furious with Stuart Fries for the failure of his tanks to take part in the attack. He also demanded a report in writing from Edward Gill of the 3rd Battalion to explain why he had 'abandoned his mission'. This bullying attitude was becoming too much for many of his officers and men. It is said that some of the veterans called him a 'corps commander with a division in the field, a division in hospital and a division in the cemetery'.[30]

By now both Gerhardt's Corps commander, Corlett, and even Uncle Charlie himself realised that the Blue and Gray needed a rest. It was also clear that despite Gerhardt's original hope, the Germans had no intention of withdrawing from Hill 122 to avoid being outflanked, and equally clear that the exhausted 29th Division could not take both Hill 122 and St Lô at the same time. Corlett decided therefore to rest Gerhardt's men on the 14th and bring in a Regiment of the flanking 35th Division to take on Hill 122. This suited Gerhardt well because by slipping the inter-Divisional boundary a kilometre to the south-east his attack frontage was again shortened.

During the night of 13/14 July the Dandy Fifth took over full responsibility for the St Lô–Bérigny road positions, allowing the 116th Regiment to be pulled back into reserve. At the same time the 134th Regiment of the 35th Division relieved the 1st and 2nd Battalions of Ordway's 115th Regiment on the right flank, leaving just the 3rd Battalion in position near the St Lô–Isigny road south-west of la Luzerne. Ordway's men moved to an assembly area near la Fossardière and Sidney Bingham's 2nd Battalion of the 116th to an assembly area near St André-de-l'Epine. There it received 125 replacements but this still left it 40% below its authorised strength.[31]

The German 3rd Parachute Division had now suffered a staggering 4,064 casualties since D-Day[32] and it too badly needed a rest. Fortunately for the survivors there was little action on 14 July because the weather was so bad that according to the Germans, 'it was possible to relieve units during daylight'. The Germans continued to improve their defensive positions and the Americans prepared for Corlett's 'Sunday punch' – a coordinated Corps attack by his three Divisions ordered for the following day. The Blue and Gray remained responsible for the main attack on St Lô. The centre of the city was less than 4km away but for its battle-weary GIs it seemed as far away as ever. As one GI put it later St Lô 'was already a legend, an unattainable objective. I'll never hear that name again without seeing dead men in ditches and smelling the decay-filled Norman air'.[33]

The only thing that kept them going was Uncle Charlie's promise that they were be properly rested after its capture.

15 July

Author's Note

It is impossible to be certain of the details of the 29th Division's attack on 15 July. The US Official History[34] is imprecise, the 116th Regimental After

Action Report does not even have the correct date for the attack and the account in the US War Department's American Forces in Action Series[35] is at variance with the Regimental After Action Report and other accounts. What follows is the author's best attempt to describe what happened and at least it makes sense from a military point of view.

By 15 July the difficulties of trying to advance along the St Lô–Bérigny road ridge had become all too obvious and Gerhardt decided that the main effort in the renewed attack was to be made on a 500m front in the centre – along the Martinville ridge. He chose the Stonewallers under their new commander, Colonel Philip Dwyer, for this task, supported by A and B Companies of the 747th Tank Battalion. The 116th, as we have just heard, had been pulled out of the line after dark on the 13th and had spent the 14th reorganising, resting and receiving reinforcements. Its initial objective was the tiny hamlet of Martinville, but it was hoped that Dwyer's men would then advance south-west through la Madeleine[36] to the outskirts of St Lô itself. The Dandy Fifth was to assist in the attack by providing 'supporting fire' from its current positions on the St Lô–Bérigny road ridge – although exactly how it was to do this is unclear. Ordway's 115th Regiment, now on a much narrower front and with C Company of the 747th Tank Battalion in support, was to advance at the same time, south-west from la Luzerne, thus protecting the Stonewallers' right flank. The attack was to be supported by heavy artillery bombardments and air strikes by the IX Tactical Air Command. On the Blue and Gray's right flank the untried 134th Regiment of the 35th Infantry Division was to assault Hill 122.

The attack by Ordway's 115th Regiment from the la Luzerne sector was launched at 0600 hours in column of Battalions with Glover Johns' 1st Battalion leading. According to the US Official History[37], which quotes the Divisional G-3 Journal of 15 July:

> The 115th lost several hundred yards as the result of confusion. Intermingling battalions and misplaced tanks disrupted regimental control. Lack of proper coordination with the 35th Division caused misunderstanding and an exchange of fire among US troops. The firm action of an artillery liaison officer, who took command of an infantry company and restored order and discipline, prevented a panicky withdrawal. A tank platoon nearby might have helped the regiment to regain the lost ground, but the tank commander could not locate a key infantry officer. While the tankers waited for instructions, the tanks remained idle.

On the 29th Division's right flank, the 1st Battalion of 134th Regiment of the 35th Division advanced 2km and by 2300 hours had managed to reach the northern slopes of Hill 122.

What of the main effort by Gerhardt's Division on this day? At 0515 hours the 1st and 2nd Battalions of the 116th advanced astride the Martinville ridge. Resistance in front of the 1st Battalion was fierce and by the afternoon less than 500m had been gained. A supporting attack by the 3rd Battalion, launched south-west along the St Lô–Bérigny road ridge and designed to take the pressure off Major Thomas Dallas's 1st Battalion, ran into heavy enfilade fire from the 101 ridge and made little progress. The picture on the Regiment's right flank was much the same with Major Sidney Bingham's 2nd Battalion group making little progress and losing seven Sherman tanks to German anti-tank and artillery fire, the latter also severely disrupting communications to the forward Companies.

In the early evening Gerhardt ordered Dwyer to renew the attack. 'Divisional artillery had thirteen battalions hitting eleven targets. Air strikes by twelve P-47s carrying 500-pound bombs had hit enemy 88mm gun positions, Hill 101 and the high ground around la Madeleine.'[38] The 1st and 2nd Battalions advanced again at 1930 hours and finally began to gain ground, but as darkness approached Uncle Charlie began to worry that they would become isolated and gave orders for them to halt and dig in. The 1st Battalion did so after an advance of some 400m, but Major Bingham was out of contact with two of his forward Companies and was unable to pass on the order. When he eventually caught up with E and F Companies and part of his heavy weapons Company, a total of only about 200 men, he found they had in fact broken through the German defences and were virtually on their objective – astride the St Lô–Bérigny road just east of la Madeleine and less than 3km from the centre of St Lô. They had bypassed Martinville and were now isolated a kilometre ahead of the rest of the Battalion and about the same distance west of the nearest unit of the Dandy Fifth at la Boulaye. Bingham set up a perimeter defence and informed his Regimental Headquarters of his situation by using his accompanying 111th Artillery liaison officer's radio. The group had only four light mortars, four light MGs and seven HMGs. It was also burdened with thirty-five wounded and had virtually no medical supplies. The remainder of the unit, with G Company in Martinville, remained on the ridge and was later attached to the 1st Battalion. The Company of Shermans that had been operating with Bingham's Battalion had not accompanied the Stonewallers in their breakthrough and together with another Company operating with Dallas's 1st Battalion, 'was detached at 2200 hours and returned to the Battalion bivouac area'.[39]

In this situation one would have expected Dwyer to reinforce the 2nd Battalion's success with everything available to him; unfortunately, his proposal to do just this and send Dallas's 1st Battalion forward during the night was rejected by Gerhardt. Uncharacteristically, Uncle Charlie decided to wait for daylight and then try to break through to Bingham with Ordway's 115th Regiment. In the meantime the 116th Regiment was to send out a strong patrol to re-supply Bingham and the Division's artillery spotter planes were to drop blood plasma for the wounded.

The German account of events on 15 July is interesting in that it paints a slightly different and more intense picture of what happened:

> The Americans attacked again in the direction of St Lô after [a] very heavy artillery bombardment. By evening the 3rd Parachute Pioneer Battalion had beaten off eleven attacks under repeated artillery fire. The twelfth enemy attack succeeded in gaining ground after inflicting casualties on the Pioneer Battalion. The enemy penetrated the main line of resistance and advanced up to Martinville. Although we counter-attacked we were unable to break through owing to nightfall and the weakness of our reserves. A counter-attack during the night by the 8th Parachute Regiment was also without success.[40]

The Blue and Gray lost another 363 men, including fifty-four killed, on this day.[41]

16 July

According to the US Official History: 'There was little improvement on 16 July. While the 35th Division fought to retain Hill 122, the 29th Division seemed virtually paralysed.'[42] This statement does little justice to Gerhardt or his Division. Despite the fact that the Corps commander, Major General Corlett, had ordered that the day was to be spent consolidating the gains made on the 15th and preparing for a coordinated attack by the 29th and 35th Divisions on the 17th, the Division was not inactive. In the case of the Stonewallers and Dandy Fifth, consolidation was out of the question anyway since they were to spend most of the day repelling German counter-attacks.

Colonel Godwin Ordway was uneasy at the idea of attacking again on the 16th. If he had gained little more than a kilometre in the previous five days, what chance had he of reaching Bingham 2km away to the south-west at la Madeleine? His Regiment had already suffered grievously; indeed, according to the Operations Journal of the 29th Division, one of his Battalions on 16 July had no more than a platoon of riflemen left in each of its rifle Companies. Nevertheless, at 0600 hours, in accordance with Uncle Charlie's orders, the 2nd Battalion of the 115th advanced against an enemy entrenched astride the St Lô–Isigny road. It soon ran into heavy resistance and although the 1st Battalion joined in the attack on the right flank, 'mortars, with some aid from mobile 88s, and machine-gun fire brought the attack to a stop'.[43] Although the assault was renewed at midday, little headway was made and at 1430 hours both units dug in – they had advanced less than 300m and lost sixty-six men.

Meanwhile, on the Martinville ridge the Americans were very much on the defensive. According to the After Action Report of the German 3rd Parachute Division:

With daybreak on 16 July we attacked again and slowly cleaned the enemy out of Martinville. [In fact the Americans had withdrawn from the hamlet.] We were unable, however, to reach the old MLR. . . More attempts during the afternoon to clean the enemy out of his break-through [area] were of no success.

Surprisingly, the Germans did not attack the Bingham force near la Madeleine but instead concentrated their efforts on the 1st Battalion, 500m east of Martinville, and the gap between it and the Dandy Fifth a kilometre away to the south-east at la Boulaye. Dallas's Battalion took the brunt of the attacks receiving heavy fire from its left flank and left rear. The Americans say that three tanks (in fact they were StuGs) and about 100 paratroopers, some armed with flamethrowers, made the first assault. It was held, but a second attack mounted from Martinville with a single StuG very nearly rolled up the Battalion from the north and was held only with the greatest difficulty. The right-hand Company received thirty-seven casualties.

Meanwhile near la Madeleine, the Bingham group received considerable mortar and artillery fire during the day but as already mentioned it was not attacked.

17 July

As well as ordering Dwyer to reinforce the beleaguered Bingham group at la Madeleine and then to push on into St Lô, Gerhardt told Ordway to strike south-west yet again on the 17th and Reed's Dandy Fifth to push west along the St Lô–Bérigny road past Hill 108. It was the same medicine again and he knew full well that the infantry Battalions of his Division were reaching a point of total exhaustion. He needed a new tactic and he therefore told his assistant Divisional commander, Brigadier General Norman 'Dutch' Cota, to form an armoured task force of tanks, armoured cars, TDs and engineers for use against the city. TF C (Cota) was to be assembled north of St André-de-l'Epine and was to be prepared to strike either through the 115th Regiment down the Isigny–St Lô road or along the road from la Madeleine to St Lô.

During the night of 16/17 July, 250 reinforcements joined the 116th Regiment. The soldiers were assigned to the 1st Battalion and the officers divided between the 1st and 3rd. Even so, the 3rd Battalion still numbered only 420 men – half its authorised strength. Its new commanding officer, Major Thomas Howie, was told that while Dallas's 1st Battalion held firm just to the east of Martinville, he was to break through to la Madeleine and that he and Bingham were then to push on into St Lô. The advance was to begin before dawn and he was to infiltrate rather than fight his way forward.

Howie followed his orders to the letter and by 0600 hours, having taken advantage of a misty morning, he had penetrated the German MLR and joined up with Bingham just to the east of the hamlet. He found that despite the American presence the enemy 'was even attempting to use the north–south road through la Madeleine to move supplies'.[44] The state of the Bingham group soon convinced Howie, however, that it was incapable of offensive action and that he would have to advance alone. He reported this to Dwyer who at 0730 hours confirmed that the depleted 2nd Battalion was to stay in its current defensive position and the 3rd Battalion was to push on into St Lô on its own. Shortly afterwards Howie was killed by enemy mortar fire. Captain William Puntenney, the Battalion Executive officer, took command and gave orders for the advance to continue. But to no avail. The Germans were now fully aware of the large American presence in the area and covered it with artillery and mortar fire, preventing any further movement towards St Lô. The 3rd Battalion went firm next to the depleted 2nd, east of the hamlet and astride the St Lô–Bérigny road.

The 1st Battalion was now charged with getting ammunition and medical aid to the two forward units of the 116th. Dallas's first action was to set up a forward outpost with a small task force of about sixty men, a TD and an anti-tank gun, just to the east of Martinville. Later in the day he tried to send half-tracks loaded with supplies and protected by anti-aircraft half-tracks down the Martinville road but the steep and twisting lanes leading to la Madeleine were found to be impassable due to abandoned enemy vehicles, dead horses and the general litter of a battlefield. Another way of getting through would have to be found.

In the meantime, enemy artillery and mortar fire had continued to fall on the area held by the 2nd and 3rd Battalions. Then, at 1800 hours, the Germans launched a full-scale counter-attack. It was beaten off but not before some twenty Germans had penetrated the American lines. Later in the evening the sound of tank or StuG engines was heard and it became clear that another, much stronger, attack was being prepared. Protective artillery fire was called for and at 2105 hours an air strike by the 506th Fighter Bomber Squadron broke up the German force. It was said that some of the Germans even ran into the American lines to escape the bombs.

Colonel Dwyer eventually decided that the only way to get supplies through to the la Madeleine group was to send out carrying parties on their feet under the cover of darkness. The After Action Report of the 116th Regiment says:

Two volunteer patrols of twenty men and one officer apiece from the Cannon and Anti-Tank Companies moved out to take medical supplies, rations and water . . . Lieutenant Williams was killed leading his patrol. All the others got through.

Both patrols then stayed with the forward battalions. Williams had unfortunately been shot by a member of a 2nd Battalion outpost who had failed to recognise his relief party.

And what of the attacks by the 115th and 175th Regiments on the 17th? The 1st and 2nd Battalions of the Dandy Fifth attacked towards la Madeleine at 1430 hours. Why this attack was delayed so long and not coordinated with Major Howie's is unclear. The CO of the 1st Battalion, Lieutenant Colonel William Terry, was killed soon after the attack started (his predecessor, Lieutenant Colonel Whiteford, had been wounded on 18 June) and within a short time the three rifle Companies of Bowen's 2nd Battalion mustered no more than four officers and 200 men – F Company had no officers left at all. Colonel Ollie Reed obtained permission to use his 3rd Battalion, which was being held in Divisional reserve, to reinforce the assault but this did not affect the outcome. The Regiment was finally ordered to go firm for the night and try again the next day.

Over on the right flank it was the turn of the 115th Regiment. With the 35th Division finally in control of Hill 122, Gerhardt hoped the attack by Ordway's Regiment might still succeed where those of the other Regiments had failed. At 1500 hours the 1st and 3rd Battalions advanced towards la Planche, one kilometre north of la Madeleine, but yet again they failed.[45] Their attacks did, however, help the 2nd Battalion to make a wide turning manoeuvre that brought it to a position about 500m north of Martinville by 1600 hours. Gerhardt and Ordway hoped this move into the 116th Regiment's sector would so threaten the Germans holding up its sister Battalions that they would pull out. Unfortunately, whilst the Battalion waited for the friendly air strike to go in near la Madeleine, it was hit by an enemy mortar concentration and suffered numerous casualties, particularly amongst the Heavy Weapons Company. This ended its advance. Gerhardt was furious. He had apparently told Ordway to 'expend the whole Battalion if necessary but it's got to get there'. For some reason the Battalion radio link to Ordway's Headquarters was not working and it had run out of telephone cable during its long move. When the Regimental commander finally caught up with the Battalion at midnight he found it digging in. He immediately ordered the advance to continue and after meeting almost no resistance it reached la Planche at 0230 hours. But still Gerhardt was dissatisfied and the following morning he sacked Ordway and appointed Colonel Alfred Ednie – he was to be the Regiment's third commander in just six weeks! The 115th was exhausted and severely weakened, but it was still well poised for an advance into St Lô.

One has to question why the attacks by Gerhardt's three Regiments were apparently so uncoordinated on 17 July – a day that cost the Division another 324 casualties.[46] The Stonewallers went in before dawn, the Dandy Fifth's attack was delayed until the early afternoon and the 115th did not advance until 1500 hours. One possible explanation is that there was a temporary shortage of artillery ammunition which meant that three simultaneous attacks could not be properly supported; another possibility is that Gerhardt was convinced that the Stonewallers' early morning attack would succeed. One also has to question why some fifty Shermans and eighteen light tanks of the 747th Tank Battalion remained idle in their bivouac area throughout the entire day.

The Enemy

By the morning of 17 July, it was obvious to SS General Paul Hausser, the commander of the German Seventh Army, that his troops west of the Vire were no longer capable of holding back the American advance on that front and that those north of St Lô were in danger of encirclement. He therefore asked for permission to pull back to the heights south and west of St Lô as a matter of urgency. That afternoon his superior at Army Group 'B', Field Marshal Erwin Rommel, was seriously injured when his car was attacked by an RAF fighter and CinC West, Günther von Kluge, was forced to take command of Army Group 'B' as well. His immediate reaction was to refuse Hausser's request, but at 2200 hours, when he found he could offer no extra troops to hold the St Lô–Coutances front (Map 1), he reluctantly agreed.[47] Outposts were, however, to be left north of St Lô to delay the US advance.

Mission Accomplished

18 – 19 July

Charlie Gerhardt had no idea that during the night of 17/18 July the Germans had pulled back leaving only outposts in and to the north of St Lô, and he was under firm orders from his Corps commander to: 'Take St Lô and secure it.'[48] He had by now given up hope of advancing into the city from the east and so, having told the Stonewallers and Dandy Fifth to go firm in their present positions, he turned once again to the ill-fated 115th Regiment under its new commander Colonel Alfred Ednie. He had just arrived in the Division from the 30th Infantry to understudy Cota. Gerhardt told him his mission was to 'open the north-east entrance to the city'[49] for TF C, which comprised the jeeps and Greyhound armoured cars of Lieutenant Edward Jones' 29th Divisional Cavalry Reconnaissance Troop (company), the 1st Platoon of C Company (Shermans) of the 747th

Tank Battalion, twelve M-10s of Captain Sydney Vincent's B Company of the 821st TD Battalion, two 105mm howitzers of the 1st Platoon of the Dandy Fifth's Cannon Company and some engineers of the 121st Engineer Battalion – all under the command of Dutch Cota. For once, however, Gerhardt was cautious. He told his Corps commander: 'We may go into St Lô but we don't want anyone to get cut off in there'.[50]

Following the usual artillery barrage, Glover Johns' 1st Battalion led the way and within an hour it had advanced 700m. There was no opposition. A further 800m was gained in the second hour and at about midday, by which time the leading troops had reached the first large bend in the road 1,500m north-east of St Lô, Gerhardt decided to alert TF C. He told Cota to be prepared to advance down the Isigny–St Lô road and gave orders that Johns' Battalion was to provide the necessary infantry support for the TF.

Shortly after alerting TF C, Gerhardt issued an extraordinary order. As a symbol of all those who had fallen in the painful advance from OMAHA Beach, he wanted Major Thomas Howie's body to accompany the first American troops into St Lô! It will be recalled that Howie had been killed after only five days in command of the Stonewallers' 3rd Battalion; he was, however, a long-standing member of the Division.

At 1430 hours Cota told Gerhardt he was ready to advance and at 1500 hours the first vehicles left the assembly area. Three hours and 7km later, on the eighth day of the offensive, the leading armoured car entered the eastern outskirts of St Lô. It was as well the main German force had withdrawn, for the route taken by the armoured TF comprises ten major road bends, has woods on its flanks and a steep drop on its east side. According to the US Official History and the US War Department Publication *St Lô*, the TF linked up with Glover Johns' Battalion near the large bend in the road at St Georges-Montcocq, and the joint force then advanced with infantrymen on each side of the road flanking the armoured vehicles. Some harassing mortar and artillery fire was encountered, especially around the bridge at Moulin Berot, but the only real opposition was a single anti-tank gun that was soon knocked out and some scattered rifle fire. Glover Johns in his book *The Clay Pigeons of St Lô*,[51] has a completely different version of events. He claims that his Battalion continued its advance on its own from the high ground near St Georges-Montcocq. It followed the track leading south-west towards St Lô, but after some 500m was halted by heavy machine-gun fire. He then received orders to pull back to the main road and *follow* the TF into the city. At this point he says he immediately turned to one of his officers and said, 'Come on, Hoff, let's go to St Lô!'.[52] As they advanced down the last hill into the city he says his 'Clay Pigeons' were in full view from the high ground on the south side of St Lô and came under regular artillery fire.

Whatever the precise details of the final advance into the city the

Americans were astounded by the sight that met them as they came over the brow of the hill hiding St Lô. All they could see was a wasteland of rubble with almost no undamaged buildings and hardly any distinguishable roads. They found it hard to understand why they had been fighting and dying for such a place. Nevertheless, and despite some misgivings, they pushed on and after a short and sharp skirmish in the area of the cemetery near the Carrefour (crossroads) de la Bascule, the joint force turned west down the rue de Neubourg. Less than a kilometre in front of them the GIs could see the ruined city centre and the Notre-Dame Cathedral. Fortunately only scattered pockets of resistance and some individual snipers remained to be cleared up. The men of the Blue and Gray set about their task with a vengeance; small groups of infantry led, followed by the armoured cars and Shermans. Blocked streets meant that many of Edward Jones' troopers had to dismount and join Glover Johns' infantrymen, but by 1900 hours the Americans were in control of all the important road junctions and even the main road bridge over the Vire which was still standing. It had been hit during an early Allied air raid but the Germans had made sure it was quickly repaired and brought into operation using a one-way system.[53] The joint force then set up defensive positions in preparation for a German counter-attack.

> Important areas . . . were reinforced to constitute formidable strongpoints, composed of an armored car, two tanks, two TDs, and an anti-tank gun. Other outposts were held by small groups of infantrymen armed with bazookas and anti-tank grenades.[54]

Concurrent with the drive into St Lô by TF C and Glover Johns' Battalion, one Regiment[55] of the 35th Division reached the Vire between its giant loop and bend while another[56] moved from Hill 122 to the northern edge of the city.[57] Fearing a possible Blue on Blue incident, Major General Corlett refused to allow either to enter the built-up area and St Lô remained the prize of the Blue and Gray.

Despite their withdrawal the Germans kept the city under regular and heavy artillery and mortar fire causing a number of casualties. The commander of the TF TD Company, Captain Sydney Vincent, was killed and Brigadier General Dutch Cota hit in the arm by a piece of shrapnel. He had to be evacuated that evening and spent more than a week in hospital.

The battle for St Lô was over and Uncle Charlie was going to make the most of the occasion. He ordered his Chief of Staff, Colonel Edward McDaniel, to have the blue and gray flag of the Division flown over the city. Sergeant Gerald Davis and Pfc Francis Bein of Glover Johns' 1st Battalion raised it above the café housing his Headquarters near the cemetery. The Americans claimed that it immediately attracted heavy enemy mortar and artillery fire to a point where Johns decided to move his

Headquarters to the crypt of the Famille Blanchet mausoleum in the nearby cemetery!

Uncle Charlie also sent a message to Charles Corlett on the evening of 18 July:

I have the honor to announce to the Corps commander that TF C of the 29th Infantry Division has secured the city of St Lô after forty-two days of continuous combat from the beaches to St Lô.[58]

The 'Recommendation for a Presidential Unit Citation' for the 29th Division includes the following statement relative to its actions in the period 13–19 July:

Thus, the important communication center and strongpoint fell and made the famous 'breakthrough' [COBRA] possible. The victory was not cheap, for the Division, during this period, lost 2,495 officers and men.

The ease with which the city had been taken surprised both Corlett and Gerhardt and in order to find out just how far the Germans had pulled back the Corps commander attached the 113th Cavalry Group to the 29th Division late on the 18th. Soon after first light the following morning C Troop moved out on the roads leading south and south-east from the city. Within a kilometre it had run into intense anti-tank, mortar and artillery fire and suffered over thirty casualties including its commander and first sergeant. A Troop on the left flank of the 29th also met heavy resistance. The German withdrawal was clearly very limited.

Although the commander of the German Seventh Army, SS General Paul Hausser, had sanctioned the withdrawal from the city, he was surprised and shocked by the speed of the American advance and ordered an immediate counter-attack. He would not, however, commit the 275th Infantry Division which had just arrived from Brittany and the only troops available were the exhausted remnants of the Blue and Gray's original enemy – the 352nd Infantry Division. According to the US Official History: 'The 352nd Division, which had tried to hold the Vire bridges . . . with too few men, mounted a counter-attack but was too weak to expel the Americans'.[59] As the Chief of Staff of the German Division said later: 'An opportunity of changing the situation by counter-attacks from our side no longer existed on 18 July'.[60]

Gerhardt's order that the body of Major Thomas Howie should accompany the leading troops of his Division into the city was executed at dusk on 18 July. A jeep of the 104th Medical Battalion carried the body. It was placed on a pile of rubble of what had once been the southern wall of the Sainte Croix church near the Carrefour de la Bascule and remained there throughout the 19th. Many of the Americans in St Lô had no idea who Major Howie was. When one officer asked, he was told:

He was a helluva a nice guy who had been with the Division for a long time. Somebody says he said 'See you in St Lô', and walked out of his command post right into a mortar burst. When the General heard about it he ordered them to get a coffin and carry Howie into town after the Task Force so his word would be good, or something like that.[61]

The whole incident inspired a poem in *Life* magazine by Alexander Auslander called 'Incident at St Lô' and to this day there is a memorial with a bust of Howie at the crossroads – since renamed 'Place Major Howie'.

Conclusion

Beginning at 0200 hours on 20 July, Gerhardt's Division was relieved in the St Lô sector by the 35th Infantry Division and moved back to the area of St Marguerite-sur-Elle and St Clair-sur-Elle. The men of the Blue and Gray remained in XIX Corps reserve but were to be rewarded with a week out of the line. But Uncle Charlie was determined that the Division should honour its dead and on the 23rd the Divisional Cemetery was dedicated at la Cambe (Map 5) – now the site of the largest *German* cemetery in Normandy.[62] A notice board at the entrance, proudly displaying the blue and gray symbol, read:

This cemetery was established on 11 June 1944 by the 29th Infantry Division, United States Army, as a final resting place for officers and men of that Division who made the supreme sacrifice on the battlefields of Normandy. . . In command of this valiant legion of the Blue and Gray is Lt. Col. William T. Terry, Infantry, who was killed in action on 17 July 1944.

This author has found it impossible to determine the exact number of men killed in the period from D-Day to the capture of St Lô. The After Action Reports of the three Infantry Regiments and the 747th Tank Battalion total 1,488. To this latter figure one has to add those of the artillery, engineer, TD and medical Battalions, so it would not be unreasonable to suggest a figure of more than 1,500.[63] Total battle casualties, excluding 'sick', were well in excess of 6,000 – roughly half of the authorised strength of the Division including attached units.[64]

Why so many casualties? First because, as mentioned in an earlier Chapter, the men of the Blue and Gray were not trained for the conditions they encountered on OMAHA and in the bocage. Second, because of the extraordinary fighting qualities of the German soldier; and third, because the Division was kept in action in some of the most difficult terrain this author has ever seen, for a period of time that in most military circles would be considered unreasonable.

The men of the Blue and Gray paraded at the la Cambe cemetery on 23 July and following a short address by Gerhardt the names of the dead were read out. 'Taps' and 'The Star Spangled Banner' followed and then Uncle Charlie stepped on to the dais once more. He wanted one more thing from his men and he got it – thousands of voices echoed his order: 'Twenty-Nine, Let's Go!'. With that the Blue and Gray marched off to 'The Beer Barrel Polka'.

NOTES

1. CMH Pub 100-13, *St Lô*, p.17.
2. Dupuy Institute.
3. From this high ground one can see some 25km to the south and south-west.
4. 5 FSD.
5. Zetterling, *Normandy 1944*, p. 384.
6. Ibid.
7. CMH Pub 100-13, p. 37.
8. Bradley, *A Soldier's Story*, p. 330.
9. Part of 353 Inf Div.
10. XIX Corps Arty AAR dated Jul 44.
11. CMH Pub 100-13, p. 41.
12. According to the AAR of 3 Para Div the attack by 5 Para Regt in the Bérigny sector was carried out by two para coys supported by pnrs. It can be reasonably assumed that the attack against 115 Inf Regt was similar in strength.
13. CMH Pub 100-13, p. 54.
14. A dramatic account of the German counter-attack against his Bn can be read in Glover Johns' own book, *The Clay Pigeons of St Lô*, pp. 111–39.
15. 116 Inf Regt AAR for Jul 44.
16. 747 Tk Bn AAR dated 4 Aug 44.
17. CMH Pub 100-13, p. 67.
18. Published as Annex 1 to G-2 Periodic Report No. 55, HQ First US Army dated 4 Aug 44.
19. 115 Inf Regt AAR dated 31 Jul 44.
20. Johns, op. cit., pp. 150–1.
21. Dupuy Institute: seventy-three killed, 328 wounded & fifty-four missing.
22. 747 Tk Bn AAR dated 4 Aug 44.
23. 115 Inf Regt AAR dated 31 Jul 44.
24. Dupuy Institute: seventy-two killed, 381 wounded & twenty-seven missing.
25. CMH Pub 100-13, p. 77.
26. Blumenson, *Breakout and Pursuit*, p. 158.
27. Balkoski, *Beyond the Beachhead*, p. 250.
28. CMH Pub 100-13, p. 79.
29. Bringing the Div total for the day, according to the Dupuy Institute, to 348.
30. Balkoski, op.cit., pp. 253–4.
31. CMH Pub 100-13, p. 79.

32. Zetterling, op. cit., p. 218.
33. Gordon, *One Man's War*, p. 69.
34. Blumenson, op. cit., p. 164.
35. CMH Pub 100-13, pp. 102–5.
36. Long since disappeared under a modern commercial development.
37. Blumenson, op. cit., p. 164.
38. CMH Pub 100-13, pp.103–4.
39. 747 Tk Bn AAR dated 4 Aug 44.
40. 3 Para Div AAR.
41. Dupuy Institute.
42. Blumenson, op. cit., p. 166.
43. CMH Pub 100-13, p. 108.
44. Ibid, p. 110.
45. In *The Clay Pigeons of St Lô*, p. 183, Glover Johns claims his Bn attacked at 0635 hrs and 'by noon hadn't gained an inch although they had suffered a lot more casualties'. This statement is not supported by the US Official History or CMH Pub 100-13.
46. Dupuy Institute.
47. Army Group 'B' War Diary dated 17 Jul 44.
48. 29 Inf Div G-3 Journal dated 18 Jul 44.
49. Blumenson, op. cit., p. 170.
50. 29 Inf Div G-3 Journal dated 18 Jul 44.
51. Pages 200–2.
52. Johns, op. cit., p. 201.
53. Lantier, *Saint-Lô au bûcher*.
54. CMH Pub 100-13, p. 117.
55. 137 Inf Regt.
56. 134 Inf Regt.
57. According to the Dupuy Institute the 35 Inf Div suffered 2,226 casualties in the period 9–19 Jul 44.
58. CMH Pub 100-13, p. 118, and a number of other sources quote 'forty-three days' rather than 'forty-two'. The latter is correct, however, because 29 Inf Div did not operate as a complete Div under Gerhardt's command until late on D+1.
59. Blumenson, op. cit., p. 174.
60. Ziegelmann, MS # B-490.
61. Johns, op.cit., pp. 234–5.
62. According to the G-1 Report of 29 Inf Div dated 11 Jun 44, 'Cemetery at 557880 [grid reference] opened 10 June 1944'. The bodies in this cemetery were later reburied at the US Normandy cemetery above OMAHA Beach. Many of them were later repatriated to the USA.
63. The Dupuy Institute gives a much lower figure of 1,138.
64. The Dupuy Institute gives a total casualty figure of 8,841.

Epilogue

Recognising that most readers will have come to their own conclusions concerning the senior commanders in the American 29th and British 3rd Infantry Divisions and the tactics they employed, and that some people consider it invidious to catalogue mistakes or apportion blame with the benefit of hindsight, this author will restrict himself to considering just four aspects of the two campaigns described in this book – training, tactics, strategy and command styles.

Before attempting to sum up, however, one has to remember that in June and early July 1944 our two Divisions were facing totally different ground and circumstances. OMAHA was much more strongly defended than SWORD and the terrain between the two beaches and the two objectives could not have been more dissimilar. Once across OMAHA the Americans had no more strongpoints in their path and no real likelihood of an armoured counter-attack, but they faced some of the most difficult country it is possible to fight through – country that was unsuitable for armour and unlikely to lead to rapid advances. On the other hand the British after crossing SWORD beach still had four major strongpoints to overcome and the real possibility of an early enemy armoured counter-attack. The distance to their major objective was half that of the Americans but the ground was basically open and in many places ideal for tanks. In summary, the Americans faced German infantry in a 'battle of the hedgerows' whilst the British faced Panzers and Panzer-Grenadiers in 'good tank country'.

Let us consider first the question of training. In this respect it is clear that while both Divisions were obviously well trained for their task of establishing beachheads on the Normandy coast, neither was properly trained for what followed – the Americans for the battle of the hedgerows nor the British for a rapid thrust inland using armour. With hindsight it is obvious that, perhaps understandably, far too much emphasis was placed on getting through the immediate coastal defences and not enough on what was to follow. In this respect the Americans were let down by the failure of intelligence staffs to point out to their commanders the potential problems of the bocage.

At the tactical level one has to wonder why both Divisional commanders failed to integrate their infantry, tanks, engineers and artillery into effective battlegroups, closely supported by ground attack aircraft.

The Germans had demonstrated the advantages, indeed the necessity, of doing so in 1939 and again in 1940 and Allied intelligence staffs had described their methods in detail. One short quotation will suffice:

> One of the outstanding characteristics of the German military system is unity of command. All units engaged on a single task are under one commander, who is responsible for the execution of that task. . . Great emphasis is placed on . . . co-operation amongst the arms. . . It should always be borne in mind . . . that there is a marked predilection in the German Army for the combination of the services [including the Luftwaffe], of all the arms [armour, infantry, engineers and artillery] and of any number of units for any specific task into one task force or battlegroup under one single commander.[1]

It seems that neither Crocker nor Rennie thought of imposing such a system on their subordinates and fiercely independent Regiments. Gerhardt and Cota did of course achieve some degree of integration in an attempt to solve the bocage problem, but neither the 29th nor the 3rd Divisions ever created proper battlegroups or led their major attacks with armour, even when the ground was suitable. Both repeatedly practised WWI tactics – massive artillery barrages, followed by infantry moving forward in lines. Once the artillery lifted the PBI, as in WWI, was at the mercy of the German artillery and machine-guns. The tanks of the Blue and Gray and Iron Divisions, if they were used at all, usually supported the infantry from a flank or acted in a counter-penetration or anti-tank role. Moreover, in the case of the British, no attempt was made to concentrate the three armoured Regiments (battalions) of the 27th Armoured Brigade as specified in the original plans.

At the strategic level it is noteworthy that the Second Army commander, Lieutenant General Miles Dempsey, wrote to Tom Rennie on 11 June as follows: 'You have formed a strong and vital hinge on which the rest of Second Army can turn.'[2] In fact, as stated by Monty before D-Day, the hinge was meant to be much farther forward, on the high ground well to the south of Caen, and it was the Americans rather than the British who were meant to make the major turning movement. It is also worth noting that in an attempt to move the hinge forward from the area secured at the end of D+1, it became necessary for the British and Canadians to launch four costly operations – EPSOM, WINDSOR, GOODWOOD and ATLANTIC – the latter being the Canadian operation concurrent with GOODWOOD to bridge the Orne and capture the southern part of Caen. Had Caen been taken on D-Day or D+1, the first two of these operations at least would have been unnecessary.

But *could* the British have reached Caen on D-Day or D+1? Brigadier K P Smith, whose 185 Brigade was given this mission, wrote later that it might have been taken if: one, strongpoints MORRIS and HILLMAN had been captured earlier; two, the Staffordshire Yeomanry tanks had married up with the KSLI sooner than they did, and three, his Brigade and the Staffordshire Yeomanry had reached Caen before the 21st Panzer Division 'arrived on the scene'.[3] But whilst there seems little doubt that HILLMAN should have been captured much earlier, it is this author's view that this would have made little difference to the final outcome – after all, HILLMAN had no detrimental effect on the advance of the KSLI although they passed within 1km of it seven hours before it was neutralised. On the other hand it was clearly expecting too much for a single Battalion mounted on tanks, with two other Battalions on their feet, to reach Caen before the arrival of the 21st Panzer Division in the sector to the north of that city. It also has to be said that the additional mission given to Rennie in the original I Corps Operation Instruction to 'support 6 Airborne Division operating east of [the] Orne having relieved the Airborne troops and taken over the defence of the Bénouville–Ranville crossings', seems to have detracted from his main mission of taking Caen and led to a significant proportion of his command being deflected away from the original Divisional centre-line. Furthermore, it is this author's belief that if the basic plan had been reversed and instead of planning to advance with three infantry battalions supported by one tank battalion, the 150 tanks of the 27th Armoured Brigade (less the 13/18 H) with two infantry battalions under command had been given the task of thrusting for Caen on the axis: Périers-sur-le-Dan–la Londe–Epron, there might have been some chance of success on D-Day. And certainly the failure of Rennie to concentrate the Staffordshire and East Riding Yeomanry under the 27th Armoured Brigade on D+1 ended any hope of achieving his D-Day mission in the short term. In summary it has to be said that the British plan for breaking out of the beachhead and capturing Caen on D-Day was flawed and certainly not in accordance with Montgomery's demand that 'Armoured columns must penetrate deep inland, and quickly, on D-Day'. The blame for this has to be placed at his door as well as those of Dempsey, Crocker and Rennie.

Readers will inevitably have noticed the different command styles of the Divisional commanders. Rennie and Whistler had been brought up to conserve manpower and at this stage of the war to avoid casualties whenever possible. In their case caution rather than panache ruled the day. Gerhardt on the other hand was more interested in results and sometimes showed a frightening indifference to casualties; exhortations such as: 'We're going to get on that objective or else', 'There will be no turning back' and 'Expend the whole battalion if necessary, but it's got to get there',[4] did not endear him to his officers or men. It should not be forgotten though that while the British spent a long period in an ordered holding operation, the Americans were almost constantly required to attack. Nevertheless, one has to wonder whether, had the roles been reversed the British, with their cautious attitude over casualties, would ever have penetrated the bocage and captured St Lô in the time frame achieved by the Blue and Gray.

Another example of American and in particular Gerhardt's ruthlessness is evident in the number of officers removed from command – two Regimental and seven Battalion commanders. In the case of the British 3rd Division only one senior officer, Brigadier K P Smith, lost his job during the period covered by this book.[5]

But for all the mistakes made and the agonies suffered in securing the beachheads and the cities of St Lô and Caen, the outstanding feature of our story has to be the courage and fortitude of the junior leaders and the GIs and Tommies of our two Divisions. This is not to belittle the performance of the Battalion and Company commanders – the Blue and Gray lost six commanding officers and eight Company commanders killed and wounded in action and the Iron Division seven commanding officers and thirteen Company commanders; but it was the junior leaders and individual infantrymen who had to close with and kill or capture the enemy. *They* were the ones who had to obey the orders from above, no matter how puzzling they may have seemed at the time, *they* were the ones who had to use their initiative in the absence of orders, and *they* were the ones who had to go on advancing or attacking when their comrades were falling all around them. When considering *their* performance one can do no better than quote (and add a couple of words to) Alfred Lord Tennyson's description of other valiant soldiers in a bygone age: 'Theirs not to reason why, theirs but to do and [too often] die!'.[6]

NOTES

1. Director of Military Intelligence, *German Order of Battle*, The War Office, Jan 44, pp. J4–5.
2. 3 Inf Div War Diary, Jun 44.
3. Smith, *Adventures of an Ancient Warrior*, p. 109.
4. Balkoski, *Beyond the Beachhead*, pp. 248 & 265.
5. Brigadier Orr, the commander of 9 Inf Bde, was also sacked but *after* the liberation of Caen.
6. *The Charge of the Light Brigade at Balaclava.*

Sequel

The Blue and Gray

Gerhardt's men enjoyed nine days in a rest area before being committed in Operation COBRA, the American breakout from Normandy, following which they took part in the liberation of Brittany and the capture of the key port of Brest on 18 September 1944. The bitter winter of 1944–45 was spent on the Roer river just to the east of Aachen, but on 1 March 1945 the Division crossed the river and captured the important town of Julich in bloody fighting. It then took part in the reduction of the Ruhr Pocket. On 29 April the Blue and Gray was the first American formation to reach the Elbe river where it dug in to await the arrival of the Red Army. This happened on 2 May and, following the end of the war in Europe on 8 May, the 29th became part of the Allied occupation force in the Bremen–Bremerhaven area; by strange coincidence the British Iron Division was in the same sector of Germany. After being shipped back to the United States in December 1945, the 29th was de-activated at Camp Kilmer in New Jersey on 17 January 1946 and its draftees returned to civilian life. Few of the men who had landed on OMAHA on D-Day were left. Between 6 June 1944 and 8 May 1945 the Division suffered 20,111 casualties – 3,720 killed, 15,403 wounded, 462 missing and 526 taken prisoner.

Although various units of the old 29th Infantry Division were reformed later in 1946 as part of the National Guard, the Blue and Gray as a whole was not reactivated until 6 June 1984 – the fortieth anniversary of D-Day. Today it is the only light infantry Division in the reserve component of the US Army. It has units in Virginia, Maryland, Massachusetts, New Jersey and Connecticut.

Charlie Gerhardt's post-war military career was undistinguished. He received no further promotions and his final appointment was as US Military Attaché in Brazil. He died in 1976, aged 81.

After leaving the Blue and Gray, Dutch Cota was given command of the 28th Infantry Division. He led it during the fighting in the Hürtgen Forest in Germany and in the Battle of the Bulge and retired as a major general in 1946. In civilian life he became Executive Director of the Philadelphia Defense Council. He died in 1971, aged 78.

As the Assistant Divisional commander of the 8th Infantry Division, Charles Canham took the surrender of the German garrison in Brest on 18 September 1944. When the commander of the 2nd German Parachute Division, General Hermann Ramcke, asked for his credentials Canham is said to have pointed to the GIs with him and said, 'These are my credentials!'. After the war Canham, who had been awarded the British Distinguished Service Order by Montgomery, became in turn, the assistant commander of the 82nd Airborne Division, commander of the 3rd Infantry Division and XI Corps and finally deputy commander Third Army. He retired in 1960 and died three years later at the early age of 62.

The Iron Division

Within a week of the capture of Caen, Bolo Whistler's men were fighting in Operation GOODWOOD, described by Montgomery as 'a real showdown on the eastern flank'.[1] It cost the British 3,474 casualties, nearly 600 of which were from the Iron Division, but it achieved its aim of holding the bulk of the German armour on that flank and away from the American breakout. The operation ended on 21 July and nine days later the 3rd Division was attacking again – this time as part of VIII Corps in Operation BLUECOAT. Monty had demanded that the Second British Army should 'hurl itself into the fight in the Caumont area so as to make easier the task of the American armies fighting hard on the western flank'.[2] BLUECOAT ended on 15 August and in early September the Division crossed the Seine. Its next task, as part of VIII Corps, was to protect the right flank of the thrust towards Arnhem in support of the ill-fated airborne operation code-named MARKET GARDEN. In October the Division lost another 1,400 men in taking the towns of Overloon and Venraij in Holland, following which it spent the winter on the Maas river line. February 1945 saw the Iron Division, still under Bolo Whistler's command, participating in the Rhineland offensive and the subsequent advance across the Ems river to Bremen where it found itself alongside the Blue and Gray. Its total casualties were also grievous, although not in the same category as those of its American counterpart: 11,254 – 1,579 killed, 8,039 wounded and 1,636 missing or taken prisoner.

Soon after the end of the war in Germany the Iron Division was withdrawn to Belgium to begin preparations for a move to America to take part in a seaborne assault on the mainland of Japan. Following the surrender of that country, however, the move was cancelled and in early October the Division, as part of the British regular Army, left Europe for duty in Egypt and Palestine. During the past fifty-seven years its units have continued to serve in many active duty stations, most recently in Afghanistan in 2002.

Tom Rennie was killed by a mortar round on 24 March 1945 during the Rhine crossing operation. At the time he was commanding the 51st (Highland) Infantry Division. Bolo Whistler continued to command the Iron Division until the end of the war in Europe. He went on to a distinguished peacetime career and retired as a four star general in 1957. He died six years later at the early age of 65.

203

Brigadier Copper Cass of 8 Brigade was badly wounded after accidentally driving into a minefield whilst partridge shooting on the Maas river-line in Holland in October 1944. He left the Army in 1948 and became Secretary of the Army Rifle Association – he had been a pre-war champion shot. He died in 1968, aged 70. Brigadier Kipper Smith, after being replaced as the commander of 185 Infantry Brigade in early July 1944, was sent out to command the East Africa Command Sub Area which included Madagascar, Mauritius and the Seychelles. He went on to command the 29th East Africa Brigade in Tanganyika before retiring from the Army in 1946. He died in 1985, aged 86, after spending thirty years working for the Royal British Legion and the Conservative Party.

NOTES
1 Directive No. M 511.
2 Directive No. M 515.

Appendix A:
US 29th Infantry Division

6th June 1944

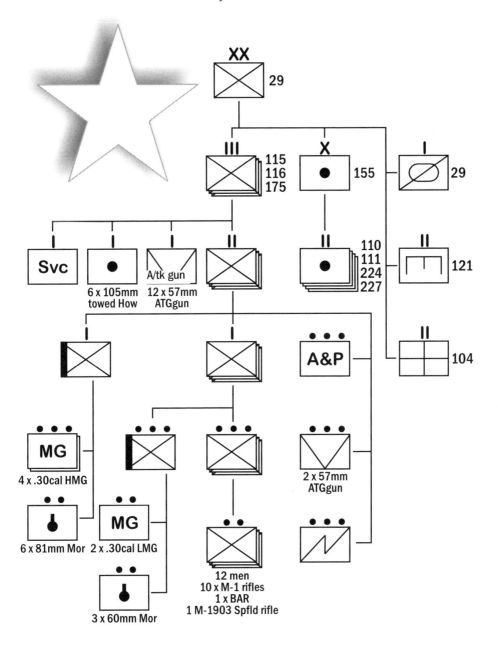

Appendix B:
US 743rd Tank Battalion

6th June 1944

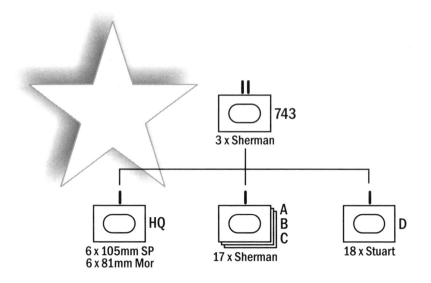

Appendix C:
UK 3rd Infantry Division
6th June 1944

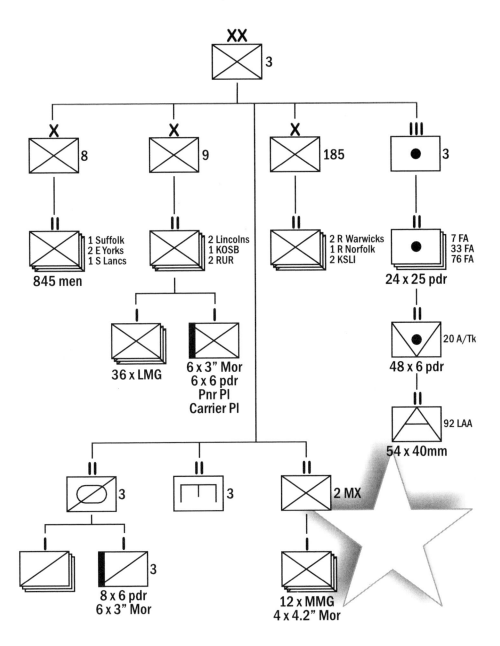

Appendix D:
UK 27th Armoured Brigade
6th June 1944

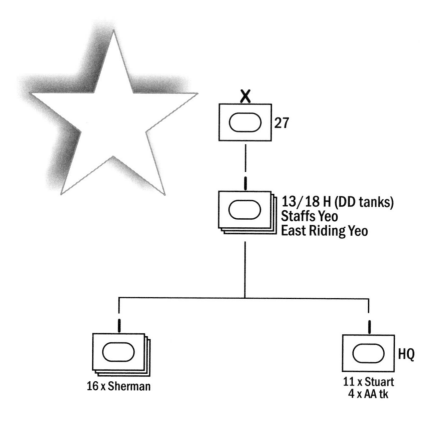

Appendix E:
716th Infantry Division
6th June 1944

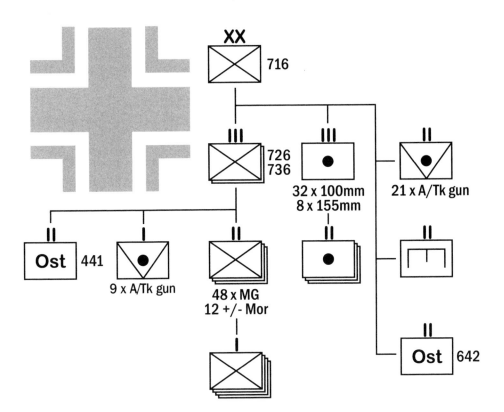

Appendix F:
352nd Infantry Division
6th June 1944

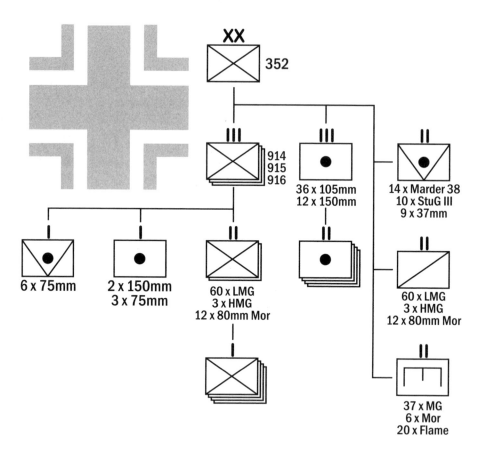

Appendix G:
German Defences
at
Les Moulins Draw

▲	Pillbox or concrete shelter
⚓	Gun emplacement
░	Minefield
[X│X]	Steel obstacles
⌇	Trench
–	Wire
⊔⊔⊔	Fire Trench

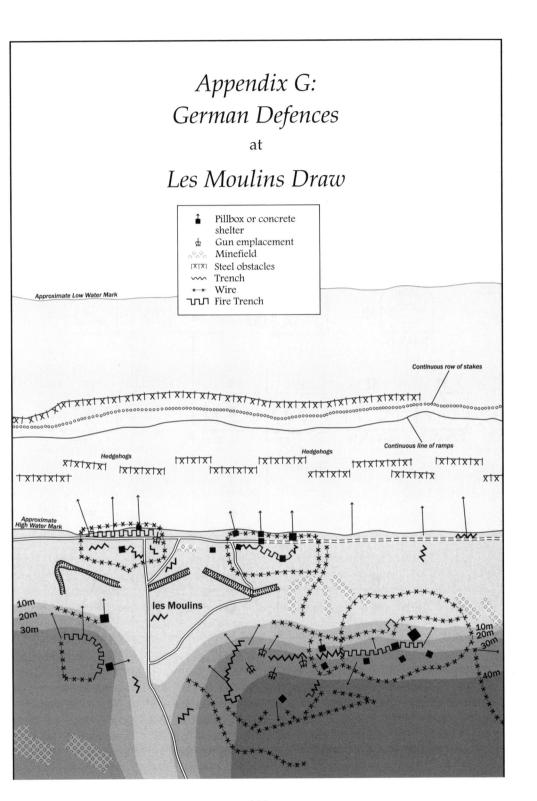

Approximate Low Water Mark

Continuous row of stakes

Continuous line of ramps

Hedgehogs

Hedgehogs

Approximate High Water Mark

les Moulins

10m
20m
30m

10m
20m
30m
40m

211

Appendix H:
21st Panzer Division
6th June 1944

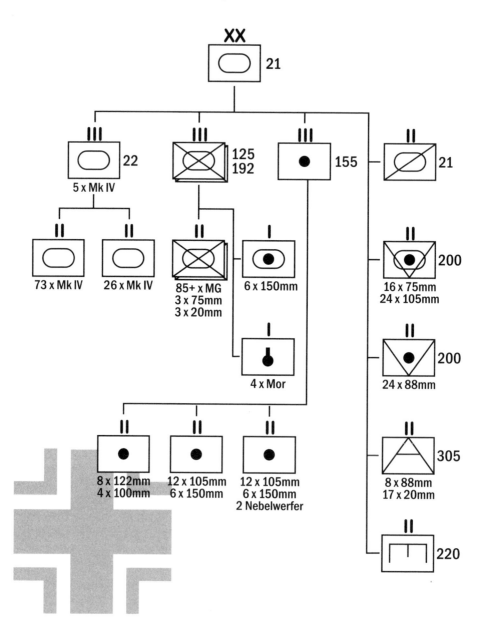

Appendix J:
12th SS Panzer Division
6th June 1944

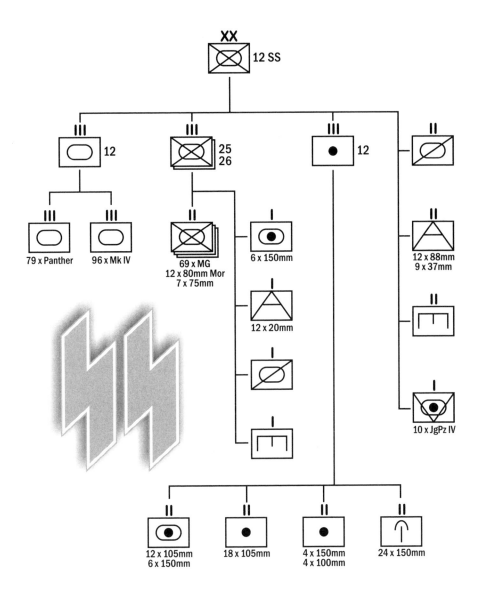

Appendix K

Sequence of Events in the 3rd Division Sector on D-Day

Time	Event
0510	Naval bombardment commenced
0530	Infantry Companies of 8 Brigade embarked assault craft
0615	DD tanks entered water; destroyers joined in naval bombardment
0640	First air raid on Caen
0650	Run-in shoot by Divisional artillery
0715	Rocket firing LCTs joined in bombardment
0720	5 ARRE and engineer assault teams started landing on QUEEN beach
0725	H-Hour; DD tanks and assault infantry Companies of South Lancs and East Yorks (8 Brigade) started landing
0745	South Lancs follow-up Companies landed; second air raid on Caen
0755	No. 4 Commando and two Free French Commando Troops started landing
0800	Majority of German 88mm guns left Périers Ridge
0805	East Yorks follow-up Companies, C Squadron 13/18 H, South Lancs and East Yorks 6-pdrs and 3-inch mortars and Middlesex MMGs came ashore.
0820	Suffolks (8 Brigade) started landing
0830	QUEEN WHITE clear with four vehicle exits
0840	SP guns of 76 Field Regiment, HQ 1st SS Commando Brigade and Nos 6 and 41 Commandos started landing
0900	Hermanville secured by South Lancs (8 Brigade)
0910	Nos 3 and 45 Commandos started landing
0915	Three vehicle exits cleared on QUEEN RED
0930	Free French Commandos cleared Riva Bella Casino strongpoint
0945	Brigadier Cass, commander 8 Brigade, came ashore
1000	Brigadier Smith came ashore and 185 Brigade started landing; Colleville-sur-Orne cleared by Suffolks (8 Brigade); East Yorks (8 Brigade) reported COD clear; German counter-attack (part of 736 Regiment) started towards Lion-sur-Mer
1030	Major General Rennie came ashore

1100	185 Brigade complete in Assembly Area; QUEEN RED closed due to congestion and backlog of vehicles
1130	Stalemate in Lion-sur-Mer
1200	MORRIS cleared by Suffolks (8 Brigade); 9 Brigade started landing; Warwicks ordered to switch to eastern flank
1230	KSLI (185 Brigade) started their advance without tanks
1300	SOLE cleared by East Yorks (8 Brigade)
1310	Suffolks (8 Brigade) launched first attack against HILLMAN
1315	Lead platoon of KSLI (185 Brigade) came under fire on Périers ridge
1330	Third air raid on Caen; Commandos reached Caen canal and Orne bridges
1330/1400	9 Brigade ordered to switch from west to east flank; Brigadier Cunningham, commander 9 Brigade, wounded shortly afterwards
1345 (+/-)	C Squadron Staffordshire Yeomanry (185 Brigade) reached Point 61
1400	Warwicks and Norfolks (185 Brigade) in Colleville-sur-Orne waiting for HILLMAN to be cleared
1425	C Squadron Staffordshire Yeomanry caught up with KSLI (both 185 Brigade)
1430	KSLI held up in Beuville
1440	East Riding Yeomanry (9 Brigade) ashore and ready to move
1450	CO KSLI (185 Brigade) ordered the main body of his Battalion to bypass Beuville
1545	KSLI reached Biéville
1615	21st Panzer Division began its counter-attack
1625	Fourth air raid on Caen
1700	Suffolks (8 Brigade) launched second attack on HILLMAN
1730	Y Company KSLI (185 Brigade) reached northern outskirts of Lébisey wood
1800	Norfolks (185 Brigade) reached Bellevue
1830	East Yorks (8 Brigade) cleared DAIMLER; Warwicks (185 Brigade) reached Benouville
2000	German resistance at HILLMAN ended; 21st Panzer Division counter-attack reached the coast in the Lion-sur-Mer sector; main body of KSLI (185 Brigade) dug in at Biéville
2115	Suffolks (8 Brigade) started digging in south of Colleville
2200	KOSB (9 Brigade) reached St Aubin-d'Arquenay
2315	Y Company KSLI (185 Brigade) withdrew from Lébisey wood area
2359	Warwicks (185 Brigade) reached Blainville

Appendix L:
3rd Parachute Division
22nd June 1944

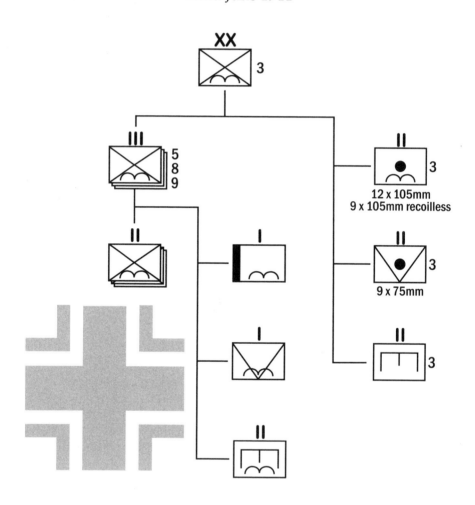

Bibliography

American Forces in Action Series, *Omaha Beachhead* and *St Lô*, Center of Military History Publications 100-11 and 100-13, United States Army, Washington DC, 1945 and 1946.

Balkoski, Joseph, *Beyond the Beachhead*, Stackpole Books, 1999.

Bennett, Robert L, *Les Journaux de Caen*, La Faculté des Lettres et Sciences Humaines de l'Université de Caen.

Birt, Raymond, *XXII Dragoons, 1760–1945*, Gale & Polden, 1950.

Blumenson, Martin, *The United States Army in WWII: Breakout and Pursuit*, Office of the Chief of Military History, Washington, DC, 1961.

Bradley, Omar, *A Soldier's Story*, Eyre & Spottiswoode (Publishers) Ltd, London, 1951.

Brown, David, *The Bombing of Caen*, Colloque International, Caen Mémorial.

Caen Municipal Information Bulletin, *Caen Normandie 44*, June 1984.

Carrell, Paul, *Invasion – They're Coming!*, George G Harrup & Co Ltd, 1962.

Chandler, David & Collins, James Lawton, *The D-Day Encyclopaedia*, Simon & Schuster, Academic Reference Division, New York, 1994.

Commander and Officers, *The Story of the 79th Armoured Division*, printed in Hamburg, July 1945.

Cunliffe, Marcus, *History of the Royal Warwickshire Regiment 1919–1955*, William Clowes & Sons Ltd, 1956.

Delaforce, Patrick, *Monty's Iron Sides*, Alan Sutton Publishing Ltd, 1995.

Detour, Françoise, *The Liberation of Calvados, 6th June 1944–31st December 1944*, Conseil Général Calvados, 1994.

Dupuy, Trevor N, *Numbers, Predictions and War*, Hero Books USA, 1985 and *A Genius for War*, Hero Books USA, 1984.

Eisenhower, David, *Eisenhower at War 1943–1945*, Ransom House, New York, 1986.

Ellis, L, *Victory in the West, Vol. I, The Battle of Normandy*, HM Stationery Office, 1962.

Gardiner, Juliet, *D-Day – Those Who Were There*, Collins & Brown Ltd, London, 1994.

217

Gordon, Harold J Jr, *One Man's War*, The Apex Press, New York, 1999.

Hamilton, Nigel, *Monty Master of the Battlefield, 1942–1944*, Hamish Hamilton Ltd, London, 1983.

Harrison, Gordon A, *The United States Army in WWII: Cross-Channel Attack*, Office of the Chief of Military History, Washington, DC, 1951.

Hastings, Max, *Overlord*, Pan Books Ltd, 1985.

Hewitt, Robert, *Work Horse of the Western Front*, Washington Infantry Journal Press, 1946.

Illing, H C, *'No Better Soldier'*, Royal Regiment of Fusiliers Museum (Royal Warwickshire), 2001

Kilvert-Jones, Tim, *Omaha Beach* and *Sword Beach*, Pen & Sword Books Ltd, 1999 & 2001 respectively.

Johns, Glover S, Jr, *The Clay Pigeons of St Lô*, The Military Service Publishing Company, Harrisburg, 1958.

Kemp, P K, *The Royal Norfolk Regiment, 1919–1951*, Vol. III, The Regimental Association of the Royal Norfolk Regiment, 1953.

Lantier, Maurice, *Saint-Lô au bûcher*, 1984.

Luck, Hans von, *Panzer Commander*, Praeger, London, 1989.

Lummis, Eric, *From Sword to the Seine*, unpublished.

Man, John, *The Penguin Atlas of D-Day and the Normandy Campaign*, Penguin Books, 1994.

McKee, Alexander, *Caen Anvil of Victory*, Pan Books Ltd, London, 1964.

McNish, Robin, *Iron Division*, Ian Allen Ltd, London, 1978.

Meyer, Hubert, *History of the 12th SS Panzer Division Hitlerjugend*, J J Fedorowicz Publishing Inc., Manitoba, Canada, 1994.

Meyer, Kurt, *Grenadiers*, J J Fedorowicz Publishing Inc., Manitoba, Canada, 1994.

Miller, Charles, *History of the 13th/18th Royal Hussars 1922–1947*, Chisman, Bradshaw Ltd, London.

Miller, Commander M O W, *Combined Operations*, unpublished.

Miller, Russell, *Nothing Less Than Victory*, Michael Joseph Ltd, London, 1993.

Montgomery, B L, *Memoirs of Field Marshal the Viscount Montgomery*, Collins, 1958.

Nicolson, N, *Alex*, Weidenfeld & Nicolson, 1973.

Nightingale, P R, *The East Yorkshire Regiment in the War 1939/45*, Mr Pye (Books), East Riding, 1998.

Radcliffe, G L Y, *History of the 2nd Battalion The King's Shropshire Light Infantry 1941–1945*, Oxford, Basil Blackwell, 1947.

Ruppenthal, Roland G, *Logistical Support for the Armies*, Vol. 1, CMH US Army, Washington DC, 1995.

Scarfe, Norman, *Assault Division*, Collins, London, 1947.

Shaw, Frank and Joan, *We Remember D-Day*, Echo Press (1983) Ltd, London.

Shulman, Milton, *Defeat in the West*, Masquerade, 1995

Smith, Brigadier K P, *Adventures of an Ancient Warrior*, Stones Printers, Milford-on-Sea, Hampshire,1984.

Smith, Michael & Erskine, Ralph, *Action The Day*, Bantam Press, London, 2001.

Smurthwaite, Nicholls & Washington, *Against All Odds: The British Army of 1939–1940*, National Army Museum, London, 1989.

Stacey, C P Col, *Official History of the Canadian Army in the Second World War, Vol. III, The Victory Campaign*, Queen's Printer, Ottawa, Canada, 1960.

Whistler, General Sir Lashmer, *Personal Diary*, unpublished.

Wilmot, Chester, *The Struggle for Europe*, Collins, 1952.

Zetterling, Niklas, *Normandy 1944*, J J Fedorowicz Publishing Inc., Manitoba, Canada, 2000.

Zuckerman, Solly, *From Apes to Warlords*, Collins, 1988.

Index

PLACES

Abbeville: 20
Agneaux: 60
Amy: 140–1
Anguerny: 90, 92, 97, 107, 154
Anisy: 115
Argentan: 13
Arras: 20
Arromanches: 15, 22, 58–9, 96
Aunay-sur-Odon: 156
Aure: 16, 121, 123–5, 128–9
Authie: 107, 169
Auville-sur-le-Vey: 128
Avranches: 176
Balleroy: 127, 154
Barnstaple: 3
Bayeux: 12, 14, 16, 22, 58, 96, 121, 156
Beauregard: 104, 113
Bedford: 2, 56
Belle-Fontaine: 180, 182
Bellevue: 84, 86, 91, 104
Bénouville: 37–9, 69, 83, 87, 103, 109, 113, 164, 200
Bény-sur-Mer: 79
Bérigny: 150, 178, 196
Beuville: 18, 24–5, 79, 85–6, 90–1, 113, 117, 158
Biéville: 18, 23, 78, 84–6, 90–1, 103–6, 113, 117, 158–9
Blainville: 24, 87, 92, 102–4, 113, 158
Bodmin: 3
Bognor Regis: 10
Bourg d'Enfer: 182–3
Bourguébus: 157
Bretel, Bois de: 139, 147
Bretteville-sur-Laize: 107, 156
Bricqueville: 22, 57, 129–30
Brighton: 8

Buron: 81, 102, 107, 115, 163, 169
Caen: xiii, 12–14, 18–19, 23, 25, 37–9, 75, 77–8, 80–2, 85–6, 89–93, 97–8, 100–4, 109–12, 115, 117, 132, 153, 156–7, 159–60, 163–71, 199–201
Caen canal: 18, 37–8, 57, 73–4, 82, 86–7, 92, 96, 102–4, 109. 113, 158
Calette wood: 129
Cambes-en-Plaine: 89, 102–4, 106–7, 112, 115–6, 158–9, 164
Canchy: 125, 129
Cardonville: 123
Carentan: 16, 21, 57–8, 96, 126–7, 131, 136
Carpiquet: 82, 85, 100, 102, 156, 163, 169
Carrefour de la Bascule: 193–4
Catz: 129
Caumont: 12, 16, 131–2, 154
Cazelle: 114
Ceresty forest: 127, 131
Charlottesville· 2
Chartres: 99
Cherbourg: xiii, 12, 17, 42, 57, 131, 137–8
COD: 19, 23, 67, 69–75, 94
Colleville-Montgomery: 72, 94
Colleville-sur-Mer: 15, 35, 53, 56, 58–9
Colleville-sur-Orne: 18, 23–4, 72–4, 80, 84, 86, 88, 91, 94
Colombelles: 165, 167–8, 171
Colombières: 22, 57, 125, 129–30

Colomby-sur-Thaon: 97
Cotentin: 57, 131, 137, 176
Coutances: 16, 149, 191
Couvains: 132–4, 139, 144–5, 151, 181
Couvrechef: 23, 81, 99, 108
Cresserons: 24, 38, 73, 75, 81, 83, 87, 103, 105, 109
Cussy: 89
DAIMLER: 37, 69, 83, 85, 87
Deux-Jumeaux: 125
Dives river: 164
Douvres: 24, 90, 100, 105, 153, 157
Dunkirk: 8
Ecrammeville: 125
Elle: 16, 128–33, 136
Englesqueville: 121–2
Epron: 89–90, 92, 102, 159–60, 163–4, 168, 171, 200
Evrecy: 98, 111–2, 153, 171
Falaise: xiii, 13, 25, 112, 157
Falmouth: 5
Flers: 98
Fleury: 111
Formigny: 53, 55, 59–60, 118, 121–2, 125
Franqueville: 169
Frome: 8
Galmanche: 104, 115–16, 169–70
Géfosse-Fontenay: 130
Grandcamp: 57, 121, 124–6
Granville: 13
Gruchy: 119–20, 122
Hauts-Vents: 174
Hermanville-sur-Mer: 18, 23, 37, 70–2, 74–6, 78–9, 82–3, 85, 91–2, 103, 106, 109
Hérouville: 18, 24, 89–90, 102, 106, 164, 166–8, 170

228

Maps

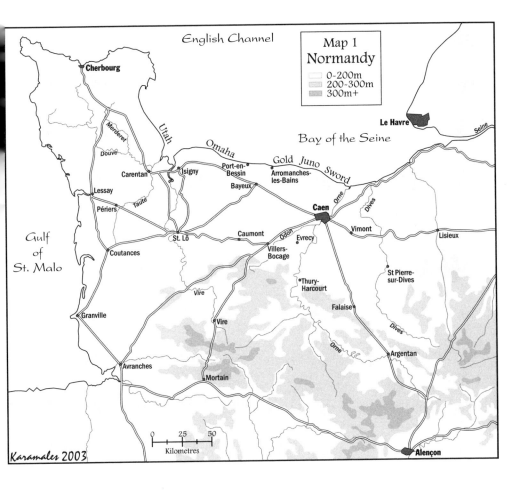

English Channel

Map 1
Normandy
0-200m
200-300m
300m+

Cherbourg

Le Havre

Seine

Merderet

Utah

Omaha

Bay of the Seine

Douve

Port-en-
Bessin

Gold   Juno   Sword

Carentan

Isigny

Arromanches-
les-Bains

Lessay

Bayeux

Orme

Caen

Dives

Périers

Taute

Lisieux

Gulf
of
St. Malo

St. Lô

Caumont

Odon

Evrecy

Vimont

Coutances

Villers-
Bocage

St Pierre-
sur-Dives

Vire

Thury-
Harcourt

Granville

Vire

Falaise

Dives

Orne

Argentan

Avranches

Mortain

0   25   50
Kilometres

Alençon

Karamales 2003

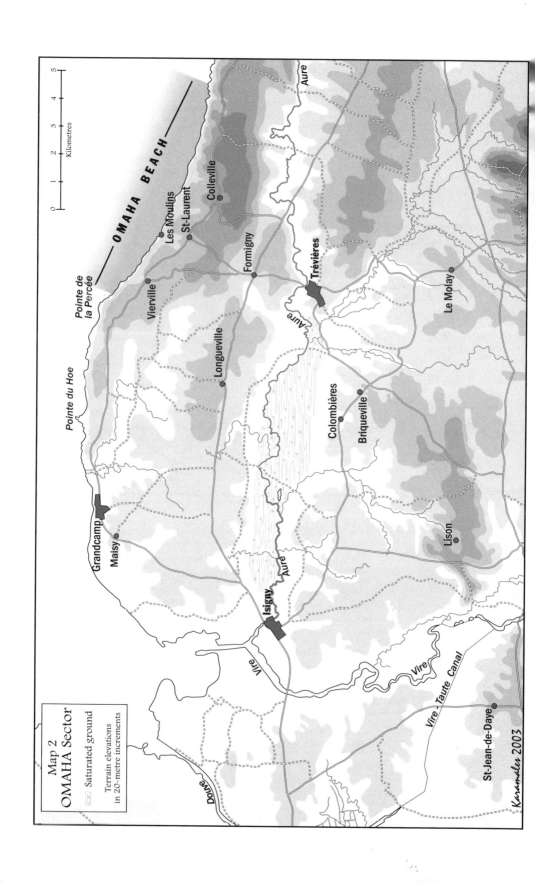

Map 2
OMAHA Sector

Saturated ground

Terrain elevations
in 20-metre increments

0 1 2 3 4 5
Kilometres

Karandas 2003

OMAHA BEACH

Pointe de
la Percée

Pointe du Hoe

Les Moulins
St-Laurent
Colleville
Formigny
Trévières
Le Molay

Vierville
Longueville
Colombières
Briqueville
Lison

Grandcamp
Maisy
Isigny

Aure
Aure
Aure

Vire
Vire

Douve

Vire - Taute Canal

St-Jean-de-Daye

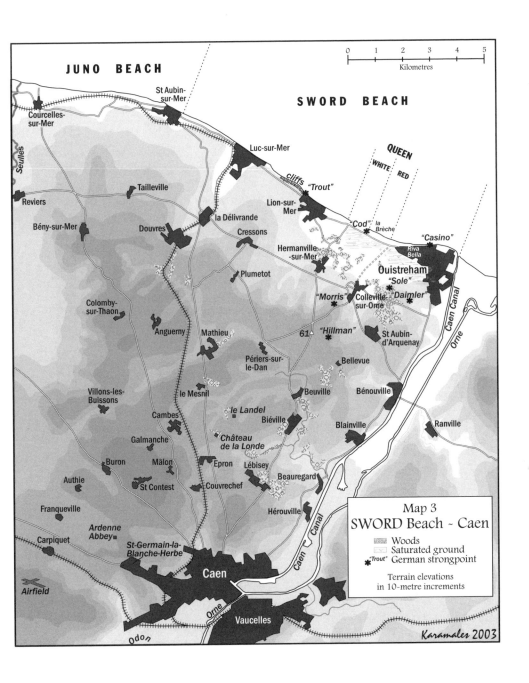

JUNO BEACH

SWORD BEACH

QUEEN
WHITE
RED

0 1 2 3 4 5
Kilometres

St Aubin-
sur-Mer

Courcelles-
sur-Mer

Luc-sur-Mer

Cliffs
"Trout"

Lion-sur-
Mer

Seulles

Reviers

Tailleville

"Cod" la
Brèche

"Casino"

Bény-sur-Mer

Douvres

la Délivrande

Cressons

Hermanville
-sur-Mer

Riva
Bella

Ouistreham

"Sole"

Plumetot

"Morris"

Colleville
sur-Orne

"Daimler"

Colomby-
sur-Thaon

Anguerny

Mathieu

61 "Hillman"

St Aubin-
d'Arquenay

Caen Canal

Orne

Périers-sur-
le-Dan

Bellevue

le Mesnil

Villons-les-
Buissons

le Landel

Beuville

Bénouville

Cambes

Biéville

Blainville

Ranville

Galmanche

Château
de la Londe

Buron

Mâlon

Epron

Lébisey

Authie

St Contest

Couvrechef

Beauregard

Franqueville

Hérouville

Ardenne
Abbey

Carpiquet

St-Germain-la-
Blanche-Herbe

Caen

Caen Canal

Map 3
SWORD Beach - Caen

Woods
Saturated ground
"Trout" German strongpoint

Terrain elevations
in 10-metre increments

Airfield

Orne

Vaucelles

Odon

Karamales 2003

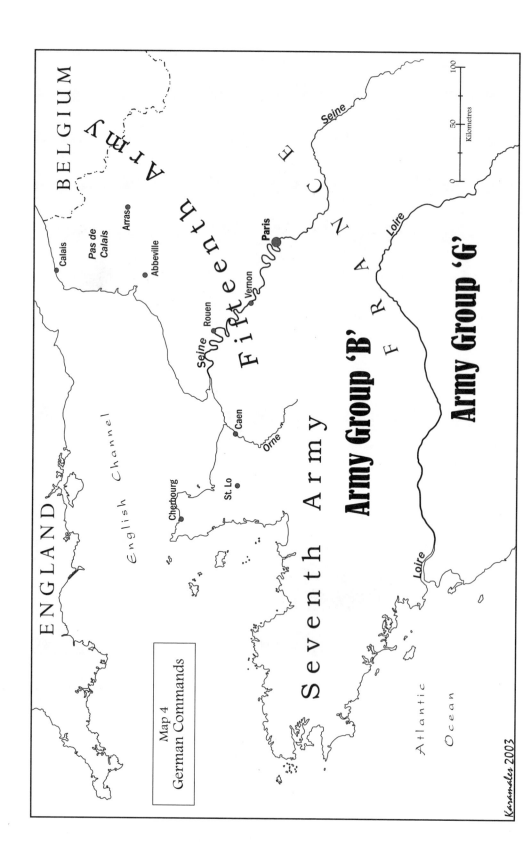

Map 4
German Commands

ENGLAND

BELGIUM

English Channel

Calais
Pas de Calais
Arras
Abbeville

Fifteenth Army

Seine
Rouen
Vernon

Seine

Paris

FRANCE

Cherbourg
St. Lo

Caen
Orne

Seventh Army

Army Group 'B'

Army Group 'G'

Loire

Atlantic
Ocean

0   50   100
Kilometres

Kershaw 2003

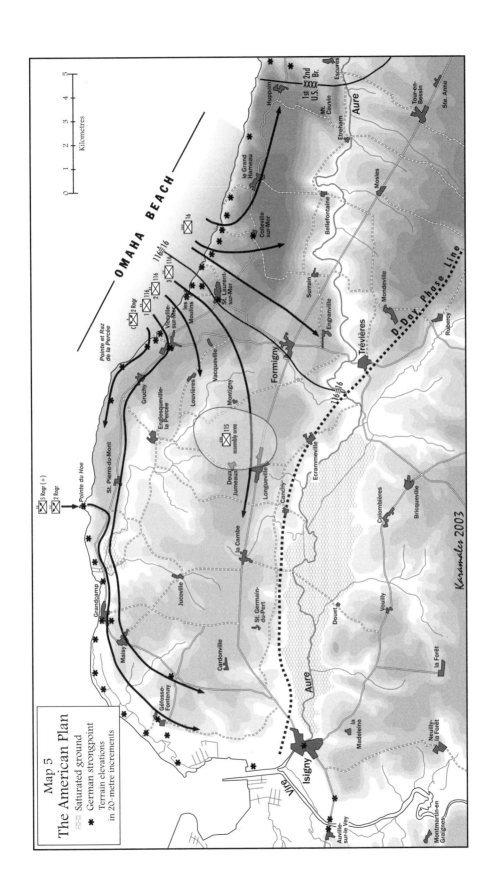

Map 5
The American Plan

Saturated ground

German strongpoint

✱ Terrain elevations
  in 20-metre increments

Kilometres
0 1 2 3 4 5

OMAHA BEACH

Pointe et Raz
de la Percée

Pointe du Hoe

St. Pierre-du-Mont

5 Rngr (+)

2 Rngr

Grandcamp

Maisy

Géfosse-
Fontenay

Cardonville

Jucoville

St. Germain-
du-Pert

la Cambe

Deux
Jumeaux

Longueville

Cauchy

Isigny

la
Madeleine

Auville-
sur-le-Vey

Montmartin-en-
Graignes

Neuilly-
la Forêt

la Forêt

Voire

Aure

Douet

Vouilly

Colombières

Bricqueville

Ecrammeville

Formigny

Trévières

116 16

D-Day Phase Line

Engranville

Ruberey

Surrain

Mondeville

Bellefontaine

Mosles

Tour-en-
Bessin

Ste. Anne

Etreham

Mt.
Cauvin

Aure

Escures

Huppain

1st 2nd Br.
XXXX
1st U.S.

le Grand
Hameau

Colleville-
sur-Mer

St. Laurent
sur-Mer

les
Moulins

Vierville-
sur-Mer

Vacqueville

Louvières

Montigny

Englesqueville-
la Percée

Gruchy

C 2 Rngr
1 116
2 116
3 116
116 16

115
assembly area

Kanander 2003

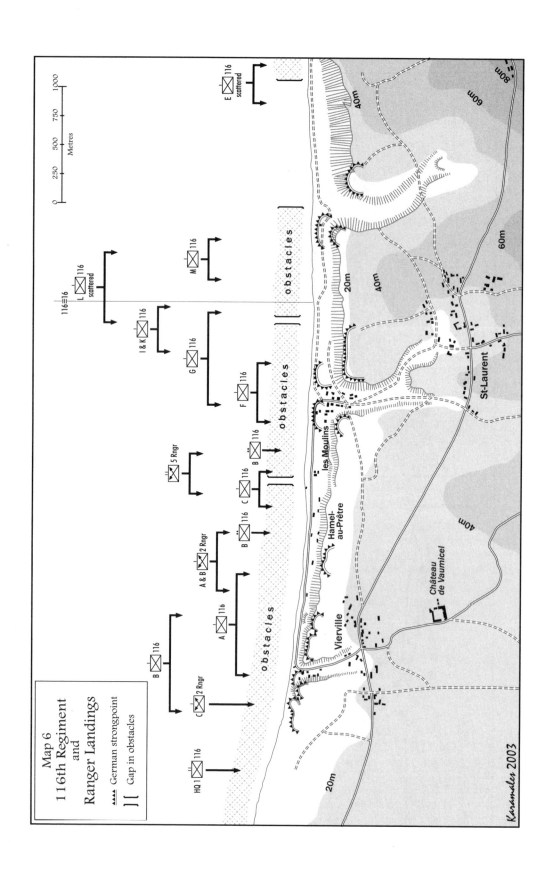

Map 6
116th Regiment
and
Ranger Landings

▲▲▲ German strongpoint
][Gap in obstacles

Metres
0   250   500   750   1000

HQ 1 116

B 116

C 2 Rngr

A 116

A & B 2 Rngr

B 116

C 116

5 Rngr

B 116

L 116 scattered
116 16

I & K 116

G 116

F 116

M 116

E 116 scattered

obstacles

obstacles

obstacles

Vierville

Hamel-au-Prêtre

les Moulins

St-Laurent

Château de Vaumicel

20m

40m

60m

80m

20m

40m

60m

40m

Karamaker 2003

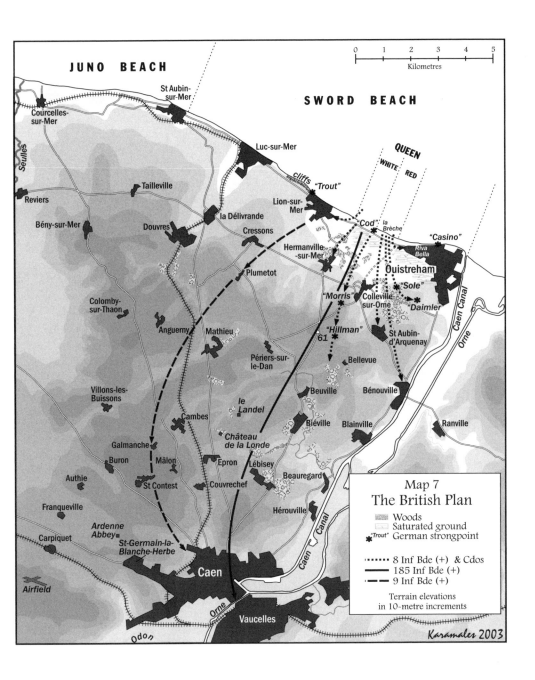

JUNO BEACH

SWORD BEACH

Courcelles-
sur-Mer

St Aubin-
sur-Mer

QUEEN

WHITE   RED

Luc-sur-Mer

Tailleville

Cliffs

"Trout"

Reviers

Lion-sur-
Mer

"Cod"   la
Brèche

"Casino"

Bény-sur-Mer

la Délivrande

Douvres

Cressons

Hermanville
-sur-Mer

Riva
Bella

Ouistreham

Plumetot

"Morris"   Colleville   "Sole"
sur-Orne

"Daimler"

Colomby-
sur-Thaon

"Hillman"
61

St Aubin-
d'Arquenay

Anguerny

Mathieu

Périers-sur-
le-Dan

Bellevue

le
Landel

Beuville

Bénouville

Villons-les-
Buissons

Cambes

Biéville

Château
de la Londe

Blainville

Ranville

Galmanche

Buron   Mâlon   Epron   Lébisey

Beauregard

Authie

St Contest   Couvrechef

Franqueville

Hérouville

Ardenne
Abbey

| Map 7 |
| The British Plan |

Carpiquet

St-Germain-la-
Blanche-Herbe

Woods
Saturated ground
"Trout" German strongpoint

Caen

Airfield

········ 8 Inf Bde (+) & Cdos
——— 185 Inf Bde (+)
– – – 9 Inf Bde (+)

Orne

Vaucelles

Terrain elevations
in 10-metre increments

Odon

Karamales 2003

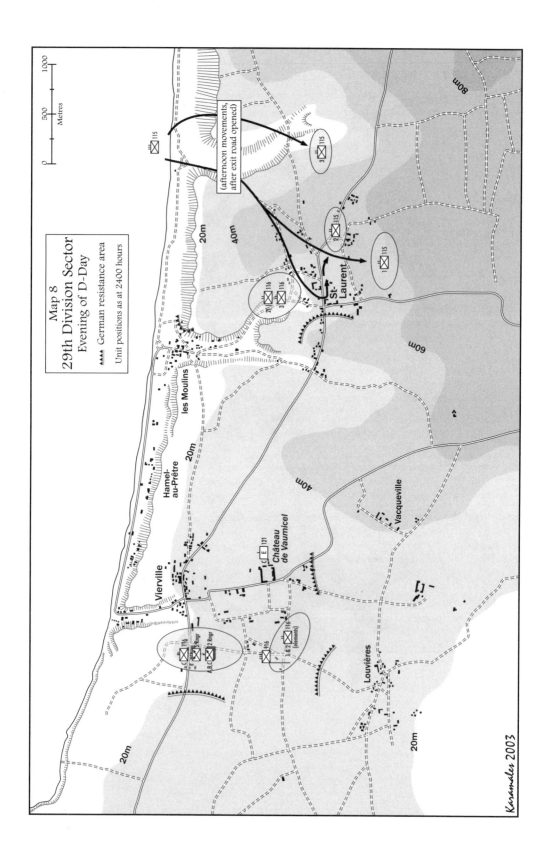

Map 8
29th Division Sector
Evening of D-Day

▲▲▲ German resistance area

Unit positions as at 2400 hours

(afternoon movements, after exit road opened)

St-Laurent

Vierville

Hamel-au-Prêtre

les Moulins

Château de Vaumicel

Vacqueville

Louvières

0   500   1000
Metres

Karslake 2003

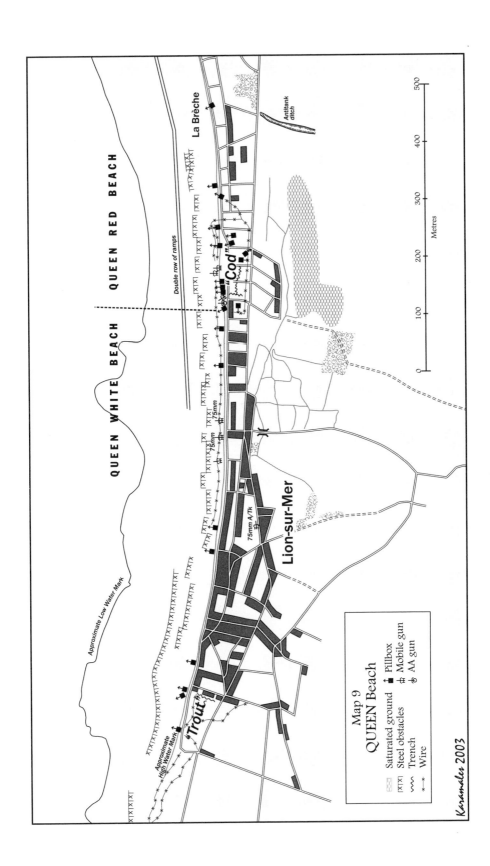

QUEEN WHITE BEACH   QUEEN RED BEACH

Approximate Low Water Mark

Approximate High Water Mark

"Trout"

"Cod"

La Brèche

Double row of ramps

Lion-sur-Mer

75mm

75mm

75mm

75mm A/Tk

Antitank ditch

Map 9
QUEEN Beach

Saturated ground
Steel obstacles
Trench
Wire

Pillbox
Mobile gun
AA gun

0   100   200   300   400   500
Metres

Karamler 2003

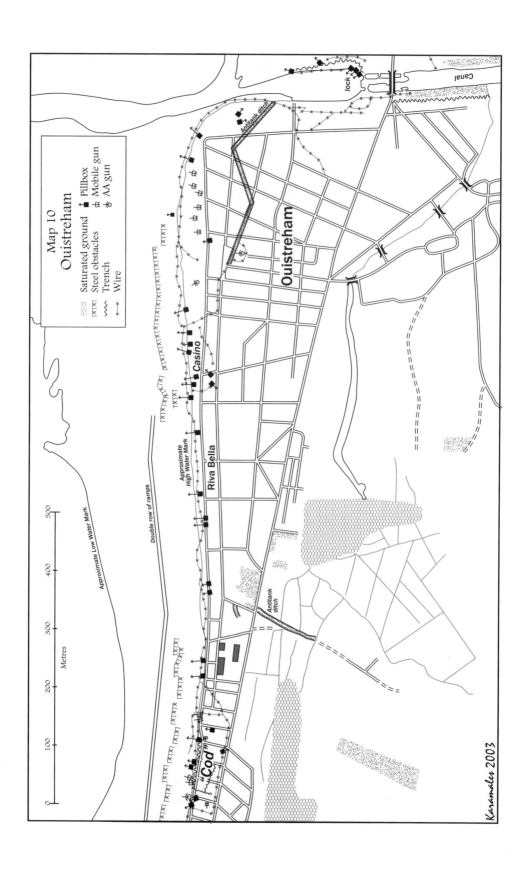

Map 10
Ouistreham

Saturated ground   ▪ Pillbox
Steel obstacles   ▲ Mobile gun
Trench   ⚓ AA gun
Wire

Approximate Low Water Mark

Metres
0   100   200   300   400   500

Double row of ramps

Approximate
High Water Mark

"Cod"

Riva Bella

Casino

Anti-tank ditch

Ouistreham

Anti-tank ditch

lock

Canal

Kanamdier 2003

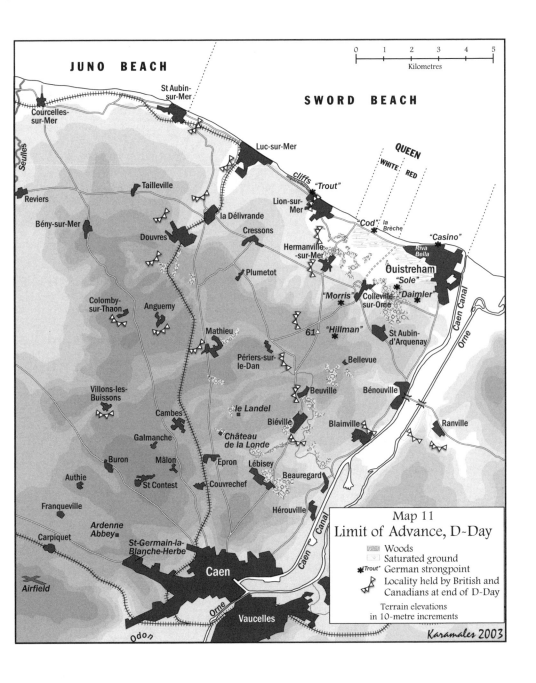

JUNO BEACH

SWORD BEACH

QUEEN

WHITE RED

St Aubin-sur-Mer

Courcelles-sur-Mer

Luc-sur-Mer

Cliffs
"Trout"

Tailleville

Reviers

Lion-sur-Mer

Bény-sur-Mer

la Délivrande

"Cod"   la Brèche

"Casino"

Douvres

Cressons

Riva Bella

Plumetot

Hermanville-sur-Mer

Ouistreham
"Sole"

Colomby-sur-Thaon

Anguerny

"Morris"

Colleville-sur-Orne   "Daimler"

Mathieu

61   "Hillman"

St Aubin-d'Arquenay

Périers-sur-le-Dan

Bellevue

Villons-les-Buissons

Beuville

Bénouville

Cambes

le Landel

Biéville

Blainville

Ranville

Galmanche

Château de la Londe

Buron

Mâlon

Epron

Lébisey

Beauregard

Authie

St Contest

Couvrechef

Franqueville

Hérouville

Ardenne
Abbey

Carpiquet

St-Germain-la-Blanche-Herbe

Caen

Seulles

Caen Canal

Orme

Caen Canal

Orme

Airfield

Vaucelles

Odon

Map 11
Limit of Advance, D~Day

Woods
Saturated ground
"Trout" German strongpoint
Locality held by British and Canadians at end of D-Day

Terrain elevations in 10-metre increments

Karamales 2003

0 1 2 3 4 5
Kilometres

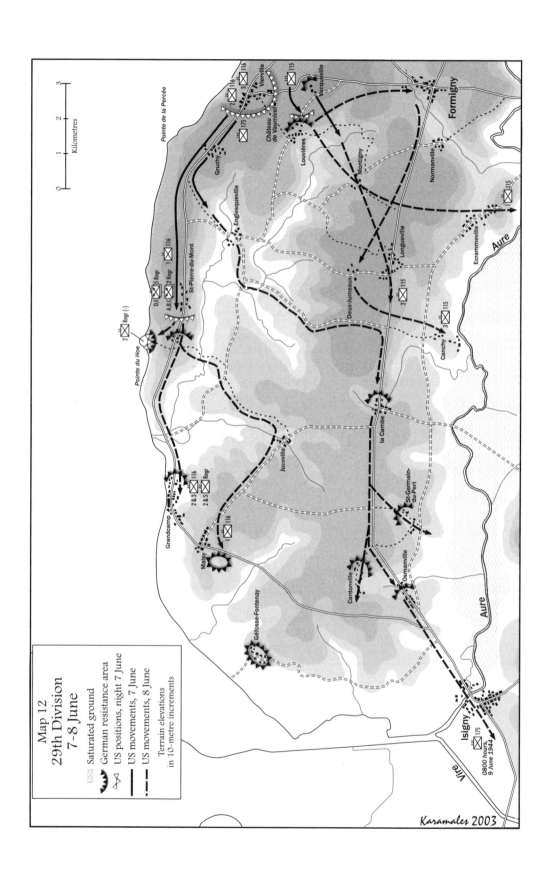

Map 12
29th Division
7–8 June

Saturated ground

German resistance area

US positions, night 7 June

US movements, 7 June

US movements, 8 June

Terrain elevations
in 10-metre increments

Kilometres
0   1   2   3

Pointe de la Percée

Vierville
Château de Vaumicel
Jacqueville
Louvières
Montigny
Normanville
Formigny
Gruchy
Englesqueville
St-Pierre-du-Mont
Deux-Jumeaux
Longueville
Canchy
Aure
Écrammeville
Pointe du Hoe
la Cambe
Jucoville
St-Germain-du-Pert
Grandcamp
Maisy
Géfosse-Fontenay
Cardonville
Osmanville
Aure
Isigny
Vire

2 Rngr (-)
D,E,F Rngr   A,B,C Rngr
5 Rngr   2 Rngr
2 ⊠ 116   3 ⊠ 116
2 ⊠ 115
3 ⊠ 116   1 ⊠ 116
3 ⊠ 175
1 ⊠ 115
2 ⊠ 115
3 ⊠ 115
1 ⊠ 115
2 & 3 ⊠ 116   5 Rngr
2 & 5 Rngr
1 ⊠ 116
3 ⊠ 175

0800 hours,
9 June 1944

Karamales 2003

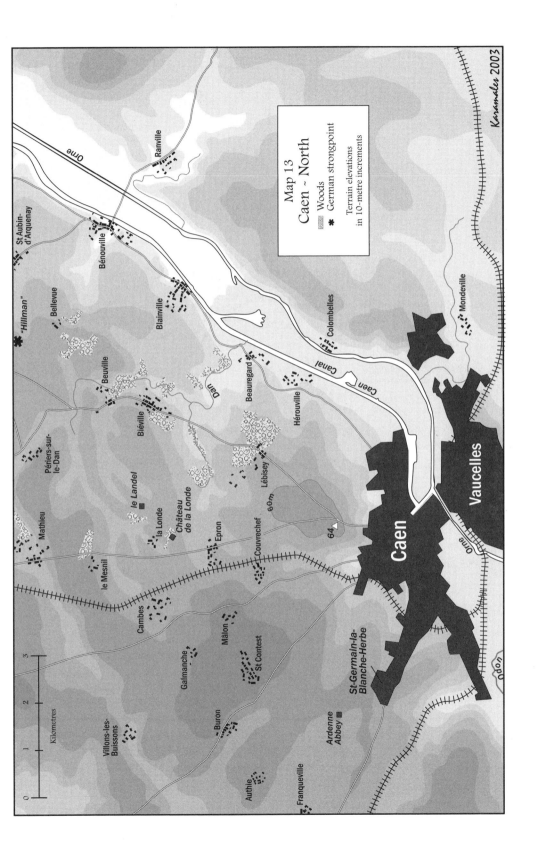

Map 13
Caen ~ North

Woods

* German strongpoint

Terrain elevations
in 10-metre increments

Kansander 2003

Orne

St Aubin-
d'Arquenay

"Hillman"

Bellevue

Bénouville

Ranville

Beuville

Blainville

Caen Canal

Colombelles

Mondeville

Périers-sur-
le-Dan

Dan

Biéville

Beauregard

Hérouville

Mathieu

le Landel

Château
de la Londe

la Londe

Lébisey

60m

le Mesnil

Epron

Couvrechef

64

Cambes

Mâlon

St Contest

Caen

Vaucelles

Orne

Galmanche

Buron

Villons-les-
Buissons

St-Germain-la-
Blanche-Herbe

Ardenne
Abbey

Odon

Authie

Franqueville

Kilometres
0   1   2   3

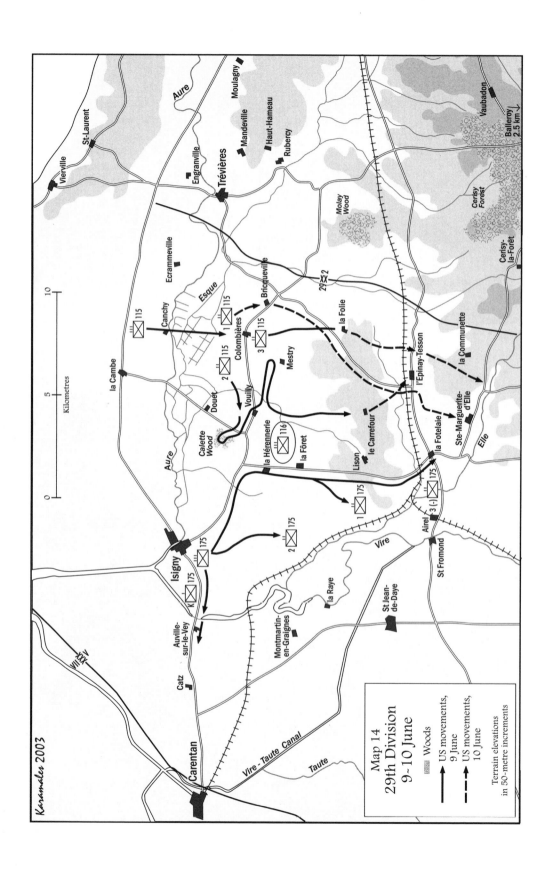

Kananlia 2003

Map 14
29th Division
9–10 June

Woods

US movements,
9 June

US movements,
10 June

Terrain elevations
in 50-metre increments

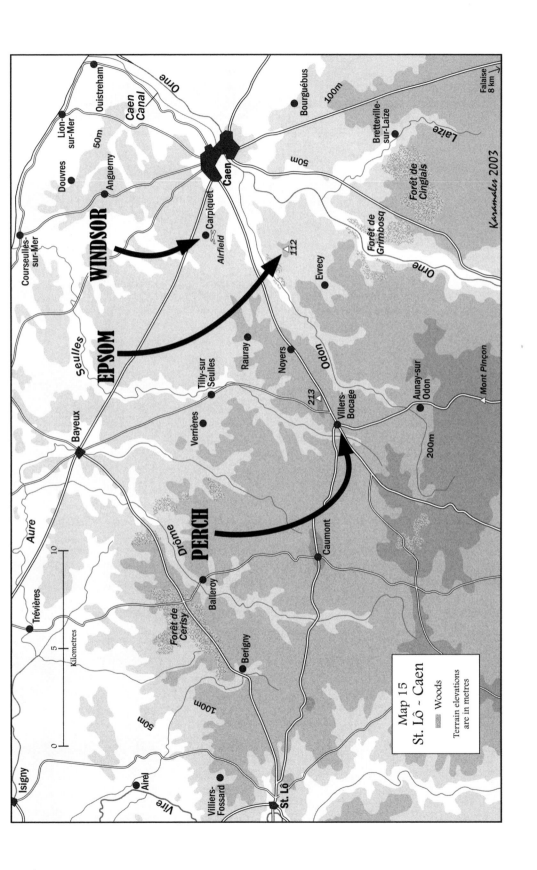

Map 15
St. Lô ~ Caen

Woods

Terrain elevations are in metres

Karswater 2003

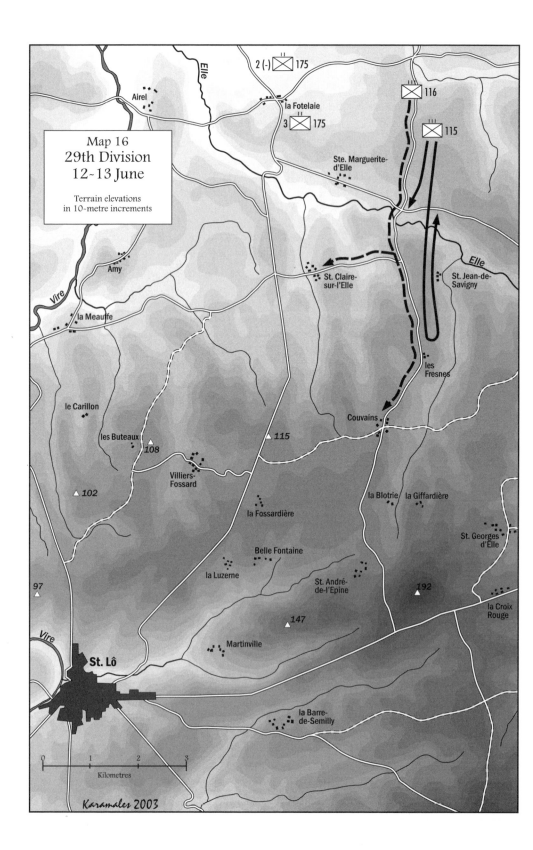

Map 16
29th Division
12~13 June

Terrain elevations
in 10-metre increments

Elle

Airel

2 (-) ⊠ 175

la Fotelaie

3 ⊠ 175

⊠ 116

⊠ 115

Ste. Marguerite-
d'Elle

Amy

St. Claire-
sur-l'Elle

Elle

St. Jean-de-
Savigny

Vire

la Meauffe

les Fresnes

le Carillon

les Buteaux
▲ 108

Couvains

▲ 115

Villiers-
Fossard

▲ 102

la Fossardière

la Blotrie   la Giffardière

St. Georges
d'Elle

Belle Fontaine

la Luzerne

St. André-
de-l'Epine

▲ 192

la Croix
Rouge

97
▲

147
▲

Vire

Martinville

St. Lô

la Barre-
de-Semilly

0   1   2   3
Kilometres

Karamales 2003

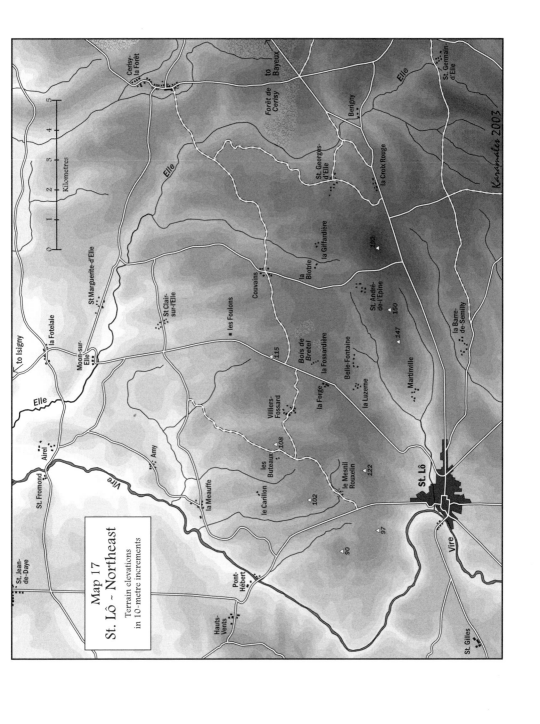

Map 17
St. Lô ~ Northeast
Terrain elevations
in 10-metre increments

Kaufmann 2003

Kilometres
0 1 2 3 4 5

St Jean-de-Daye

to Isigny

Elle

St Fromond

Airel

Amy

la Meauffe

le Carillon

les Buteaux

Pont-Hébert

Hauts-Vents

St Gilles

Vire

102

90

97

122

le Mesnil Rouxelin

la Luzerne

Belle-Fontaine

la Forge

108

Villiers-Fossard

Bois de Bretel

la Fossardière

115

ies Foulons

la Fotelaie

Moon-sur-Elle

St Marguerite-d'Elle

Elle

St Clair-sur-l'Elle

Couvains

la Blotrie

la Giffardière

St André-de-l'Epine

147

150

Martinville

St. Lô

Vire

la Barre-de-Semilly

la Croix Rouge

Bény

St Georges-d'Elle

192

Forêt de Cerisy

to Bayeux

Elle

St Germain-d'Elle

Cerisy-la-Forêt

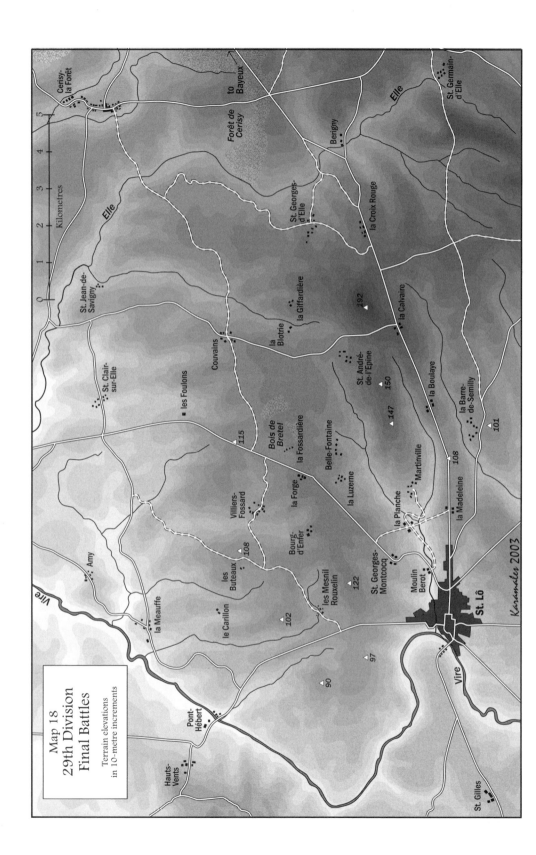

Map 18
29th Division
Final Battles

Terrain elevations
in 10-metre increments

Cerisy-
la Forêt

to Bayeux

Forêt de Cerisy

Elle

St. Germain-
d'Elle

Berigny

St. Georges-
d'Elle

la Croix Rouge

St. Jean-de-
Savigny

Elle

la Giffardière

la Calvaire

192

St. Clair-
sur-Elle

Couvains

la Blotrie

la Boulaye

les Foulons

115

la Fossardière

Bois de
Bretel

Belle-Fontaine

St. André-
de-l'Epine

150

147

la Barre-
de-Semilly

101

Amy

Villiers-
Fossard

la Forge

la Luzerne

Martinville

108

la Meauffe

108

Bourg-
d'Enfer

les Buteaux

les Mesnil
Rouxelin

St. Georges-
Montcocq

la Planche

la Madeleine

le Carillon

102

122

Moulin
Berot

Vire

97

St. Lô

90

Pont-
Hébert

Vire

Karameler 2003

Hauts-
Vents

St. Gilles

Kilometres

0 1 2 3 4 5